The Althouse Press
Faculty of Education, The University of Western Ontario
Frank and Davison, MASCULINITIES AND SCHOOLING:
INTERNATIONAL PRACTICES AND PERSPECTIVES

MASCULINITIES AND SCHOOLING

INTERNATIONAL PRACTICES AND PERSPECTIVES

Edited by
Blye W. Frank and Kevin G. Davison

THE ALTHOUSE PRESS

First published in Canada in 2007 by
THE ALTHOUSE PRESS
Dean: *Allen Pearson*
Director of Publications: *Greg Dickinson*
Faculty of Education, The University of Western Ontario
1137 Western Road, London, Ontario, Canada N6G 1G7

Copyright © 2007 by The University of Western Ontario, London, Ontario, Canada. No part of this publication may be reproduced, stored in a retrieval system, or transmitted in any form or by any means, electronic, photocopying, mechanical or otherwise, without the prior written permission of the publishers.

Editors: *Greg Dickinson, David Radcliffe*
Editorial Assistant: *Katherine Butson*
Cover Design: *Louise Gadbois*

Library and Archives Canada Cataloguing in Publication

    Masculinities and schooling : international practices and perspectives / edited by Blye W. Frank, Kevin G. Davison.

Includes bibliographical references and index.
ISBN 978-0-920354-65-0

    1. Young men—Social conditions. 2. Men—Socialization. 3. Masculinity. 4. Young men—Education. I. Frank, Blye, 1949- II. Davison, Kevin G. (Kevin Graham), 1971-

HQ1088.M38 2007   305.242'108837   C2007-902491-2

Printed and bound in Canada by Hignell Book Printing Ltd., 488 Burnell Street, Winnipeg, Manitoba, Canada R3G 2B4

Contents

Acknowledgements   *i*

Contributors   *iii*

Preface   *ix*
    Kevin G. Davison and Blye W. Frank

Chapter 1   *1*
    Researching Schooling and the Making of English Boys
    Mairtin Mac an Ghaill and Chris Haywood

Chapter 2   *13*
    "Dangerous Pedagogies": Exploring Issues of Sexuality and
    Masculinity in Male Teacher Candidates' Lives
    Wayne Martino and Deborah P. Berrill

Chapter 3   *35*
    On a Knife's Edge: Masculinity in Black Working-Class
    Schools in Post-Apartheid Education
    Robert Morrell

Chapter 4   *59*
    Confronting Masculinity at the University of Zimbabwe
    Marc Epprecht

Chapter 5   *75*
    Men's Violence Against Women: An Urgent Issue
    for Education
    Jeff Hearn and Hans Wessels

Chapter 6   *93*
    High School Masculinities: Unheard Voices
    Among "the Boys"
    Michael D. Kehler

Chapter 7   *111*
    Boys on the Road: Masculinities, Car Culture, and
    Road Safety Education
    Linley Walker, Dianne Butland, and Raewyn Connell

Chapter 8   *129*
    The Thin Line Between Pleasure and Pain: Implications
    for Educating Young Males Involved in Sport
    Lindsay J. Fitzclarence, Christopher Hickey, and Bruce Nyland

Chapter 9   *153*
    Sites of Asian American Masculinities in School:
    "In-citing" Difference
    Kevin K. Kumashiro

References   *171*

Index   *193*

Acknowledgements

I would, first and foremost, like to acknowledge and thank Kevin Davison for his dedication and time consuming work on this co-edited book. Greg Dickinson and Katherine Butson of The Althouse Press, thanks! A sincere thanks to the chapter authors. Kevin and I both thank Meagan Hasek-Watt and Paula Cameron for their secretarial and editorial assistance with the various versions of the manuscript.

Blye W. Frank

I would like to acknowledge the noble patience of all the contributing authors of this collection who endured the many years it took to bring this book to fruition. I would also like to express my sincere appreciation to Greg Dickinson and Katherine Butson, at The Althouse Press, for all the time they invested in editing, proofing, and typesetting this book. Dedicating oneself to cleaning up others' words can be a frustrating and thankless task, and I am indebted to you for your labour and commitment to this collection. Lastly, I am grateful to Blye for working with me over the years on this book, and many other collaborative research projects and publications.

Kevin G. Davison

Contributors

Deborah P. Berrill is a Professor in and Founding Director of the School of Education and Professional Learning, Trent University, Peterborough, Canada and has been involved in issues of gender and schooling for her entire teaching career. Her research, in Canada and internationally, is grounded in her work with teachers and teacher candidates and the insights they provide as they negotiate the professional teaching landscape. Her most recent publications address issues of gender and literacy, and teacher professional integrity.

Dianne Louise Butland has been a Lecturer in Education at the University of Sydney and a member of the New South Wales Board of Studies and its Gender Project Steering Committee. Her fields of research include curriculum, gender, and equity. She has extensive practical experience in the school system and has been a member of the New South Wales Department of Health's Advisory Committee associated with the Survey of Drug Use by NSW Secondary School Students. She has also been involved in extensive community consultation around the purposes and process of schooling and is an activist interested in its social transformation.

Raewyn Connell is a Professor at the University of Sydney. She is author, co-author, or editor of nineteen books, including *Masculinities* (University of California Press, 1995, 2005); *Ruling Class, Ruling Culture* (Cambridge University Press, 1977); *Making the Difference* (Allen & Unwin Australia, 1982); *Gender and Power* (Polity Press, 1987); *Schools and Social Justice* (Our Schools Ourselves, 1993); *The Men and the Boys* (Allen & Unwin Australia, 2000); *Gender* (Polity Press, 2002); and *Southern Theory* (Allen & Unwin Australia/Polity Press, 2007). Dr. Connell has also contributed to research journals across a number of disciplines, including sociology, education, political science, gender studies, and related fields. Her current research concerns social theory, changing masculinities, neo-liberalism, globalization, and intellectuals.

Kevin G. Davison is a Lecturer in Education and Research Development Coordinator, Department of Education, The National University of Ireland, Galway. He teaches graduate courses in sociology of education, gender and education, and qualitative research methodologies and researches and publishes in the area of masculinities, bodies, boys and literacies, and research methodologies. His recent research on substance abuse, suicide, and academic disengagement in rural Ireland engaged young men in filmmaking and digital storytelling. Guest co-editor of three special issues on boys, masculinity and education for *The Journal of Men's Studies, The Canadian Journal of Education*, and *The McGill Journal of Education*, he is the author of *Gender Gravity and The Postmodern Push: The Pressure of Gender and Bodies on Curriculum*, forthcoming from The Edwin Mellen Press.

Marc Epprecht is an Associate Professor in the Development Studies Program at Queen's University, Kingston, Canada. He has published extensively on the history of gender and sexuality in southern Africa, including *'This Matter of Women Is Getting Very Bad': Gender, Development and Politics in Colonial Lesotho, 1870-1965* (University of Natal Press, 2000). His *Hungochani: The History of a Dissident Sexuality in Southern Africa* (McGill-Queens University Press, 2004) was the winner of the 2006 Joel Gregory Prize for best book on Africa published in Canada in 2004-05. His forthcoming book, *The Making of "African sexuality": An Intellectual History*, traces the development of received wisdom about "African sexuality" back through time. He has taught in high schools and at universities in Lesotho, Zimbabwe, and South Africa.

Lindsay J. Fitzclarence is an Associate Professor in the Faculty of Education, Monash University (Gippsland). Previously he worked in the Division of Education, Arts and Social Sciences at the University of South Australia, in Education at Deakin University, and before that, as a physical education teacher. He maintains an interest in the study of sport and physical activity but, at the same time, has published in the areas of education and violence, and youth culture. He has studied the importance of male peer culture within sport and education and has been involved in a research project about the Rock/Croc Eisteddfod—the use of popular music in educational programs for schools.

Blye W. Frank is a Professor and Head of the Division of Medical Education in the Faculty of Medicine at Dalhousie University, Halifax, Nova Scotia, Canada. Since 1990, when he completed a PhD in the Sociology of Masculinity entitled "Everyday Masculinites," he has held four Social Sciences and Humanities Research Council of Canada grants in the area of masculinity, the most recent of which is entitled "Homophobia and Heterosexism in Medical Education" (2000-2009). Dr. Frank's extensive research and publications in the area of sociology of masculinity are informed by a feminist post-structural theoretical approach and focus on the intersection of multiple identities of men.

Chris Haywood currently works in the Faculty of Education at the University of Newcastle, England. He has written on young people, sexuality, and masculinity. His interests include research methodologies and the epistemology of identities.

Jeff Hearn is a Professor at Linkoping University, Sweden; the Swedish School of Economics, Helsinki, Finland; and the University of Huddersfield, UK. From 1990 to 1995 he was co-convenor of the Research Unit on Violence, Abuse and Gender Relations, University of Bradford, UK; from 1999 to 2005 he was the co-convenor of the Sexualized Violence Research Consortium, Finland; and from 2000 to 2003 he was the Principal Contractor, EU Research Network on Men in Europe. His books include *Men in the Public Eye* (Routledge, 1992); *Men, Gender Divisions and Welfare* (Routledge, 1998); *Violence and Gender Relations* (Sage, 1996); *The Violences of Men* (Sage, 1998), *Gender, Sexuality and Violence in Organizations* (with Wendy Parkin, Sage, 2001); *Handbook of Studies on Men and Masculinities* (co-edited with Michael Kimmel and R. W. Connell, Sage, 2005); and *European Perspectives on Men and Masculinities* (with Keith Pringle, Palgrave Macmillan, 2006).

Christopher Hickey is an Associate Professor in the School of Education at Deakin University (Geelong), where he teaches the undergraduate teacher preservice course and supervises masters and doctoral candidates. His teaching duties are complemented by a strong research interest in the education and development of young males. He has undertaken extensive work in masculinity studies as applied to issues related to sport and physical activity, in particular, the behaviours and rationalizations of young males as members of peer groups. This work has focused on the links among identity formation, masculinity, sport, physical activity, and popular culture. With Lindsay Fitzclarence and Russell Matthews, he has edited *Where the Boys Are: Masculinity, Sport and Education* (Deakin University Press, 2000).

Michael D. Kehler is an Associate Professor teaching in the preservice and graduate education programs in the Faculty of Education at The University of Western Ontario. His research interests include the counter-hegemonic practices of high school young men, literacies, negotiating the masculine body, masculinities, and the ongoing negotiations involved for young men resisting heteronormativity. His research has been published in a range of journals including *Journal of Curriculum Theorizing, Discourse, McGill Journal of Education, Educational Review, Taboo,* and *The International Journal of Inclusive Education*. He is co-author, with Wayne Martino and Marcus Weaver-Hightower, of a forthcoming book, *The Problem with Boys: Beyond the Backlash in Boys' Education* (Haworth Press). He has also contributed a chapter to *Boys, Girls and the Myths of Literacies and Learning* (Canadian Scholars' Press, forthcoming).

Kevin K. Kumashiro is an Associate Professor of policy studies in the College of Education at the University of Illinois-Chicago, and the founding director of the Center for Anti-Oppressive Education. He has taught in schools in the United States and abroad, and has served as a consultant for colleges, educational organizations, and state and federal agencies. Most recently, he was a senior program specialist in human and civil rights at the National Education Association of the United States. He is the author of several books, including *Troubling Education: Queer Activism and Anti-oppressive Pedagogy* (RoutledgeFalmer, 2002), which received the 2003 Gustavus Myers Outstanding Book Award. His most recent book is *Against Common Sense: Teaching and Learning toward Social Justice* (RoutledgeFalmer, 2004).

Mairtin Mac an Ghaill works in the Sociology Department at the University of Birmingham, England. With Chris Haywood, he has written *Men and Masculinities* (Open University Press, 2003) and *Gender, Culture and Society: Contemporary Femininities and Masculinities* (Palgrave Macmillan, 2006).

Wayne Martino is an Associate Professor in the Faculty of Education, The University of Western Ontario, Canada. His research has involved extensive investigation into the impact of masculinities and homophobia on the lives of boys and male teachers in schools. His books include *What About the Boys? Issues of Masculinity and Schooling* (Open University Press, 2001); *So What's a Boy? Addressing Issues of Masculinity and Schooling* (Open University Press, 2003); *'Being normal is the only way to be': Boys' and Girls' Perspectives on Gender and School* (UNSW Press, 2005); *Gendered Outcasts and Sexual Outlaws: Sexual Oppression and Gender Hierarchies in Queer Men's*

Lives (Haworth Press, 2006). His latest books include *Boys' Education: Beyond the Backlash* (Haworth Press, in press) and *Boys and Schooling: Contexts, Issues and Practices* (Palgrave, in press). He is currently working on a Social Sciences and Humanities Research Council-funded project with Dr. Goli Rezai-Rashti, entitled, "The Influence of Male Teachers as Role Models in Elementary Schools."

Robert Morrell was formerly a Lecturer in history at the Universities of Transkei and Durban Westville. At present, he is a Professor of Education at the University of KwaZulu-Natal, Durban, South Africa. Robert has written and edited a number of books on issues of masculinity in Africa. These include *Changing Men in Southern Africa* (University of Natal Press/Zed Books, 2001); *From Boys to Gentlemen: Settler Masculinity in Colonial Natal, 1880-1920* (UNISA Press, 2001); *Baba: Men and Fatherhood in South Africa* (with Linda Richter, HSRC, 2006); and *African Masculinities: Men in Africa from the Late 19th Century to the Present!* (with Lahoucine Ouzgane, Palgrave/University of KwaZulu-Natal Press, 2005).

Bruce Nyland is a South Australian teacher and is married with five children. He has been a classroom teacher, student counsellor, faculty coordinator, and Assistant Principal in a career spanning more than 35 years with the South Australian Education Department. His academic qualifications include a BA (Adelaide), AVA in physical education and a diploma in teaching. His sporting achievements range across Australian Rules football, cricket, squash, athletics, swimming, and boxing. He is currently trying to write his first novel.

Linley Walker has been a Lecturer in Sociology at the University of Western Sydney, Australia. She has conducted a longitudinal ethnographic study of high school girls and their families in a working-class comprehensive school in suburban New South Wales and has extensive experience in teacher education and curriculum development at the tertiary level. A pioneer of ethnographic research on masculinity among working-class youth in the area of motor vehicle use and road safety, drug use, and sexually transmitted diseases, she is the author or co-author of numerous journal articles and government reports on education, gender equity, social class, race and ethnicity, and road safety.

Hans Wessels is a qualified teacher. He graduated with a BA in Teaching and an MA in Musicology from the University of Utrecht in The Netherlands. During these studies he focused particularly on gender, masculinity, and feminisms. At present he is working as a classroom teacher and a teacher of music and ethics in a primary school in Finland. His current interests lie in gender, education, and cultural studies, and he is currently researching in this area. He has also recently published on masculinity, music, and popular culture. He was the founding Chair of Profeminist-imiehet ry, Finland, the Finnish profeminist men's registered organization.

Preface

Since the 1970s, inspired in part by the second wave feminist movement and the gay liberation movement, Western scholars have been questioning boys' and men's "traditional" practice of masculinity. The field of masculinity research has stretched across disciplines from Film Studies (Silverman 1992) and Jungian Psychology (Bly 1990) to Sociology (Kimmel 1997) and History (Walvin and Mangan 1987). These studies often problematized the way men perform their masculinity. This literature on masculinity, not all of which has been theorized from a profeminist point of view, together with the feminist literature in gender and schooling, prepared the foundation for educators to examine specifically the experiences of boys and men in schooling. As critical research into men and masculinity grew, Connell pointed out in 1995 that "there [was] surprisingly little discussion of the role of education in the *transformation* [emphasis added] of masculinity" (238).

Over the past fifteen years the educational literature focusing on masculinities has grown significantly (Alloway and Gilbert 1997; Browne and Fletcher 1995; Connell 1987, 1989, 1995, and 1996; Epstein et al. 1998; Frank 1987, 1990, 1993, 1994, and 1997; Gilbert and Gilbert 1998; Kenway and Willis 1998; Mac an Ghaill 1994a, 1994b; Martino 1996, 1997, and 2000; Salisbury and Jackson 1996). The majority of this research has been conducted by scholars in Australia and the United Kingdom. For example, *Project Arianne* examined masculinities and schooling across eight European countries in order to broaden adolescent male education as well as to improve boys' understanding of women's changing position in society (Arnot 1997).

Over a decade of research in the area of boys, masculinity, and schooling has both created a strong theoretical base and offered practical advice for teachers confronted by problematic masculine practices in the classroom. It is well documented that boys' bullying, harassing, homophobic, and violent behaviour threatens the safety of teachers and students in schools (Browne and Fletcher 1995; Letts and Sears 1999). Because of this awareness, in Canada for example, Halifax Men for Change, a profeminist men's group, has developed a three-volume curricular guide entitled *Healthy Relationships* (1994) that takes up similar themes, but focuses on masculinity in the media and relationship issues for young men. Over the last ten years, some universities in Canada and the United States have begun to offer programs in gender studies that take up an analysis of masculinity (Connell 1995). Furthermore, courses in a variety of disciplines, including education, are beginning to focus on masculinities and schooling.

This growing awareness of gender and masculinity has prompted educators and parents in Australia, the United Kingdom, and recently in North America, to demand that more attention (and funding) be given to boys' issues. Magazines and other media publications have fueled interest in the issue with headlines such as "'The War on Boys' (*Men's Health* October 1994), 'Girls doing well while boys feel neglected' (*Guardian* 26 August, 1995), 'The trouble with men' (*Economist* 28 September, 1996), 'How boys lost out to girl power' (*New York Times* 12 December, 1998), and 'Boy burn out' (*The Australian* 27 July, 1995)" (Lichter 2002). Thus, "What about the boys?" has become a popular catchphrase drawing attention to boys' literacy and numeracy rates, underachievement, and drug abuse and suicide rates (Epstein et al. 1998).

A study from 2001 in Quebec, Canada focused on the importance of fathers' involvement in addressing the gender gap and the underachievement of boys. The Durham District School Board and the Ministry of Education in Ontario, Canada have attempted to address boys' lower literacy rates (in relation to girls') by introducing "male role models, bringing in male authors to conduct readings, attempting to find more books and magazines geared to boys' interests and [by] finding new, less girl-centered teaching methods" (Fine 2001, A6). Further, two *New York Times* bestselling books have taken up the emotional lives of boys (Pollock 1999; Kindlon and Thompson 1999).

This shift in gender analyses has come about from both a concern for, and interest in, the practice of masculinities (Frank 1990, and 1994; Davison 1996, 2000a and 2000b), as well as in response to gender initiatives which have not often included an exploration of the complexities of the lives of young men (Epstein et al. 1998; Cohen 1998; Connell 1996). Educators and social commentators have noted that as "we enter the next millenium it is the under-achievement of boys that has become one of the biggest challenges facing societies today" (Wragg 1997 cited in Cohen 1998, 20). However, Griffin and Lees warn that during this time of "panic" over boys' underachievement, educators must not forget that "such panics [may] confound issues concerning gender, 'race' and class in ways that do little service to boys *or* girls" (1997, 1).

What is often left out of contemporary concerns regarding boys, masculinity, and schooling is that the panic over boys and schooling is not a new phenomenon (Cohen 1998). Foucault reminds us that "we have to know the historical conditions which motivate our conceptualization. We need a historical awareness of our present circumstance" (1982, 777). The British colonial history of public institutional education has focused regularily on the underachieving boy (Lichter 2002). Pedagogical approaches, curriculum selection, disciplinary interventions, educational policy, and funding have been re-evaluated continually to address the educational needs of particular boys (Cohen 1998). At the turn of the twenty-first century concerns over boys and schooling have been raised yet again. Situating the current debate in a greater historical context helps to position such research, including the work contained in this book, as a part of an on-going, fluid, ever-changing, dynamic of gender, rather than an inevitable static construction.

Pointing to the *differences* in the way masculinity is performed individually, within the contexts of both families and broader cultures, we hope that readers can identify the complexity of the interplay of masculinities and schooling and their influence upon the everyday social world. All too often boys and masculinity "have been situated as a monolithic, unitary, fixed construct that has been culturally and socially defined within a matrix of cogent gender norms and has been vehemently positioned in opposition to anything feminine" (Lichter 2002, 189). If, as Connell (2000) explains, "the making of masculinities in schools…is a process with multiple pathways, shaped by class and ethnicity, producing different outcomes" (163-4), then this collection aims to dismantle, re-think, and re-theorize various practices of masculinities in schools from trans-disciplinary and international perspectives.

The goal of this collection is to problematize the ordinary ways in which masculinities often escape the critical eye. The absence of a critique often stems from the assumption that masculine gender performances are similar. Thus, simplistic solutions are often applied to issues such as bullying, violence, and sexual harassment in schools with the belief, and sincere hope, that these harmful acts might be eliminated. Yet, there seems to be a recurring feeling of disillusionment when some masculine performances do not change after the practices of *individuals* are examined in relation to what is believed to be "boy-like" behaviour. There is a need to re-focus the issue of boys and schooling toward a more progressive social and political analysis. Rather than framing the debate within a psychological analysis, the chapters of this collection locate the investigation of boys and schooling within a long tradition of feminist scholarship, thus positioning boys and schooling in the context of gendered, social, and educational relationships.

This collection of essays encourages a critical analysis of masculinities and schooling. The difference here is difference itself: acknowledging difference we are not simply pointing to diversity. We are attempting to reveal how masculinities work in and through educational institutions—not as a unified and coherent practice. Performances of masculinity are a very messy mix of multiple ways of enacting gender *as individuals*, while at the same time acting within various *public* discourses of masculinity. Highlighting some of the ways masculinities are practised in different contexts and from various cultural perspectives, this collection encourages more than simple, quick-fix solutions.

This book arises out of the daily experiences of boys and those who work directly with them in schools. Their voices not only provide insight into the struggles and contradictions of their lives, but also speak to the possibility of change. Through an examination of socio-economic class, sport, violence, harassment, and homophobia, the book examines the "messiness" of the daily gendered practices of boys. As a reflection of individual practices, the theories and the analyses of lived lives are also complex, as each chapter illustrates. As a gender performance, masculinity is therefore not limited to biologically male bodies. In acknowledging the distinction between gender and biological sexed bodies, and the lack of stability between the two, we also want to acknowledge that masculinities are often played out on, or in reference to, female bodies, especially in schools. With this said, it is necessary to address what may seem like an absence of research in this collection that directly involves girls or women. As the editors of this collection, we drew together these scholarly works to focus on masculinities, not simply the sexed bodies that are often associated with masculinity. More importantly, however, there was a conscious choice made to actively resist positioning boys and men *against* girls and women as it often has the effect of creating a zero-sum equation where one party inevitably loses out or absorbs greater critique. Instead, we argue that an examination of masculinities and schooling on its own, with all the complexities that it entails, will help to build a stronger theoretical foundation to rethink gender, not in the absence of women, but very much *for* the benefit of women *and* men in schools today.

In Chapter One, Mairtin Mac an Ghaill and Chris Haywood situate the debates over boys and schooling in the British context, examining what they refer to as "moral geographies" of contemporary England. By focusing on the contextual politics, they illustrate the interconnectedness of masculinities and schooling cultures as "masculinity making devices." They open this collection by locating masculinities as contingent upon various complex and interrelated discourses at play.

Chapter Two examines the experiences of two men (one gay and one straight) who teach in elementary schools in Canada. Martino and Berrill illustrate how the recent demand for more men in elementary schools to serve as role models for boys is saturated with tensions and contradictions. The authors focus upon the various ways in which the two men "police" their subjectivities to fit "normalized" discourses of masculinity in schools, and how their teaching practices are affected by such self-regulation. Martino and Berrill's research asks readers to reconsider the challenges and struggles that male elementary school teachers face, and, in turn, to reflect upon the intersections of gender, sexualities, and schooling.

That masculinities and sexualities are further intersected by the enfolding of race, culture, and history is illustrated by the research discussed in Chapters Three and Four. These chapters offer a rare insight into African masculinities that is usually absent in Western academic work. Through an analysis of working-class masculinities in post-apartheid South Africa, Morrell examines the continual presence of patriarchy and violence in the lives of boys. His examination of educational policy and contemporary practices of masculinity in South African schools illustrates the various possibilities for positive change, while pointing out that such possibilities are "balanced on a knife's edge." Epprecht's "Confronting Masculinity at the University of Zimbabwe" reflects on masculinities and profeminist education at the University of Zimbabwe. Epprecht highlights the connections between violence, crime, homophobia, sexual assault, and post-colonial economic underdevelopment and particular patriarchal structures embedded in social practices of masculinities. This chapter features the difficulty involved in contesting potentially harmful gendered practices and various levels of resistance to feminist theory by university students in Zimbabwe.

In Chapter Five, "Men's Violence to Women: An Urgent Issue for Education," Hearn and Wessels give an account of profeminist action and anti-sexist pedagogy in schools. They argue that men's violence against women and critical examinations of gendered sexual power relations should be completely integrated into school curricula and not just temporarily inserted into or added onto existing curriculum structures. The authors view schools as having great potential for effecting social change and present strategies for schools to address men's violence against women.

Kehler, in "High School Masculinities: Unheard Voices Among 'The Boys,'" argues that schools can indeed be places where young men can unlearn, resist, and repurpose masculinity. Chapter Six presents stories of boys engaging with profeminist discourses to demonstrate how a particular group of boys, marginalized by their profeminist actions, negotiate the often narrow and shifting terrain of hegemonic masculinity. These boys' voices help to illustrate the various ways feminism and profeminism may be incorporated into, and may ultimately change, contemporary practices of high school masculinities.

In Chapter Seven, Connell, Walker, and Butland present a number of educational considerations in re-thinking masculinities. The focus of their research is young Australian men's involvement in car culture as a point of entry into cultures of hegemonic masculinity. By examining young men's relationships with cars and road safety, the authors draw attention to some very real dangers that arise when gender collides with the inorganic.

The social and performative aspects of masculinity leave behind physical and psychological residue, whether in the form of car parts or as remembrances of self and nationhood, as Fitzclarence, Hickey, and Nyland illustrate in their autobiographical accounts of the pleasure and pain of engaging in school sport. Chapter Eight links "boy culture" to legends of bravery in sport and military history and offers advice for coaches and educators who work with boys and masculinities and are often in a position to challenge young men to rethink their "intolerance of differences." The authors suggest that discourses of masculinity can be interrogated and reformulated through the same institutions that spawn and perpetuate them.

Their suggestion is explored further in Chapter Nine which examines masculinities in the Asian-American context. Kumashiro outlines the multiple discourses available to Asian-American boys as they construct and practise masculinities in schools. Kumashiro interrogates "different stereotypes, representations, and self-representations [...], different discourses of masculinity, including such discourses as hypomasculinity, hypermasculinity, deviant heterosexuality, White masculinity, Black masculinity, traditional Asian masculinity, Orientalism, and butch lesbianism to highlight the complex ways masculinities are "cited" by students.

This book offers a different way of thinking about the "panic" of boys and schooling. It is intended to challenge, unsettle, and disrupt some of the taken-for-granted, everyday practices of masculinities and schooling. The international scope of the research included in this collection should render it a useful resource for educators across disciplines and across geographic boundaries. Lastly, the intention of this book is not to provide answers, but to provoke greater interrogations into the various contextual and contingent discourses of masculinities in the lives of men and boys in schools. Critical engagements and dialogue regarding masculinity, both inter-cultural and inter-disciplinary, have the potential to transform harmful social and gendered practices such as violence, bullying, sexual harassment, and homophobia. We hope this collection will contribute to positive social change for men and women, and boys and girls, in schools.

Kevin G. Davison and Blye W. Frank

Chapter 1

Researching Schooling and the Making of English Boys

Mairtin Mac an Ghaill and Chris Haywood

Introduction

A series of moral panics about boys and boyhood have been emerging recently across Europe, each with its own local (national) inflections. For example, a visitor to England in the early 21st century might have assumed that there were no girls in the population. The visitor might also have assumed that boys were both a great risk to themselves and a threat to the rest of society. More specifically, English state-led anxieties over "failing boys," where boys (in relation to girls) are seen as underachieving at school, are locating the assumed problem within gender relations and, in particular, as expressive sex attributes of "boyness." Examining the range of literatures available to make sense of what was going on would not have helped. On the one hand, most educational literature failed to engage with contemporary social and cultural theory that might have offered frameworks of explanation. On the other hand, the latter—as illustrated in queer theory and post-colonial studies—has disconnected from empirical investigations of state institutions, such as schools. One might add that further confusion for the visitor emerges from the fact that the social, cultural, and economic specificities of England remain unexplored.

In contrast to the absence of the "failing boys" discourse in academic texts, pervasive media reports have highlighted a major concern among parents, teachers, and government officials about boys' low academic achievement and its links to increased alienation and anti-social behaviour (OFSTED 1996; Carvel, 1996; Bennett, 1996). The dominant media explanation for boys' underachievement suggests that these findings are evidence of equal opportunities policies having gone too far, making schools less boy-friendly. In turn, educationalists have argued the need to locate the dynamics of underachievement primarily in relation to available role models, curriculum content, teaching styles, and classroom management. However, such responses fail to acknowledge that schooling processes are intricately connected to a broader field of social discursive power relations. In the light of the continued failure of educationalists to go beyond examining gender as a technical variable or effect, this chapter argues the need to view masculinities as part of a dynamic process within a specific local context—that of English schooling. We outline the current moral geographies that surround this state institutional context, highlight a number of conceptual absences in educational research on English boys, and explore a number of strategies that we have found productive in our own research on understanding boyhood.

The Moral Geographies of English Schooling

In recent years a radical reconstruction of English state schooling has taken place, largely as part and parcel of the New Right's having fractured its public-sector character during the 1980s and early 1990s (Chitty 1999). Neo-Liberal interventions have cultivated commercially oriented schools within quasi-private markets, contractually identifying the state as purchaser and the parent as consumer. Such restructuring is situated within the more fundamental sociopolitical changes following the breakdown of the post-Second World War educational settlement, whose purpose was to develop economic growth, equality of opportunity, and social justice. Presently, in English schools, the combined effects of the changing labour process of teaching and the emergence of an entrepreneurial curriculum can be understood as a direct attempt by the state to re-masculinize schooling (Mac an Ghaill 1994a). The cumulative effect of the restructured authority system, with accompanying intensified surveillance, disciplinary codes, curriculum and testing stratification technologies, subject allocation, and knowledge selection, is serving to demarcate a range of new hierarchically ordered masculinities. As a consequence, English schooling is subject to competing moral imperatives, with definitions of "good" schooling practice being contested according to individual school histories, regional specificities, teacher experiences, student catchment areas, and statutory regulators (such as OFSTED).[1]

The broader English political context of schooling is integral to explaining what part schools play in making young English masculinities. Unlike the static representations emerging from the "failing boys" crisis, it is argued here that schooling is a dynamic social process constituted by a set of social relations charged with formal and informal meanings. These meanings offer not only interpretations about what it is to be male or female, but also institutional and self-definitions of being a good (real) boy or good girl. The shifting meanings of "good" schooling practice have involved a series of expectations about what "proper" boys should and should not do. Importantly, these normatively loaded ascriptions are dispersed across a diverse area that includes discipline and control, the formal and hidden curriculum, streaming and prefectorial systems, teaching staff appointments, and auxiliary staff. In effect, because schools are located within a complex interplay of social, economic, and political pressures, they situate, shape, and make available spaces for different styles of masculinity. More specifically, schooling processes can be seen to form gendered identities, marking normatively ascribed styles of being (Butler 1993).

At the same time, the moral geography of English schools has been intersected by the partial implementation of gender and race equal opportunity policies and the more general impact of feminism and anti-racism (Weiner 1994). In particular, during the 1970s and early 1980s, feminism provided a major contribution to explaining gender in the schooling arena. A key concern was identifying the structure of gendered hierarchies in which specific social practices were used to reproduce social divisions and inequality. A major success of early feminism was its explanatory power (and its mobilizing force) in uncovering the logic behind the organization of social inequalities. It also provided a social vocabulary that could be deployed in recognizing and naming systematic oppression. Much of this research has identified boys as being responsible for a whole range of misogynistic and homophobic effects.

Epistemologically, we have tried to make sense of the meanings and practices of boyhood by examining those effects (Haywood and Mac an Ghaill 1997). A key concern for us is the way in which gender research in schools tends to hold onto a one-dimensional conception of power, where social collectivities either have power or they do not. In other words, there is no empirical, analytical, or theoretical space beyond a powerless and powerful couplet.

Situating Moral Geographies: The Formation of Young English Masculinities

We suggest that English schools do not simply reproduce gendered power relations, but that changing political and ideological conditions have fundamental generational effects on the formation of masculinities and corresponding relations of power (Mannheim 1952; Cohen 1984). The formation of boyness is intricately, yet not necessarily intentionally, connected to the wider social and political changes outlined above. For example, in his study of secondary schools in the 1990s, Mac an Ghaill (1994a) does not assume that gender/sexual identities have not been present in schools, but that the changing institutional structures and attendant technologies of power, such as changing curriculum planning, subject knowledge, and training regimes, are helping to re-shape young masculinities. Until recently, schools were divided along a high status/academic and low status/vocationalist binary. Mac an Ghaill suggests that this division has been challenged recently and is in the process of being reconstructed. The impetus for reconstruction has been the increased funding for vocational projects, marking a shift from a liberal-humanist schooling paradigm to a technical training paradigm. New resources for the fulfilment of career aspirations emerged as students entered subjects such as business studies, technology, and computer studies. Mac an Ghaill found that the emergence of a new vocationalism signalled the change in the constitution of stratified knowledge.

One result of the re-stratification of knowledge is that male student identities take on new dimensions. Rather than seeing male groups in terms of a simple pro-school or anti-school dichotomy, Mac an Ghaill proposes a more complex approach to capture these new dimensions. He identifies four types of male students, who represent the styles of masculinity present in the secondary school: the Macho Lads, the Academic Achievers, the New Entrepreneurs, and the Real Englishmen. These four groups of students were positioning their masculinities in relation to the school organization, and in particular, the curriculum. The working-class Macho Lads rejected formal schooling. In contrast, the Academic Achievers legitimized and affirmed the schooling process, locating themselves within academic subjects, whereas the working-class New Entrepreneurs located themselves within the new high-status technical and vocational subjects as a resource for developing their masculinities. The Real Englishmen represented a group of middle-class students, who, like the Macho Lads, rejected schooling but remained ambivalent about its significance. Key elements of their masculinity included honesty, difference, individuality, autonomy, and authenticity, all of which they claimed were absent from the school's middle-class culture. Significantly, it is within these peer group networks that collective masculinities were socially and spacially regulated, maintained, and contested. Each group attempted to impose its own definition of masculinity, thus reinforcing its own social position. Consequently, the form and content of the students' schooling experiences became mediated.

Connecting generational specificities to an understanding of the formation of English boyness highlights a number of limitations present in contemporary studies of English masculinities. First, current cultural representations of young men in England tend to focus on sensational images of road protesters, football hooligans, or aberrant fathers. Similarly, accounts of boys in schools tend to represent them as spectacular social actors, often captured in terms of repeated episodes of misogyny, homophobia, and racism. Such sociological representations frequently portray English boys as sexually dangerous, aggressive, uncooperative, anti-school, and violent. Second, what appears missing in the English context is an account of ordinary boys, whose meanings and practices are not necessarily reduced to a dominant and subordinate dichotomy (Brown 1989). In relation to both these questions, much feminist work has explored the range of different masculinities. Such accounts often utilize Connell's (1987) hegemony of masculinity as a means of illustrating the various forms of male oppression. Although the representation of boyness changes, the underlying power structures of boys' oppressive practices do not. At a local level, those boys who do not engage in spectacular forms of masculinity, transfer their patriarchal privilege by *complicitly* sanctioning the more spectacular (abusive) masculine styles. Such a framework allows research from America or Australia to be compared to English research as contextual differences simply surround the culturalized forms of male power, rather than its articulation. This is illustrated in the current educational literature with the representation of English boys dominating the playground by playing soccer and thus marginalizing girls; American boys carrying out similar sporting practices through American football; and Australian boys doing so through Australian rules football. Part of connecting a research framework to the making of a national boyhood requires a reflexive consideration of the contextual specificities. A key question is whether the changes in cross-cultural forms of masculinity correspond with changes in power relations.

This problem is further highlighted by another absence in studies on English boys, namely, the relationship between age and gender, which remains conceptually underdeveloped by sociologists of education. As a result, research findings appear to assume that there is little differentiation of age-related masculinities. For instance, those working on masculinities in primary schools tend unproblematically to adopt a concept of masculinity. We need a critical analysis of younger boys' identities that captures the confusions, fears, and frustrations of investing in masculine styles, whilst simultaneously being located within schooling institutions that situate them as children (non-male). Research we have carried out suggests that younger boys' gender harassment of girls tends to be overconcerned with breast growth and menstruation (see also Walkerdine 1990; Skelton 1998; Renold 2000; Mac an Ghaill and Haywood 2000). At the same time, the emergence of these cultural signifiers of adulthood in girls and their accompanying anxieties have important implications for the formation of young boys' subjectivities. Further work in this area might investigate these complexities in relation to broader sex/gender regimes.

A further limitation in the sociological literature on English boys is the absence of sexuality. From the 1980s, sexuality has developed a high media and political profile (Durham 1991). In contrast, contemporary English accounts of school masculinities and boyhood tend to downplay issues of sexuality. Where it does appear, sexuality is added on as part of a panacea of analytic tools that include gender, race/ethnicity, class, and age relations. However, the emergence of a discourse of child abuse (Davies and Hunt 1994) alongside the implementation in the early 1990s of Section 28 and the age of consent for homosexual acts has, in part, regenerated the ambivalence surrounding teaching boys.[2] Safety and protection have been invoked as key themes of these debates, resulting in relations between teachers and students taking on sexual significance. Presently, not only are boys discursively constructed as desexualized (not male), but adult masculine sexuality in popular representations is also embodied by perverts, strangers, homosexuals, and child abusers. As a result, teaching practice has come into sharper critical focus, with a range of publicly documented incidents problematizing previously acceptable professional conduct in schools.

In our own research, we have endeavoured to address such limitations. We will focus here on three aspects of post-structuralist theorizing, namely, the imbrication of gender and sexuality in the search for "real" boyness, multiplicity and the making of sexual subjectivity, and finally, inversions and the disruption of the sexual normative. These analytic devices have provided an important stimulus in examining the making of boyhood in English primary and secondary schools.

Explaining English Boys: The Search for "Real" Boyness

In earlier work we have tried to clarify some of the connections between schooling and "proper" gender designations (Haywood and Mac an Ghaill 1995, 1997). Using ethnography, we aimed to analyze some of the ways in which inhabiting particular forms of heterosexual masculinity enables male students to negotiate wider gender relations and the formal and informal cultures of schooling. However, the research does not immediately explain why these "proper" forms of masculinity are heterosexual. A question arises: What is it about occupying "proper" forms of masculinity that almost inevitably implies a heterosexual identity? The answer seems to lie in the fact that, in mainstream contemporary English cultures at least, heterosexuality and gender are profoundly imbricated.

For example, Judith Butler (1993) argues that gender is routinely expressed through a "heterosexual matrix" in which heterosexuality is presupposed in the expression of "real" forms of masculinity or femininity. Thus, she writes:

> Although forms of sexuality do not unilaterally determine gender, a non-causal and non-reductive connection between sexuality and gender is nevertheless crucial to maintain. Precisely because homophobia often operates through the attribution of a damaged, failed, or otherwise abject gender to homosexuals, that is, calling gay men 'feminine' or calling lesbians 'masculine', and because the homophobic terror over performing homosexual acts, where it exists, is often also a terror over losing proper gender ('no longer being a real or proper man' or 'no longer being a real or proper woman'), it seems crucial to retain a theoretical apparatus that will account for how sexuality is regulated through the policing and the shaming of gender. (238)

Eve Kosofsky Sedgwick's (1991) work on changes in Anglo-American male-male relations has begun to fill in some of the historical background to this imbrication of gender and sexuality. She argues that the current exclusion of male-male erotic contact from "proper" forms of masculinity has its origins in an eighteenth-century shift from the religious to the secular discursive construction of sexuality, and that an important consequence of this pervasive and enduring panic over homosexuality has been the fact that homophobia is used to police the boundaries of acceptable heterosexual male behaviour and identity as well as more overtly (and often violently) being used to police homosexual behaviour and identity. Hence, in structuring the attributes of "real" boyness, the various forms of masculinity that are hegemonic in English schools can all be argued to be crucially involved in policing the boundaries of heterosexuality as much as the boundaries of "proper" masculinity.

For example, at an institutional level, English boys' identities are formed in relation to the formal curriculum and the categories it makes available, including the academic/vocational, arts/science, and academic/sporting polarities. Thus, the hard scientific version of cleverness that is validated in school exists in opposition to supposedly soft subjects, like art, music and literature, which are seen as easy options, as essentially frivolous or somehow lacking in due rigour and seriousness. They are, in effect, girlish subjects that are not for "real" boys. Similarly, to be "bad at games" can be read as a cultural index, implying a lack of manly vigour and hinted-at effeminacy, while to be deficient in the core aspects of "laddishness" (in particular school opposition, a certain level of working-class credibility, and interest in football and the pub), is to be a "bit of a poof."

The specificities of the English context are illustrated by Redman and Mac an Ghaill's 1996 article, "Schooling Sexualities: Heterosexual, Schooling and the Unconscious," in which they discuss the experiences of an English student (Peter) in "becoming heterosexual" in an all-boys grammar school in the late 1970s and early 1980s. Using an auto/biographical methodology, they explore the meaning of Peter's investment in a particular form of heterosexual masculinity that they call "muscular intellectualness." They argue that Peter's fascination with the muscular intellectualness he identified in his teacher, Mr. Lefevre, could be understood in terms of the access it promised to give him to the entitlements of conventional masculinity. The world of ideas and knowledge that Mr. Lefevre seemed to inhabit no longer appeared effeminately middle-class and thus the object of ridicule or embarrassment, but powerfully middle-class, a source of personal strength and a means to exercise control over others. Thus, as a source of "real" masculinity, muscular intellectualness "defeminized" academic work in the humanities and refused the label "bit of a poof."

Boyhood Sexuality Speaks Ethnicity, Speaks Class

As we have argued in this chapter, it is important to conceptualize subjectivity as a process of becoming, characterized by fluidity, oppositions, and alliances between particular narrative positions. Subjectivity conveys identity (Davies 1993). It allows a simultaneous relationship between analytic concepts such as age, race/ethnicity, gender, sexuality, and class. This suggests that to understand identities in educational sites, researchers and teachers need to examine the simultaneous articulations of a dispersed and localized shifting nexus of social power. It is in this sense that we need to understand how sexual identities are simultaneously racialized and gendered within specific national and regional institutions.

Sedgwick's work is beginning to question the automatic correspondence of masculinity with the "male sex" (Sedgwick 1995). Part of the analytic project of understanding the making of English boys is not only recognizing the simultaneity of social processes, but starting with the notion that within sociological accounts gender has become interchangeable with biological sex. Such work is questioning conventional social scientific "gender common sense." This shift to a notion not only of floating *signifiers* but also of an unanchored *signified*, may offer an alternative productive account of gender processes. Indeed, English educational research on gender has tended to produce "oversexed" accounts where meanings and behaviours remained inextricably linked to sexed bodies. An interesting absence in the current concerns over the underachievement of boys has been the sociological question, "Which Boys?" Empirically, it can be shown that large proportions of English boys of the non-socially mobile working class have always "failed"—leaving school with low status, low grade qualifications, and a sense of cultural exclusion. However, the historical significance of class has been overlooked and has resulted in a partial, "oversexed" account of English boys' behaviours that are simplistically compared to girls' behaviours. Borrowing Gaten's notion of the "imaginary body," we would argue that what we understand as sex/gender is historically located in cultural contexts:

> Masculinity and femininity as forms of sex appropriate behaviours are manifestations of a historically based, culturally shared phantasy about male and female biologies, and as such sex and gender are not arbitrarily connected. (Gatens 1996, 13)

When we examine masculinities we are localizing the specific way bodies intersect with cultural salience. We would similarly argue that analytically, we can collapse sex/gender distinctions. At the same time, we must acknowledge that masculinity is culturally anchored within a base of "sex." In this way, masculinity can be understood as the cultural register of anatomy.

In earlier research one of us conducted with ethnic minority male students, an issue emerged that illustrated how one category fails to capture the complexity of boys' social and cultural practices. The two main ethnic groups involved were Asians (Indian, Pakistani, and Bangladeshi young men) and African-Caribbeans. At the time (the mid-1980s) there was a racist practice called "paki-bashing," which involved White boys physically and verbally attacking Asian students. A research question emerged: Why was there no African-Caribbean bashing?[3] The research framed behaviour exclusively in terms of racialized social interaction and hence could not resolve this absence in these terms.

It became apparent that racial politics was simultaneously a sexual and gender politics and the research began to highlight how, in the White imagination, Asian boys were constructed as a weak masculinity, in relation to the tough masculinity of the African-Caribbean boys. The usefulness of exploring school boyhoods as cultural differences, spoken through each other, began to link "paki-bashing" with "poofter-bashing," that is, physical and verbal attacks by straight people on gays—another soft masculinity. So, to be a "paki" is to be a "poof" is to be a "non-proper" boy. The notion of multiplicity offers a frame for making some sense of the way boys were policing themselves, particularly within informal peer group cultures and subcultures.

Inversions and the Disruption of the Sexual Normative

Another aspect of post-structuralism that is helpful in rethinking boyhood has been to invert predictable logocentric assumptions that surround the formation of gender/sexual identities appearing in earlier forms of feminist analysis. In her paper "Challenging Masculinity and Using Sexuality," Skeggs (1991) provides a clear illustration of the explanatory power of this theoretical position. Earlier feminist approaches to the formation of identity in educational arenas have positioned females as both subordinated females and students. Skeggs's work on females within a university suggests that being female students did not necessitate a double oppression. Rather, the females in her study were able to contest the dominant institutional gender/sexual hierarchies. For example, the females would openly challenge the teachers' sexuality. In doing so, they repositioned themselves with an active and positive female sexuality and simultaneously challenged the implicit student position as being the object of teaching. Importantly, Skeggs argues that such displays of power by the young females constituted resistance. She suggests that the discursive space won by the females, in contesting the dominant gender/sexual categories, was not a momentary disruption of an all-encompassing, dominant gender/sexual discourse. Rather, the repositioning by the females was an effective means of defending and maintaining their own identities.

Similarly, our work with young Black and Asian gays and lesbians has highlighted their contradictory position within educational arenas that actively proscribe sexuality. As a consequence, the gay students articulated the isolation, confusion, marginalization, and alienation they experienced in a secondary school that privileged a naturalized heterosexuality. However, this account became more complex because their dissonant institutional location also contained a positive and creative experience (Frank 1993). In particular, the gay and lesbian students had an insight into the contradictory constitution of a naturalized heterosexuality that was structured through ambivalent misogyny and homophobia. In this way, gay and lesbian students were able to occupy social locations that allowed the contestation and inversion of heterosexual power. Matthew, a young gay man, illustrates this contestation and inversion:

> The RE teacher said one day in class that teenagers go through a homosexual phase just like earlier on they go through an anti-girls phase....I told him, I did not think that boys go through phases. I said that if boys go through an anti-girl phase, it was a long phase because men were abusing women all of their lives....The teacher went

mad. It was gays that were supposed to be the problem and I turned it round to show the way that it really is.... (Mac an Ghaill 1994a, 168)

Importantly, we have found it productive to make sense of young gays' and lesbians' experiences of marginalization and disempowerment without *necessarily* reverting to a conventional understanding of power, where responses to a naturalized heterosexuality are read as forms of "resistance." An unintended effect of this conventional approach (often called an anti-oppressive framework) is that experience is compressed within a powerful/powerless couplet. In other words, as argued above, there is no empirical, analytical, or theoretical space beyond domination and subordination. In our work with young people, we have found that social relations are in a continual constitutive process. As Foucault (1981) suggests, "Relations of power-knowledge are not static forms of distribution, they are 'matrices of transformations'"(99). In this way, we have to move towards understanding structures and hierarchies as not completely stable and forceful, and as engaged in a process where outcomes are not entirely secured.

Conclusion

Throughout this chapter we have suggested that schools are "masculinity making devices." Within this suggestion, we have argued that the formation of masculinities is nationally and culturally specific. As a result, we have emphasized that boyhood identities do not exist as exclusive categories but are constituted in complex interrelationships with other social and cultural identities. Parallel questions thus emerge: Do the contextual specificities that form and inform the formation of boyhood identities designate and result in contextually specific power relations? Or, does national context simply act as a filter for the mediation of underlying structures of power? These questions have acted as a dynamic for our work by holding onto different definitions of power (Mac an Ghaill 1999). However, this academic work is contextually located at a particular social and historical juncture. It should be noted that studies of school masculinities have the potential to collude with the current backlash against feminism by implicitly suggesting that boys are now the "real victims." Christine Skelton (1998) asks, "What are girls going to get out of the work and effort currently being invested in the focus on boys/masculinities?" (218). In response, we intend that this chapter will build on feminist, gay, and lesbian scholarship and activism, contributing to the political deconstruction of masculinities. We hope that, in turn, this will generate fresh insights into what constitutes young masculinities. More specifically, we have argued for the need to examine heterosexual masculinities critically and, in the process, to destabilize the assumed naturalness and inevitability of sex/gender schooling regimes within national contexts.

Notes

1. OFSTED (Office for Standards in Education) is the statutory regulatory inspectorate of education in England.
2. Clause 28 of the Local Government Bill (later Section 28 of the Local Government Act, 1988) states that a local authority shall not "promote the teaching in any maintained school of the acceptance of homosexuality as a pretended family relationship."
3. State-based forms of institutional discrimination included racial stereotyping of African-Caribbean young men as educationally subnormal, and their criminalization with the introduction of the SUS law that permitted the police to stop and search individuals on the basis of mere suspicion—a law that disproportionately discriminated against these young men.

Chapter 2

"Dangerous Pedagogies":
Exploring Issues of Sexuality and Masculinity in Male Teacher Candidates' Lives

Wayne Martino and Deborah P. Berrill

Introduction

In this chapter we draw on research with two male teacher candidates to explore how issues of sexuality and masculinity affect their lives.[1] We are particularly interested in analyzing how they learn to police their subjectivities and in examining the kinds of norms which govern their self-perceptions and practices as teachers. Although this research is based on a study involving student teachers from both Canada and Australia, we have chosen to focus on two Canadian subjects to highlight some of the significant issues that had an impact on their lives. Hence, we have opted for *depth* rather than *breadth* in reporting on our research for this chapter. The emphasis, therefore, is on examining in detail how notions of self-surveillance and issues of safety feature in these men's lives in terms of setting limits and possibilities for establishing certain kinds of pedagogical relations with students in schools. We draw on interviews to highlight how the fashioning of subjectivity for male teacher candidates is circumscribed by normalizing practices through which specific gendered discourses become mobilized.

Many of the men we interviewed, for instance, felt constrained by what has been termed the limits of "compulsory heterosexuality" (Rich 1980). They talked about their preference to teach in caring, nurturing ways, following pedagogy and practices traditionally associated more with females than with males. As well, they explicitly referred to their own understanding that these ways of relating to students run counter to the dictates of hegemonic heterosexual masculinity (Brod and Kaufman 1994; Frank 1987; Kimmel and Messner 1989; Salisbury and Jackson 1996; Segal 1990; Seidler 1989; Simpson 1994). They felt that these pedagogies and practices could be potentially dangerous for them as future teachers insofar as they might be perceived as sexually suspect for failing to hold tightly to hegemonic masculinities.

This issue was also tied to the need they felt to police their masculinities very carefully for fear of having their sexuality brought into question. They spoke about how this could easily incite the anxiety-provoking and dangerous discourses of sexual perversion and moral deviancy (Epstein and Johnson 1998; Squirrell 1989; Steinberg, Epstein, and Johnson 1997). Several of the male teacher candidates also mentioned that many of their supervising teachers in schools had warned them about being too friendly with students and had advised them never to be alone in a classroom with a student. These issues, we argue, are important and need to be addressed explicitly in pre-service teacher-training courses in universities and professional development programs for teachers.

In light of this focus on the pivotal role that sexuality plays in the policing of male teacher subjectivities, the focus in this chapter is on one gay and one straight male teacher candidate. This juxtapositioning will highlight how regimes of compulsory heterosexuality limit and constrain both straight and gay male teachers. However, we also draw attention to how issues of heterosexual privilege guarantee the straight teacher a position of safety that is unavailable to a gay male subject who is marked within heteronormative regimes as the "deviant other" (Redman 1996). What emerges, therefore, is the investment that heterosexual men have in embodying particular forms of masculinity and the privilege that accrues and is denied to those subordinated males who identify as gay (Connell 1995).

Framing the Issues

Foucault's work (1978; 1988a; 1988b; 1993) was particularly useful in providing us with a framework for understanding the role that sexuality played in how the male student teachers fashioned and policed their masculinities. For instance, Foucault highlights specifically how normalization and practices of self-surveillance operate in the fashioning of subjectivity. His particular theorization of subjectivity draws attention to the function of sexuality in social discourses as a regulatory mechanism for policing the self. It is in this sense that sexuality is treated as

> *a type of normativity and a mode of relation to the self*; it means trying to decipher how in Western societies, a complex experience is constituted from and around certain forms of behaviour: an experience which conjoins a field of study (connaissance) (with its own concepts, theories, diverse disciplines), a collection of rules (which differentiate the permissible from the forbidden, natural from monstrous, normal from pathological, what is decent from what is not, etc.), *a mode of relation between the individual and himself* (which enables him to recognise himself as a sexual subject amid others). [Emphasis added] (Foucault 1984, 333–4)

Foucault emphasizes that he is concerned with investigating the deployment of sexuality within a normalizing regime of practices in which the individual is incited to relate to himself or herself as a particular kind of subject. It is in this sense that the specification of sexual behaviour is tied to disciplinary regimens and apparatuses in which certain concepts, theories, and rules for governing conduct are formed according to an assemblage of historically contingent norms. Thus we are concerned with exploring how particular knowledge and power relations are implicated in the ways in which male student teachers learn to police themselves and to fashion their subjectivities within regimes of compulsory heterosexuality (Rich 1980). In other words, for the men we interviewed the imperative to display themselves as "acceptable" male teachers (e.g., heterosexual, hierarchical, assertive, non-nurturing) was closely tied to the need to consciously fashion a particular form of masculinity (Connell 1995; Nayak and Kehily 1996; Epstein 1997a). In this way, a particular safety net could be established by the male teacher candidates which protected them from being perceived as sexually or morally suspect.

The limits of such normalizing regimes of practice, therefore, are highlighted in relation to exploring the limits of hegemonic heterosexual masculinities (Frank 1987). These are imbricated in the production of a binary of sexuality which demarcates those identifying as non-heterosexual males as deviant and prone to sexually abuse or entrap children. It is in this sense that we examine how the heteronormative imperative to establish a desirable heterosexual masculinity or to pass as straight is driven by anxieties linked to the fear of somehow being seen as sexually suspect and, hence, a danger to children and young people (Epstein and Johnson 1998; Squirrell 1989; Skelton 1994; Steinberg, Epstein, and Johnson 1997).

Therefore, for some male teacher candidates, policing masculinity becomes a survival tactic to avoid attributions of sexual deviancy and, hence, categorization as a pedophile. Thus, learning to be a teacher and the actual practice of teaching are fraught with anxieties for males who are forced to grapple with a certain regime of masculinity organized around the "heterosexual matrix" and, thus, grounded in enforcing a rigid hetero/homo dichotomy of subjectivity (Rubin 1984; Richardson 1996; Britzman 1995; Martino 1999). We intend, therefore, to examine the workings of such practices of normalization and their impact on several male teacher candidates' lives in terms of the dangers that arise for those of them who do not identify as heterosexual, as well as those who wish to interrogate and challenge dominant masculinity. However, we want to stress that even for those teacher candidates who identify as straight, there is always a risk of being seen as suspect if they fail to subscribe to the norms governing what is considered to be acceptable masculine behaviour (Roulston and Mills 2000).

Methodology

A qualitative research methodology deploying semi-structured interviews was used to gather data. The analysis of the data was informed by the Foucauldian framework outlined above (Quinn Patton 1990). The following questions were used as a guideline but they were not always strictly adhered to:

- Can you tell me why you decided to become a teacher?
- What do you see as being some of the major influences affecting you as a teacher in a school/classroom? What are some of the factors impacting on the way you see yourself as a teacher?
- Can you talk about any issues that you perceive to be important for other teachers to understand or reflect on in light of your experience? What do you think prospective student teachers should know and understand about teaching? What advice would you give them?
- What in your view makes an effective teacher?
- Do you think there are any issues which males as teachers specifically have to deal with?
- Are you aware of gender reform programs or approaches to gender reform in schools? Can you talk about these programs?

- What gender issues do you think need to be addressed in schools? Are there issues specifically for boys/girls that need to be addressed?
- How do you define masculinity? What does it mean to you? What do you think it means to other men and male teachers you have met? Based on your experience as a boy growing up and with male students in school, can you talk about how boys learn to define their masculinity?
- Much research has shown that many boys learn to define their masculinity in opposition to femininity. In other words, they denigrate many things that appear to be associated with girls. Has this been your experience of masculinity as a boy growing up? Have you noticed this kind of behaviour in schools?
- What issues arise for male student teachers/teachers/students who identify as non-heterosexual?
- What are some of the issues generally that arise for men in today's society? Do you think these impact on male teachers in any way in schools?

Posing these questions created a space in the interview in which participants could explore issues of masculinity and sexuality in their lives as prospective teachers. Given that no methodology is norm free, we were quite explicit about encouraging the teacher candidates to examine specifically their own understandings of masculinity and how they affected their self-perceptions as teachers and their pedagogical relations with their students.

Sexuality and Safety: Policing the Boundaries of "Appropriate" Teacher Behaviour

The issues involved in policing the boundaries of what is perceived to be acceptable behaviour for male teachers in relating to young children are highlighted by John, aged 21, who is training to be an elementary school teacher.[2] One of his concerns relates to physical contact with young children. This leads him to engage in a practice of self-problematization and surveillance:

> Just yesterday when I was in the kindergarten classroom, by about half way through the day I'd connected with a lot of the children and because the class was very open there was a lot of hugging and things like that and I'm fine with that....[T]hat's a good thing that I'm looking forward to but it's also a worry of mine as well.

>Because I tend to be a little more, I guess, kinesthetic in my way of affection or teaching, I can sort of predict some problems in that area because...nowadays you're not supposed to touch children at all. There's just so many different stipulations around what you're supposed to do around children. *I can see how that might get me in trouble some day because I've always been like a huggy kind of person, very affectionate and warm.* For me, reinforcing a child's behaviour is more than just saying "good job" or whatever, because I'd usually pat them on the head or give them a tap on the arm or something like that. Now of course this can be construed as sexual and *it's being hammered into our heads basically not to do those types of things*, whereas I think they're important for some children—they need that, the touching and the hugging—and I think that's an issue not only for men but for women as well because no one is supposed to do anything, although *it's looked down upon more with men.* I've heard a lot of cases of males going into elementary school systems and being sort of doubted just because of those issues. [Emphasis added]

John's point that it is being "hammered into our heads" not to relate to young children in this physical way highlights the potentially dangerous nature of such a relational and pastoral pedagogy in terms of the wider implications of teachers being charged with sexual impropriety or even just being perceived as sexually suspect (Epstein and Johnson 1998; Skelton 1994). The comment that men are more likely to be *doubted* also draws attention to the intensification of anxieties produced within such discourses in which links are forged between the policing of masculinity, self-surveillance, and the avoidance of sexual deviancy. To transgress the boundaries of acceptable masculinity in schools risks attributions of not only homosexuality, but by extension, sexual deviancy. John, who identifies as gay, is aware of the dangerous and explosive nature of declaring his sexuality as a male teacher. Epstein (1997b) highlighted the consequences of such a declaration for one Head of School in the United Kingdom, who was attacked for being a lesbian and for commenting that *Romeo and Juliet* is "exclusively heterosexual" (Epstein and Johnson 1998, 31; 1997b). Epstein and Johnson (1998) also highlighted the moral panic fuelled by the media and parliamentarians over addressing issues of sexuality in schools. In fact, this regulation of social subjectivities by public discourses mobilized by the media and certain parents features prominently in the lives of many of the student teachers we interviewed in Canada and Australia (Berrill and Martino 2002). The New Right agenda in the United Kingdom and elsewhere, as pointed out by Epstein and

Johnson, has led the imperative to inculcate a particular moral order in schools that is grounded in practices of normalization, stigmatization, and a repudiation of the "monstrous other" who often emerges as the threatening non-heterosexual subject (28).

The effects of such a conservative and traditionalist moral order committed to preserving an ideal, romanticized version of the family as nuclear and heterosexual emerges in the interview with John, who identifies as gay. This is highlighted below, particularly when he starts to consider whether he will need to balance carefully the public and private dimensions of his life as a teacher.

Wayne: Do you think that there might be some risks for you [in being open about your sexuality]?

John: Yes, there's definitely some risks. Well, there's been a lot of problems in my head lately about how I'm going to confront those issues with students and parents and faculty members. *Whether I'm going to openly be gay in the school or sort of keep it as my own personal life, or sort of do a mix of the two.* Like not really have the staff know but not really advocate to the children but allow the parents...like I don't know if I want to balance it out. It's really kind of confusing how I'm supposed to get those things across. Another thing, if I'm supposed to, because I'm just wondering whether there's going to be...issues with other faculty members saying *that certain things are inappropriate.* I don't know what to expect really, I'm going to have to wait till I get there and see how I'm going to go. And then it also depends on if I have a stable partner at the time—you know, if I'm going to be inviting him in...or...going out for lunches and things and he's going to pick me up or if he might show up once in a while. That could sort of change my ideas as well. [Emphasis added]

On one level, John is concerned about trying to establish a particular comfort level with students and colleagues at school based on an awareness of the potentially dangerous implications of occupying a stigmatized sexual status within a homophobic society in which he runs the risk of being categorized as a sexual deviant and, hence, the "monstrous other" (Steinberg, Epstein, and Johnson 1997). Thus, later in his interview he talks about the need to present himself as a "normal person," despite the fact that, and especially because, he identifies as gay:

John: Yes, I would say so just because most of the teachers that I've been in the classroom with haven't really discussed their partners much at all. But every now and then they do and I realize that they feel comfortable about it and they can if they want to. Their partner can show up in the classroom if they want to and help out a little bit or pick them up for lunch, something like that, and there's no problems. Whereas I'd just like to...if I could, establish the same sort of *comfort level* with a gay partner, and just be able to have the school sort of be accepting. I realize that it's not, or it might be, but I'm sort of predicting the worst case scenario that it's not going to be good. I guess I'm just going to have to be willing to fight that, maybe not even fight it but just sort of work my way in and show them that, look, *just because I'm gay doesn't mean it's all messed up and I'm psycho or something.* [Emphasis added]

Wayne: So do you intend communicating to students your sexual identity? Do you see that as happening?

John: I don't know, that's a really, really sticky sort of area. I really don't know what I'm going to do about it. I'm planning on trying to talk to more homosexual men in...a school setting and see what they've been doing. Because I know...I've been talking to my uncle more and he teaches Grade 7 and 8, so they're a little older, but he hides his sexuality from them. He says that he doesn't feel it's as important to get those things across but I think in the same sense he's kind of hurt that he can't discuss...issues from home....There isn't that comfort level; there's always that area that you can only tell so much and then once you get to that line you can't go any further. I don't think that's really very fair to the teacher at all....I don't know if it's created by the teacher, or by the students, or a little bit of both, or the faculty itself. I can see how some teachers would create the line themselves and I guess I'm just hoping that I can cross that line and it won't be so hard. But, I don't know, I'd really like to think that it wouldn't be much of an issue and especially with younger children—I think that they're much more open to issues. They're not [that way] to start with...but once you get them used to something it doesn't become an issue anymore. So I

> think I'd really like to cross that barrier, *present myself as just a normal person and maintain that comfort level in the classroom.* Once I've established...a long-term partner, just sort of be able to say, "Well, so and so is coming in and blah, blah, blah, or when he shows up just be, like, "Oh, class, this is so and so." ...I don't necessarily have to be like, "Oh, we've been together for blah, blah, blah" because that's not appropriate either. I don't mean to throw it in their faces but I'd like to have the comfort level just to be able to say, "This [is] so and so, we're just heading out, blah, blah, blah." [Emphasis added]

These kinds of reflections appear to be motivated, on one level, by the imperative John feels to challenge the very public regulation of his sexuality as deviant or pathologized and, hence, the implication that he has a predisposition to indecent and morally illicit behaviour. He wants to work carefully, therefore, to present himself as a "normal person" and not a sexual deviant to avoid potentially disruptive situations in his classroom. However, when asked to consider how parents might respond to him as a gay teacher, he becomes worried.

> John: I guess *one of the big worries is parents pulling kids out of the classroom just because of that.* I think that would be a huge offence, I think I'd definitely get upset over that. One of the big problems I can see is that I don't really like this city much at all. I don't know if that's just because I've always grown up in the middle of nowhere, or if I just don't like it. But I don't think I want to teach in the city setting; I think I want to teach in a small town which could also add a lot more problems to it because, I don't know, just from growing up in a small town...it's very, very closed-minded and not so open to new ideas, and change isn't really very good. I can just see some problems there. I'd like to be the one to show them change and that it doesn't have to be so disruptive and upsetting. It can just happen and it can be comfortable—you don't have to worry about things being all scary. I don't know, I just worry that the parents would be really upset and take their children out of my classroom. I don't think that would be fair to the children at all because I think I'd have a lot to give to the children, a lot to teach them. [Emphasis added]

Wayne: So why would they withdraw them, what would drive them to withdraw them from your class?

John: I think the fear of, ridiculous as it is, ...[of] conversion or whatever. Just my influence on the children may make them lean towards...a gay way of life or something like that. I don't know. Just sort of that concept...and, again, the sexual part of it as well I think. That *they'd be worried just because I'm...a male but also maybe because I'm gay as well, that there'd be problems with sexual abuse and things like that*. Like, to me these things seem ridiculous but I'm just creating a lot of scenarios in my own head I think. [Emphasis added]

John is drawing attention to the links between gay sexuality and deviancy—that just because he identifies as gay, the assumption immediately would be that he is predisposed to sexually abusing children. So "coming out" in school can be potentially dangerous for teachers in terms of how such public discourses might be mobilized to cast aspersions on John's integrity as a teacher. It is such an awareness of the ways in which a demarcation between heterosexuality and homosexuality is regulated through the superimposition of binary classifications such as natural/pathological and normal/abnormal that leads this teacher candidate to engage in these practices of self-problematization and regulation. Epstein and Johnson (1998) highlight that "teachers' sexual identity is connected to the role of 'moral guardian,'" which is built on the heterosexual, traditionalist imperative to preserve family values (123). Moreover, as a result of the panoptic surveillance of schools by the media, parents, and politicians, sexuality becomes dangerous terrain for teachers, who risk discrimination on the basis of being perceived as morally suspect. This risk is highlighted when John mentions public reporting by the media of sexual impropriety in schools:

John: [I have] my own preconceptions and my own ideas go wild and create these situations and things that are just awful. I heard some stories through the news and things like that where they just seem to be carried away.

Wayne: Like?

John: Well, I have heard...some stories. There's a school near my house—actually the principal was molesting a younger boy and that sort of threw the whole area into a big, big uproar for quite a while. It kind of re-establishes a lot of those homo-

	phobic ideas and stereotypes and things, sort of makes a lot of people, I think, sort of makes them stronger. They start to believe those things a little more when something like that happens.
Wayne:	They believe what in particular?
John:	They still *have these ideas that the gay people are more likely to do that kind of thing.* [Emphasis added]

So the issue of safety emerges strongly for John as he contemplates how his sexuality will affect his life as a student teacher in an elementary school.

John:	As a student teacher, I'd say there's a lot of stress going into the job, a lot of unknowns as to what you're going to encounter and how bad or how good it could be. There is definitely a lot of doubt as to...how good it could be. If you're definitely, I am at least, prone to see the worst situations, create those in your own head so that when you do get in the position if something good comes out of it then you can appreciate it because you were expecting something awful, and if the awful does happen, at least you are already thinking of it. It's kind of a nasty way to look at things but to me *it seems like the safer* [*way*]. I'd also say as a student teacher it's rather difficult sometimes working with a teacher in their classroom because then you have yet another person thrown into the mix who could have problems with your sexuality. If it does become an issue it could also become an issue with that person as well and you could have, I guess, repercussions from that side as well—from not only the students and parents and faculty but also someone who you are working with...directly at the time, and another thing, someone who is grading your performance as a teacher. That could be a very big influence on you, so...in a way I think it could really make you work harder not expressing any of those feelings or anything about your sexuality in fear of repercussions from the actual teacher themselves, in grading or just in maybe even sort of doubting your teaching styles just because of that. [Emphasis added]
Wayne:	So it could be used to discriminate against you in some way.

John: Which could really hinder the student teacher, I would think, in their confidence of becoming a teacher because someone could just be going on personal lies and personal fears and be using that to tell someone that they're not doing a very good job....

This awareness of such practices of normalization, however, also leads John to police his own masculinity and to undertake a particular kind of surveillance of himself to avoid having his sexuality questioned and, hence, to protect himself.

John: There's a little bit of a worry there about stereotypical ideas of...males in school systems—I know that those things can be deconstructed fairly quickly with other adults but it's different in schools. I think that they would just assume...[with] a male coming in, "Oh, he'll take over the sports and blah, blah, blah." I love baseball—I'm a totally top coach of the baseball team—but basically any other sport, no, I don't think so. I don't know if they'd have any problems with any of the other things I'd be interested in maybe running, like an arts group or something like that, or taking trips to see plays and things like that. I'm pretty sure they'd be fine with things like that but *there's always these little things in the back of my head that say basically watch out for voicing some of your interests, just to make sure, sort of like test the waters first.* I guess that's always been a tactic, you just sort of grow up feeling that way and you always have to test the water where you're going and make sure that how you're feeling and your interests are going to be accepted before you even mention anything, which is kind of a sad way to go about it. You should be able to just talk about your interests and bring things up immediately, but it's sort of become like *a survival kind of tactic* I guess. [Emphasis added]

To survive in schools, therefore, it would appear that male teachers feel that they are expected to display an acceptable masculine pedagogy, one which fits within heteronormative frames for acting appropriately masculine (see Mills 2000; Roulston and Mills 2000). This is because failing to meet the expectations of others at schools in terms of how males should behave carries with it the risk of one's sexuality being questioned and pathologized. In particular, gay males are perceived to be morally suspect and, hence, a danger to children. For instance, Epstein and Johnson (1998) argue:

> Any revelation about same sex relationships outside school presents a potential threat to the job of the teacher concerned. This is not the case for heterosexual relationships where the levels of transgression, especially for men, would have to be extreme, probably even illegal, outside connections to the school. (124)

This is particularly noteworthy given that a study by Jenny, Roeseler, and Poyer (1994) found that 82 percent of accused abusers were heterosexual males (Weems 1999). However, it needs to be reiterated that dominant masculinities are heavily policed and grounded in anxiety-provoking discourses founded on a misogynist and homophobic repudiation of the feminine and deviant "other," which informs a rejection of a pedagogy of caring and nurturing (Buchbinder 1994; Mac an Ghaill 1994a; Connell 1995; Plummer 1999). In this sense, sexuality plays a key role in the panoptic surveillance and regulation of masculinities in the lives of the male student teachers we interviewed, particularly given the highly charged rhetoric informing media scandals about homosexuality and sexual impropriety of male teachers in schools.

Normalization and the Production of Masculinity

This emphasis on public surveillance and moral regulation was also discussed by another teacher candidate—Chris, aged 22, who identified as straight. He specifically mentioned the power of parents to incite a moral panic in executing a form of panoptic surveillance of teachers who choose or wish to address issues of sexuality in schools.

Chris: So, really when you're talking about sexuality, I see all the time this myth that older men are trying to recruit younger men into this sort of brotherhood of homosexuality, and it's just ridiculous. But at the same time, I think depending on which board you're with, it's a reality that you have to deal with when you start talking about sexuality. A lot of parents are very uneasy about that and don't want the option presented at all. Because really, I don't know how things are elsewhere but, in Ontario, especially in the board that I live in...there is a family action coalition so I really know whenever the word "family" is used what it means. And they're adamantly opposed even to the word "homosexuality" being mentioned because they're just desperately afraid of it for some reason. Even to present it as an option sort of gets you into this recruitment myth that you're trying to pull young boys and girls off the track, or whatever, into this. It's amazing because I just think about the silence that was given homosexuality in my high school experience, the act of love between two men or between two women was really not even mentioned. For me, I sort of breezed through a good portion of high school without really thinking about it. It's just like, well, if I go there, I'm just going to be lost in this void. Homosexuality doesn't exist in high school yet, it's not there.

Chris talks at length about the dangers involved for teachers who choose to address issues of homosexuality with their students at school. The homophobia surfaces in the form of an accusation that the teacher is trying to recruit or convert students to become homosexual. Although, on a rational level, Chris asserts that "it's just ridiculous," parents embody for him a powerful threat to a teacher's well-being and professional integrity. He elaborates on this in his reference to the role played by parents in their capacity to dictate what a teacher teaches at school.

Chris: Parents have a lot of power by just talking to the principal if they find out that teachers are teaching this stuff. It's very rare that a principal will just say, "Okay, now we've said goodbye to the parents and you just keep doing what you are doing, you're doing a great job." They're very interested in pleasing the customers and education is quickly becoming a business in Ontario for sure, so the parents are definitely in a customer role and are always right. They dictate the terms. They don't even want teaching about homosexuality to be an option, they don't want it to happen. It's amazing.

Chris is highlighting how the power of parents has been mobilized to an even greater degree within wider socio-political and economic forces which have led schools to become designated as marketplaces. The implications are that the customer who pays has certain rights and can make particular demands on schools. This, in turn, has implications for what appears to be the ongoing resurgence of a new Rightist or neo-conservative public discourse grounded in a traditonalist conception of family and parenthood (Epstein and Johnson 1998). The power of the media and parliamentarians to activate such discourses and their capacity to affect the moral surveillance and regulation of teachers' practices and subjectivities in schools are significant factors in determining thresholds of safety in executing particular pedagogies.

However, in terms of discussing the way he wants to relate to his students as a male teacher in a secondary school, Chris is committed to repudiating the performativity of normalized masculinity.

Chris: When I think about being a male teacher, I see the importance of masculinity and that there will be a lot of young males who will look to me as a sort of grown-up version of themselves, which I don't really buy into at all. But I'm aware that a lot of young kids want that, young boys want a role model or whatever and many don't have that elsewhere. But, even when I get to thinking about that, I feel like there are certain concessions I have to make to masculinity to be this role model—like I have to be coach somewhere in a school or something like that. So it's funny, because I'm running into it with my younger brother because I feel like for him to respect me—because he wants older males to look up to, and a lot of the older males he looks up to are real arseholes—I really have to be very interested in hockey....Not that I don't express interest but it seems like I have to play this role where I'm the big man who happens to be also a nice guy. I don't know, it's all such a confusing mess. I don't think it means that much to me except psychologically, and the psychology or the biology [or] whatever is almost something that I'm trying in my life to surpass, to untie myself from that.

Wayne: Interesting. It seems to me that you're torn somewhat between what you think is expected of you as a male or what younger boys might expect of you as a male, as opposed to what you want to be as a male.

Chris: Yes, and I think that in life I am pretty much what I want to be as a male. *As a teacher there are these issues of accountability, that I obviously have to be aware of the way that I present myself and it's a little bit nerve-racking because I don't like the idea....I mean in some ways I definitely want to be accountable to my students as far as the relationship that we have in our classroom and everything, but in the end with regards to my personal feelings about masculinity or whatever, it really annoys me that I'm going to have the family action coalition on my back and no one will be there on the board to support me.* [Emphasis added]

Wayne: What did you mean when you said you have to be aware of the way you present yourself?

Chris: Well, in taking a somewhat public position I suppose then I'll have to act accordingly as someone who is under the watchful eye of 120 students a year, or a semester, and maybe twice as many parents—that I will have to modify my behaviour....I guess, fortunately, as far as how I live up to gender expectations or whatever, I have these sorts of things that people often portray....Like I have a deep voice or whatever; I'm like all the things I am supposed to be. That sounds conceited.

Once again, the way in which Chris fashions his masculinity is situated within a wider social network of panoptic surveillance and self-regulation. He engages in practices of self-problematization in attempting to deconstruct the impact of dominant masculinity in his own life. He is conscious of not wanting to model this kind of masculinity for his younger brother and the students he will teach in high school, but appears to be claiming that this is the very masculinity that they find desirable and to which they subscribe. It is interesting how Chris is aware of the need to modify his behaviour under the normalizing gaze of his students and parents and to perform a masculinity that will not call into question his sexuality or practices as a male teacher in any way. In this sense, he highlights that failing to measure up to the norms of dominant normalized masculinity can also be dangerous in schools because it may provoke anxiety and homophobic denigration, which, of course, has its costs for teachers. In fact, Chris reflects at length on how he performs a hegemonic masculinity, the effects of which are to create a certain "comfort level" and degree of safety in executing what might otherwise be considered a potentially dangerous pedagogy.

Chris: I think that I fit into masculinity in some ways initially that probably set a lot of people at ease. So I guess I'm fortunate, if that's the right word, in that sense. Because if I was very flighty, like immediately there wouldn't be a sort of bridge between masculine and feminine behaviour and a lot of teachers would be, like, "Oh, is he married?" and they'd question my sexuality. But I think I've got a bit of a head start because although I don't ever see myself getting married at this stage or anything, probably I will be in a heterosexual relationship. So I feel it's a sick way to look at it but I feel like I've almost got more credibility. I hate that, but I feel like, if that's my privilege, I'd rather not feel guilty about being in a heterosexual relationship. I'd rather understand my privilege and use it.

Hence, the policing of masculinity is considered essential because apparently once a male crosses over the masculine boundary and enters territory traditionally considered to be the domain of the feminine, he is immediately perceived to be suspect. Chris seems to think that a failure to perform a normalized masculinity would prevent him from doing some of the important work around deconstucting gender regimes with his students. This raises certain issues about heterosexual privilege and the normalizing tendencies built into his embodiment and fashioning of heterosexual masculinity. For instance, as Redman (1996) argues, it is important to address "the investment, both conscious and unconscious, that heterosexual men and boys have in the forms of masculinity that they occupy" (166). What is Chris's investment as a straight teacher in challenging heteromasculinity and what might be the unintended effects on students of his commitment to do so? For example, Chris is able to escape a certain vulnerabilty and threat through embodying a particular form of heteronormative masculinity. However, this does not mean that the very homophobic discourses requiring him to consciously fashion such a normalized heteromasculinity in the first place necessarily will be questioned or challenged. In taking up such a position, to what extent will he be able or willing to challenge the very discourses that generate a hysterical fear and moral panic around the potential threat of gay men impinging on the moral and physical well-being of students placed in their care? Furthermore, although Chris wants to provide a particular role model for his students, how might such a fashioning of heterosexual masculinity affect those boys who themselves embody masculinity "differently" and, who, on the basis of this "difference," risk becoming the target of homophobic surveillance and harassment? These remain very important issues for educators to consider. In short, it is important to remember that one of the unintended effects of a commitment to using one's heterosexual privilege to challenge dominant masculinities might be an unconscious reinforcement of the heteronormative status quo.

It is noteworthy that Chris sees himself as using his power and privilege in a productive way to assist students to interrogate dominant constructions of gender in their lives. For example, he states that he is committed to "gender treachery."

Chris: Well, I think that if I can do anything as a teacher in terms of gender, I just really want to open things up because I think that as much as the girls act like girls and boys act like boys, they're not. I think there will be in every classroom many anomalies and I never used to think of anomalies, but I think the differences between one girl and the next girl can be somewhat wider than the differences between boys and girls generally. I guess I want to be able to make students comfortable enough so that I can say, "Here, look this is gender treachery" or whatever. I think Margaret Atwood uses that term. And just make a place that's comfortable enough to say that treachery is okay, it won't be punished here, and just make people aware. Because it's not as if I'd be introducing some kind of alien element to the class....I just really want to encourage students who are already subverting gender ideas, gender dichotomy or whatever, and just show it myself and applaud it....I'm not going to be trying to change them—of course I will be—but I'm not going to be giving these new units and everybody is like, "Wow!" I'm just going to work with what's there and not be, "Now, now students, you shouldn't be doing that," [or] whatever. I just don't want to deal with the negative so much. I don't want to deal with "Don't you see how typical your behaviour is?", or whatever, varying degrees of that. I think I'd like to be more positive about the times when people sort of slip out of the role that they're supposed to play and to try to be subversive about what people are most comfortable and to make them more comfortable with a wider range of behaviour. I think that's where I have to go to make it successful.

So Chris positions himself as a classroom strategist (Patterson 1997) in helping students to subvert regimes of normalization and dichotomous classifications of gender (see Martino and Pallotta-Chiarolli 2001; 2003). What is interesting here, though, is the unquestioned assumption that he can achieve such "gender treachery" only by embodying a heterosexual masculinity that will apparently remove him from the homophobic gaze and, hence, surveillance by his students and their parents.

> Chris: I think that I feel I just happen to be in a position of power, being, I guess, heterosexual identified and fitting into a certain mould. I think that I feel safe in a lot of ways in terms of my personal self, my physical self. And, in that sense, I definitely want to be able to use that and to also avoid being blind to whether it's issues of sexuality or if it's race as well....I just want to be able to use that and be also aware, always questioning, and never be completely comfortable with being a straight, White male because it's completely privileged to be comfortable. I think I want to always be looking at that and questioning it in the way that a gay male teacher will always be questioned with everything. And then in terms of the curriculum and my personal relations with students or whatever, with my English curriculum, with anything that I do with history, I really want to work against this sort of invisibility, that I have this sort of perspective on alternative cultures and lifestyles or whatever and just allow students to explore the outside without fearing that they're just going to fall [off] the edge or something and be forgotten....I want to make them aware that there are things that lie outside of their field of reference I guess. I think I'd be in a good position to do that.

Ultimately, Chris has come to a realization that, given the nature of homophobia and the heteronormative frames of reference through which gender regimes are operationalized, he can achieve much as a result of the way he embodies and enacts a particular form of masculinity. Consequently, he feels safe in undertaking a strategic pedagogical practice committed to encouraging students to subvert and to deconstruct gender regimes in their lives. In other words, in performing the kind of masculinity he performs, he does not immediately run the risk of being seen as sexually suspect, and hence, morally depraved. In this sense, he believes that he is in a position to use his privilege as a White heterosexual male—a position of safety in schools—to interrogate the impact and effects of normalization and gender with his students at school. But the extent to which he is able to challenge those homophobic discourses that led him to assert such a form of masculinity in the first place is still a crucial question that remains unanswered. As stated earlier, there needs to be further problematization of the effects of the embodiment of such normalized constructions of masculinity by straight teachers, particularly for those boys in school who do not fashion their masculinity in this way. In this sense, the question of how a straight teacher might break out of his own privilege to work for change is one that requires further investigation.

Implications of the Research

This research has major implications for placing gender and issues of sexuality on the agenda in teacher education institutions. Moreover, we believe that matters such as those discussed in this chapter need to be the subject of professional development for teachers and school administrators (Letts and Sears 1999). Such a focus for education and professional development is even more imperative given the current educational and political climate in the United Kingdom, Australia, and North America, where concerns about boys and masculinities are being fuelled by an anti-feminist backlash rhetoric that advocates the need for more male role models in schools to address the problems that boys are experiencing.[3] As Mills (2000) points out,

> One of the issues raised in boys' programs is the place of male teachers in a boy's education. Central to mythopoetic politics is the importance of men in boys' lives (Bly 1991; Biddulph 1995, 1997; Fletcher 1995: for critical assessments of such politics see Connell 1995; Kenway 1995, 1996; Kimmel 1995; Mills and Lingard 1997; Gilbert and Gilbert 1998; Lingard and Douglas 1999)....It is also regularly raised as an issue in newspapers. This can be seen in some recent headlines which suggest that men are being driven away from teaching: "Wanted: male teachers" (Meryant 14 March, 1996); "Men and young shun teaching, principals told" (Aldred and Butler 5 October, 1996); "It's goodbye Mr Chips: guys give our schools a miss" (Griffith 12 January, 1997); "No panic, guys, kiddies need you—lecturer" (O'Chee 20 February, 1997); and "Even fewer men on the roll" (O'Chee 27 November, 1997). One of the dominant arguments found within such sources is that boys need more male role models. This is often founded upon either the belief that school has become feminised domain, causing boys to miss out on acquiring the discipline necessary to control their disruptive behaviour, or

the interrelated belief that the education of boys is a form of men's business. (224)

Thus, as Mills illustrates, in much the same way as it regulates and polices social and sexual identities (Epstein and Johnson 1998), the media also has a significant role to play in promoting the view that schools have been colonized by a feminist or feminizing agenda, or both, which has driven males out of schools or prevented them from choosing teaching as a career. This has led, he argues, to the call for more male role models in schools to address the problems that boys are experiencing (Capp 2000). However, as Mills correctly points out, certain assumptions about masculinity and the kinds of male role models considered suitable to undertake this kind of work with boys have not been made explicit and, indeed, have proven to be quite troubling. This is because the very models of masculinity advocated are those which lead to the reinscription and reinforcement of certain problematic behaviours and gendered social practices for males. These are practices that leave unquestioned the role that issues such as sexuality, homophobia, the denigration of the feminine, and ethnocentrism play in the production of hegemonic heterosexual masculinities (Frank 1987; Connell 1995; Roulston and Mills 2000).

A more informed perspective on the issues facing male teachers in schools is needed—one based on an understanding of the workings of such models of masculinity. This need has been highlighted in this chapter's focus on the ways in which sexuality is deployed to police not only the limits of masculinity, but also the social and teaching practices that are perceived to be acceptable and safe given the nature of institutionalized homophobia and heterosexism. Unless these matters are addressed and discussed in schools and teacher education institutions, the ways in which hegemonic masculinities and compulsory sexuality function to detrimentally affect the social and pedagogical practices and career choices of males will persist.

Conclusion

In this chapter we have drawn on our research with male student teachers to highlight some important issues related to the impact of masculinities and sexuality on male student teachers' professional lives. Although there is a call for more male teachers and male teacher role models, particularly in elementary schools, our research suggests that very little will change in schools unless the influence of hegemonic heterosexual masculinities is examined in male teachers' lives, especially its capacity to set the limits of acceptable pedagogical practices and relations with students. Unless such models of masculinity are actively interrogated by schools, teacher education faculties, and male teachers themselves, any attempt to address the social and educational issues facing boys will not be successful. This is because the anxiety-provoking discourses of sexual abuse and pedophilia that function to police the kinds of student-teacher relations that are deemed acceptable for male teachers in schools are deployed within a wider regime of public and media surveillance to make the kind of pastoral pedagogies we are advocating dangerous and transgressive practices. However, based on our research with student teachers in both Canada and Australia, we have concluded that many men realize the limits of such models of masculinity, are aware of the need to interrogate these regimes of masculinity in schools, and are willing to do so.

Notes

1. This research was funded by a Special Australian Research Council Grant and involved interviewing six teacher candidates in Ontario, Canada who were part of a sexualities/masculinities discussion group organized by Deborah at Trent University. Teacher candidates from Murdoch University in Perth, Western Australia, were also interviewed, but those interviews are not utilized in this chapter.
2. Pseudonyms are used for the teacher candidates.
3. For critiques of these positions, see Martino and Meyenn 2001; Epstein et al. 1998; Lingard and Douglas 1999; Kenway 1995; Yates 1997; Pallotta-Chiarolli 1997.

Acknowledgment: We would like to thank Blye Frank and Kevin Davison for their invaluable feedback on earlier drafts of this chapter.

Chapter 3

On a Knife's Edge:
Masculinity in Black Working-Class Schools in Post-Apartheid Education

Robert Morrell

Introduction

Gender relations and identities change. Masculinities change. But how, where, and with what consequences? This chapter addresses these questions by examining aspects of the South African education system. It will demonstrate that important policy shifts have given gender equality a high profile but that, at the same time, levels of school violence associated with violent masculinities have remained high. This paradox will be examined in the light of evidence of how the policy shifts have affected Black working-class learners. School masculinities still contain strong misogynistic, homophobic, and violent elements; but importantly, they also contain the seeds of change. Whether the potential for change is realized is balanced on a knife's edge.

Since 1994, when a new African National Congress (ANC)-dominated government was elected, gender equity has been prominent in policies and laws. Education policy has reflected the commitment to gender transformation and schools have been the sites of state-sponsored interventions.

The boys whose voices are heard in this chapter attend fairly well resourced urban schools. Most of the boys are African and come from working-class families. They have escaped the township schools set up under Bantu Education for exclusive African use and are among the lucky few to gain access to former White schools. Yet the schools they attend have close similarities to township schools in terms of gender relations and ethos. These township schools, which serve predominantly working-class African children are considered, rightly or wrongly, to be places where little learning takes place, where crime is rampant, and where levels of violence are high. Such environments are not gender friendly (Morrell and Moletsane 2002). In these schools, hegemonic forms of masculinity are frequently associated with misogyny, homophobia, authoritarianism, and compulsory heterosexuality (Deacon, Morrell and Prinsloo 1999).

The identification of schools as sites of violence and gender inequality has caused non-oppressive features of masculinity and gender discourses to be ignored. The gaze has been so fixed upon violence that non-violent men and non-violent masculinities have effectively been overlooked.

In South Africa, especially in its transitional state, the balance between hegemonic and subordinate masculinities is particularly precarious and unpredictable. Shifts in the material and political conditions of the country produce contradictory effects on gender relations. On the one hand, political liberation has brought a Black ruling class to power. Race, as a formal mark of inferiority and rightlessness, has been redeemed and now is a major part of a discourse of national redress and citizenship. On the other hand, globalization has pushed the economy into a neo-liberal direction where previous ANC and government commitments to a redistributive socialist or welfare economy have been watered down and economic growth has faltered. In this context, constructions of masculinity are in a state of profound flux. The nature of hegemonic masculinity itself is in question. Being Black no longer automatically excludes a man from power and thus no longer obliges him to select a subject position from within oppositional, submissive, or complicit masculinity discourses. By contrast, the decline of the working class and the limited prospects of getting work have threatened the emergence of new masculinities that have wage earning as a central component.

The fluidity of broader society demands a particular vigilance when assessing the state of masculinity. A change in the social landscape is likely to affect gender configurations. In this chapter, a detailed analysis of school-based discussions reveals how violent and racialized constructions of masculinity coexist with communitarian and humanistic values, suggesting the possible emergence of alternative, non-hegemonic masculinities.

To put the school conversations of the late 1990s discussed below into context, I went back to the voices of young African boys living in townships during the 1980s. This was a period of dark repression. Virtually all township schools experienced direct forms of repressive state action—invasion by police and the closing down of schools were common. It therefore comes as some surprise to find that, in this period, not all masculinities were oriented towards the struggle to overthrow apartheid. Not all young students were in the streets throwing rocks at caspirs and thinking of nothing else than the vanquishing of the White supremacist state. Reflecting on both the poverty of their circumstances and the political turmoil of the time, a number of Soweto schoolchildren expressed their dreams for a new South Africa during the state of emergency in 1985. Mokgethi (aged 13) wrote about "Freedom in South Africa":

> People must all be educated and be filled with knowledge so that they can communicate with other countries. We must all work hard to keep Azania shining we beatiful things, and we must help one another as one nation. There must be no hating one another because God likes to see his children loving one another.... (Open School 1986, 42)

But the message of hope was most poignantly stated by Moagi (aged 8):

> When I am old I would like to have a wife and to children a boy and a girl and a big house and to dogs and freedom. My friends and I would like to meat together and tok (Open School 1986, 54–5).

These testimonies were generated in violent and poverty-stricken contexts. They remind us that the simple association of Black working-class boys with criminal or political violence is misleading. They also remind us that change can occur in the most unlikely places.

African Youth, Schooling and Violent Masculinities

Young African men rarely experienced schooling until 1955, when Bantu Education made it compulsory for Africans to attend state schools. These schools were inadequately resourced and the quality of education was poor. More importantly, a fundamental pedagogy was the norm, instilling in boys the idea of an absolute truth and authority outside of themselves. Bantu Education also taught ethnic particularism and racial inferiority. It relied heavily on corporal punishment.

Young Lions and Marginalized Youth

From 1976 onward, the nation's youth (which normally meant young African men of school age, although the term sometimes is extended to refer to men in their early thirties) took centre stage in national politics. Protests, school boycotts, and violent state repression became widespread and increasingly intense after the Soweto student uprising. "The comrades" emerged as heroes in this process. Called "young lions" in the media and by many UDF/ANC supporters (including Winnie Madikizela Mandela), they were presented as heroes, pursuing the noble goal of effecting social justice and an end to apartheid (Nkosi 1987). The research that examined this period reflected the scholars' militant engagement with the struggle against apartheid. Descriptions of the period analyzed the social origins of "the comrades" and charted their activities. Gender seldom received attention and violence was accepted as unproblematical (Everatt and Sisulu 1992; Hirson 1979; Hyslop 1999; Seekings 1993; Sitas 1991).

The gradual exposure of the violence that accompanied these struggles (particularly the murder of ten-year-old Stompie Seipei by members of the Mandela Football Club in 1989) led to a change of emphasis in the representation of, and research into, youth (Freund 1996). In the 1990s, the decline in political violence and the rise in the prominence of the now legal ANC in national politics led to the demise of "the comrades." Instead of being soldiers of the revolution, they were considered "the lost generation." They rapidly lost political influence and, with the education system still in an unreformed condition, many saw little reason to study and turned to crime (Xaba 2001). The spotlight fell on the sexual violence of gangs called "jackrollers" (Mokwena 1991) and on the activities of other anti-social gangs (Pinnock 1997). Youth were now considered to be "a problem." Dissenting views that pointed out the complexity of the situation (Marks 2001) could not escape the fact that African youth *in* school were doing badly (as evidenced by very high drop-out rates and poor matriculation performance) and that those *out* of school were often engaged in crime.

Some scholars attempted to rescue the youth from the condescension of the present. Linda Chisholm and her colleagues (1996) found that African school-leavers tended to find gainful employment, but only after five years. Valerie Moller (1990) discovered that the stereotype of loutish and violent youth needed to be qualified and that many young people were involved in a variety of club activities. And, in pioneering work, Crispin Hemson (2001) began to suggest that the apparent cul de sac of township life could be escaped by taking avenues that led into new areas of life previously blocked off to Blacks. He argued that such an escape was associated with the development of a more responsible and confident masculinity.

However, violence was identified by the state-appointed Gender Equity Task Team as a major problem for safe schools and for achieving the goal of gender equity (Wolpe, Quinlan, and Martinez 1997). Morrell (1998b) associated the violence with the prevalence of violent school masculinities. The masculinities forged by urban African township dwellers, both young and older men, have been characterized by misogynism (Mager 1998; Ratele 2001). Rob Pattman (2001) shows that even amongst teachers in training (in a Zimbabwean teachers' college), misogynism (rather than homophobia) is the key component of hegemonic masculinity. This relatedness to women can produce violence (Wood and Jewkes 1997) but, as Elaine Unterhalter points out, this is not necessarily the case. Her analysis of a non-violent discourse on masculinity, which she terms "heroic masculinity," highlights the fact that violence may not be the most important characteristic of masculinities, but even in its absence, women tend to be subordinated to a "natural" gender order in which men make decisions and dominate public space (Unterhalter 2000). Recent research has not yet, however, begun to ask how the current state of affairs in South Africa might have affected masculinities. Scholars have not asked whether new masculinities which are *not* founded on misogynism may be emerging and whether, more broadly, the political transition in the country might be accompanied by some important gender shifts, particularly in schools.

Making Sense of School Masculinities Theory

How do masculinities change? To answer this we need to have an institutional approach and a personal approach. In the first instance, we need to ask what the role of schools is in constructing masculinity and, in the second instance, how boys participate in the gender relations of a school. In practice these are closely interrelated. Mac an Ghaill's (1994a) examination of a school in the United Kingdom demonstrates that masculinities are affected by a range of complex forces that operate in and on schools—state policy, school hierarchies, and so on. State policy has a diffuse but nevertheless important impact. The effects of policy are filtered down and work to structure school discourses, interacting as they do so with the existing school gender regime. Schools can promote, condone, or oppose the presence of violent hegemonic masculinities. They are active agents as well as sites where gender relations are worked out in a relatively autonomous way, partly independent of the school itself (Thorne 1993). Gender transformation in school, therefore, happens at many levels and, according to Kenway and Fitzclarence (1997), will occur only if tackled holistically at all levels using a variety of strategies. Two questions that need to be asked of this approach in the context of the South African schools will be discussed in the next section. Can such an approach override material constraints or alter existing constructions of masculinity? And, what will be the effect if efforts at transformation are partial and do not reach all areas of a school?

James Messerschmidt's (1993) path-breaking work on crime and masculinity examined the different types of criminal behaviour of White middle-class and Black working-class schoolboys. His argument, somewhat bluntly put, was that the imperatives of masculinity—the need to establish peer credibility and to "be a man"—pushed both these groups into criminal behaviour. This behaviour took different forms because of the different life opportunities their social positions dictate. Consequently, young Black inner-city boys were likely to express their masculinity on the street in physical ways that led to interpersonal violence and confrontational antiauthoritarian acts. White middle-class boys, on the other hand, were less likely to be confrontational or physically violent in their criminal behaviour, not least because school offered them much more affirmation and opportunity than it did for their Black peers (102–5). This frame of analysis has a great deal of relevance for South African schools. Messerschmidt notes that oppositional and conformist masculinities exist side by side in schools, but he sees "criminal behaviour" as a structural inevitability. I find this model persuasive but pessimistic. Effectively, it argues that to change masculinities in a progressive way we need to change society. Thus, we are left with a model in which hegemonic masculinity can be challenged only by those outside its ambit, which, in turn, leaves "ordinary kids" as the problem and denies them agency in a project to transform hegemonic masculinity. Or, we are left with a model that suggests that a particular set of conditions inexorably drives a particular social grouping to perform masculinity in a particular way.

To address my second question requires posing four others: What if a school beset with problems receives a set of inputs (initiatives) which implicitly challenge the existing violent gender regime of the school and which directly address the social context from which students come and in which they live? What if such initiatives are not specifically directed at transforming gender relations? What if they do not address all levels of gender inequality? What might be the effect of such an initiative? In the following section, I describe the site of the research discussed in this chapter and suggest that the conditions within a particular school case have important implications for the transformation of masculinities.

The role that boys play in making masculinity is critical. Yet, Connell warns that projects of individual transformation or individualized projects run the risk of ultimately helping to "modernize patriarchy rather than abolish[ing] it" (Connell 1995, 139). For Connell, masculinity is a collective phenomenon and has to be tackled as such. It is not always easy to measure changes in gender practice. One way of identifying change is to examine the discursive construction of masculinity and to look for contradictory features which may be harbingers of emergent, progressive masculinity. Subject positions are chosen from, and gender identities constructed within, a range of existing discourses (Gilbert and Gilbert 1998). It thus becomes critical that these discourses offer positions that will not locate boys or men in violent or otherwise abusive relationships with fellow learners, teachers, and the school community.

The approach developed by social historians in examining the construction of working-class consciousness and action is instructive. English social historian E.P. Thompson's insistence that classes make themselves might usefully be applied to how masculinities are constructed in school and amongst youth. A group comes to realize and constitute itself. It accommodates, responds to, and resists social forces. It becomes involved in a process of cultural revolution (Corrigan and Sayer 1985). What young male learners are saying in schools, which are undergoing transformation themselves, provides us with one way of uncovering different school discourses. In the process of listening to them, we may not only uncover "boyz own stories" (Epstein 1997a), but we may also begin to identify possible markers that indicate shifts in school masculinities.

In the following discussion, extracts are drawn from what boys said and wrote in the course of a research study. In this discussion I shall be reflecting on Gilbert and Gilbert's (1998) view that "in criticising dominant masculinity, we need to be able to replace it with a sense of being male to which boys can aspire. Ridding the dominant images of its worse excesses is important, but it needs to be replaced by some alternative vision and sense of direction" (247).

Methodology and Research Site

The data cited below was generated in the CRISP (Crime Reduction in Schools Project) project initiated at the University of Natal, Durban in 1998. It received funding from the Department of Arts, Culture, Science and Technology in 1999 and involved a number of discrete community outreach programs. Six schools, three primary and three secondary, were the sites in which a range of initiatives were undertaken. Lecturers and university students from a broad spectrum of disciplines worked in these schools. The intention was to develop mediation and arbitration skills and attitudes of tolerance, and to give the schools the capacity to handle a variety of crises. All the schools are close to the University and serve predominantly working-class African communities.

Most of the schools were formerly reserved for Whites, but the breakdown of apartheid has not only opened their doors to all races, but has also changed residential demography so that many Black people now live in or within reach of areas formerly reserved for exclusive White occupation. In the two schools from which the testimony cited below is drawn, there was not one White student. White students elected to attend "safer" or "more orderly" schools even if they are further away. Most of the students came from distant townships. The journey (by commuter train, bus, or taxi) exposed students to crime. The numerous assaults and robberies that were reported provided a focus for CRISP's early attempts to make the schools safer.

In the sections below, I discuss material generated from a classroom exercise in which over 500 students in Grades 5 to 12 wrote an essay on the topic, "Crime I have seen." The project, organized by Ted Leggett, covered students ranging in age from 9 to 18. I have selected text from male students who were 14 years or older. A second source is group interviews on "Gender conflict amongst adolescents" conducted in 1999 by Ravani Chetty with Grade 8 schoolboys (aged 14 to 16 years). The third source of data is structured one-to-one interviews by Sheryl Walton in September 1999. Volunteers who had been involved in gangs were asked about their lives, especially how they became involved with a gang.

South African Schooling: The Current Context

The South African education system has been in a state of reform for ten years. Since 1996 the direction of transformation has become clearer (with the landmark 1996 South African Schools Act). Policy is designed primarily to address the massive racial inequalities in the system which were a legacy of the Bantu Education system and the racially skewed distribution of educational resources under apartheid. In the last few years, the Department of Education has begun to shift its attention toward tackling socio-economic class inequalities. Children in poorly resourced (often rural) schools are beginning to receive assistance to narrow the gap between themselves and their counterparts in the richer urban schools.

The process has been difficult and disheartening. Matriculation results since 1995 have deteriorated and attempts to narrow the gap between the performance of formerly White schools and that of Black schools have met with little success. Crime and violence also continue to be major obstacles to the improvement of schooling. In the light of the perilous situation, the government undertook a number of initiatives. Corporal punishment, which historically had been widely used in the schooling system, was banned by the 1996 Schools Act. Despite the fact that it continues to be in common use, corporal punishment is now much more limited and less severe (Morrell 2001a; Mkhize 2000). A second initiative was the establishment in 1997 of COLTS (Culture of Learning, Teaching and Service), a national ministerial campaign to improve the learning environment in schools. The initial goal was to transform schools, within two years, from sites of struggle to sites of learning. An explicit goal was to drive "deep into popular consciousness and behaviour some of the key values of the education process: discipline, application, determination to succeed, mutual support, community ownership" (Department of Education 1997, 1–2). There were five components to the plan; the most important was arguably the "No Crime in Schools" component. It called for, amongst other things, a ban on all weapons, drugs, rape, vandalism, and violence, and for efforts to "build solidarity to enforce the ban" and to "build and implement conflict-resolution processes" and "human rights for all" (4). These goals had not been achieved by the end of 1999. In a sense this was not surprising because much of the malaise could not be corrected overnight. A Witwatersrand University Education Policy Unit report in 1996 identified the three major causes of the collapse of learning as inadequate infrastructure, poor socio-economic environments and fragile social relations in schools (Chisholm and Vally 1996, 60). Although a national crisis of resources made and continues to make it impossible to rectify the first two elements, initiatives unleashed by the broad transformation process have already had some impact.

Provincial ministries have continued to emphasize this initiative, looking to produce role models that demonstrate "the difference between having a wish for change, and having the will to make a difference" (ELRU and Quaker Peace Centre 1999, 1). All provincial ministries have given COLTS in their areas a particular slant, but all have included "crime" as a major focus. This emphasis is understandable in the context where the cabinet generated a National Crime Prevention Strategy (1995) and COLTS was integrated into that strategy. One of the focuses of the Crime Prevention Strategy was "Public Values and Education." Its three targets were school safety, violence prevention, and victim empowerment. These goals were incorporated into the projects generated by provincial ministries and other concerned parties. Many non-governmental organizations became involved, using donor funding to drive towards these goals. The CRISP project is an example of such involvement.

Crime and Masculinities

Township schools are frequently the sites of violence (Mahlobo 2000). On occasion, gang intrusions have resulted in the murder of teachers and learners on school premises and, much more frequently, assaults and robberies. Male teachers and students are implicated in this violence in a variety of ways. From the sample examined in this study, it appears that many students have been party to violent incidents and gang activities (Reid et al. 2000). Some of the violence is centred on competition over women (Niehaus 2000), while some of it is structural—corporal punishment is still widely practised (Mkhize 2000; Morrell 2001a). The bottom line is that, in township schools, the masculinity that is hegemonic is centred on relationships of domination and competition. This description, however, oversimplifies the situation in schools. Crime and violence are not ever-present realities and gender discourses are not uniformly centred on violence and domination. Accepting the view that violence is pervasive and hence absorbed, internalized, and legitimated in constructions of masculinity conceals the fact that it is contested, tenuous, and subject to qualification.

Most of the respondents to the "Crime I have seen" exercise voiced reservations in their testimonies. They did not endorse all violence and many distanced themselves from it. Macho media images may abound (Fenwick 1996), but the criminal is not, at least in these schools, held up as the only model of masculinity.

A 15-year-old boy describes his experience with crime. Although he is not the antagonist, he is caught up in a whirl of events in which competing versions of gender-specific behaviour are pitted against one another. Aggressive and violent behaviour prevails but it is significant that more conciliatory and passive options are attempted. This example suggests that, even amongst boys living and working in violent contexts, forms of masculinity that rival violent and assertive ones exist and are deployed.

> One friyday athernoon coming from school. My friend and I were walting for the bus. When it came we rushed to sit at the back seat. It was late so the bus was full. Some boy's were sitting in front of us , they were smoking and drinking alcohol. The boy who was standing in front of me was not pleased with the boys who were smoking. One of the boys who was sitting stood up and fell on to the one who was standing, he was very angry and threatened to hit the one who fell on him. The other boy apologised but the boy who was standing slaped the other boy. Even when he was slept he still apologised. The boy slaped him again and he apologised. He apologised three times and he still got slaped. He was also very angry and punched the other boy. They hitted each other and a fight developed. The boy who was sitting next to me broke up the fighte. After a few minutes they both took out bush knifes and stabbed each other. The one who stoped the fight got stabbed four times and the other one two times. There was blood in the bus and my shirt was red. The bus driver stopped the bus and sorted out the "bloody" problem. I was very frightened that someone would have been killed in frend of me.

Many of the respondents condemned crime and criminals. A 16-year-old issued this message:

> My message to the criminals is that they must think again of what they always do, if they don't have money and doing nothing good to earn money who is there to work for them. No one but themselves....Work hard to suceed.

For many others, however, circumstances weighed heavily. In some it induced a reluctant collusion. A 17-year-old respondent described the compromise of circumstance.

> A boy we all knew...came to us and told us to act as if we didn't see him steeling a car of a person we all knew. He mannagde to

> break in the car and drive away with it. The time he was driving away, we also ran away, because we were scared the we were going to be suspects. We all knew what had happened, but we were scared to tell, because maybe someone the boy who stole the car would be told and he and his connections would come and kill us. So we just kept quiet. Not even one of us was aiming to tell the truth. It is bad because we all the proof for the boy to be arrested, but we couldn't help because we were scared for our lives.

In others it forced a strategic involvement.

An 18-year-old boy described how he became involved in drug dealing to earn money to pay for medical services for his unemployed and sick mother. After his mother had been restored to health, he stopped dealing. He looked back on his involvement with mixed feelings.

> Drug dilling is bad I did it for my mother inorder to pay for operation and buy food for us and even go to school with that amount of money likely I did not have a brother or sister to look after.
>
> Now my mother is not sick at all a I have dropped selling even mother is back at home and we are living happy after all.
>
> Stop drug dilling For the sake of people's life's.

In still others, it promoted a vengeful masculinity, tinged with the violence that they were themselves resisting. Boys at these schools are considered privileged by boys in poorly resourced township schools, resulting in tension and conflict. One 16-year-old member of a group of three friends reports that, after being attacked and stabbed, the group fought back.

> Ayanda and Senzo ensisted that we pay back (take revenge), but I stopped them and told them that they must'nt (but) [l]ast week, when Ayanda and Senzo went to Phoenix, where Ayanda lives. I went to the shop, and they stopped me and though they were going to take advantage of me, just because my friend were not there. But they were wrong. They polled out their knives and I was was forced to fight. I footh with one

of them and I hit him so badley that he started crying. I told the rest of them to come one-by-one. But they did'nt.

Fearful of criminals, the boy proposed a vengeful justice.

> In crime like this the community must work together with the police in order to solve the problem, when that doen't happens, then their neighborhoor must try and help, and when the boy's are court they must not sentence them to any years they must "kill" them (ded sentence). When even the court cannot do that and some how eccape then the community must take care of them by making sure that their killed cause if they live they would do the very same thing, so community just "kill" them.

Masculinity is shaped by context, peer pressure, material constraints, and instrumental considerations. When girls admire bravery, there is an inducement to be "brave." This can contribute to the climate of violence. An 18-year-old girl gives some sense of a masculinity represented by hegemonic understandings of appropriate male behaviour. After having observed gangs robbing and abducting girls at the Rossburgh railway station, she writes:

> Even the boys getted cowardly. Although one of the girls knew those guys who were taking them but I consider it as crime because they all did not want to go with them. Crime has tamed our braveness. This is bad especially for the boys because being brave is the main way to prove their manhood.

In and Out of Gangs

Respondents were 13 to 15 years of age. Not all of them were gang members, but all were closely acquainted with gang life. Gang involvement was a choice made generally in the context of poverty, though such factors as a desire for expensive clothes and the fast life (women and cars) were also present. According to one student, "Boys join gangs to be famous and to get nice clothes." Gang membership sometimes stemmed from the necessity to meet basic needs and, in the opinion of some boys, it was therefore defensible. One of the respondents made the following distinction: "Some people steal because they are jealous. There is a difference if you are stealing because you are starving. It is not OK to steal if you are rich." In the former case, a central aspect of hegemonic masculinity—that men should be breadwinners—was often critical. In the latter case, the desire for peer affirmation was central. Other forms of peer affirmation were available: playing soccer was the most common example. Another central feature of gender identities is the need to have a peer group. Gangs satisfy this need, though other social groupings can do so just as well. The church and soccer teams were frequently cited as alternative loci of masculine support (Scarnecchia 1997).

"Dr. Khumalo" was 15 years old when interviewed. He borrowed his pseudonym from a local cult soccer star, a choice which reflected tragically an accident that drove him into gangs. He damaged his eye playing soccer at age 11 and thereafter could not participate. This seems to have propelled him into gang life, which he described as "fun": "they used to make jokes and I enjoyed that, it was fun." As with most of the other students interviewed, Dr. Khumalo noted that gangs were dangerous. His brother, a gang member, was in jail. "It is not a good place....The police will arrest me as well if I am caught with those people, and then I will be in jail and when I get home I will get it from my grandmother, she will even hit me, he [sic] is too old, she is about 60." Apart from the costs of gang membership, the pull of an alternative source of affirmation and the existence of an alternative source of male company have caused him to abandon gang life: "I don't want to be part of a gang anymore. I have found other friends now. We go to church together, the Seventh Day Adventist."

Fourteen-year-old "Sipho" also turned his back on gang life, realizing its dangers: "Life is too short when you are a gangster." Now he plays soccer and goes to church. "If they asked me to join the gangs [again] I would say no. It is no life, they are always running. I want to be a doctor when I finish school. School is important. You can learn and get your own money, it is better to be paid your own money that you have made than to steal it." Sipho's world is now built around hard work and deferred gratification. His version of masculinity is now much closer to that of the *amaKholwa*, the early Zulu Christians who constituted themselves as "black Victorians" and who bought land, stressed the value of education, and concentrated on capital accumulation via honest industry.

The appeal of this version of masculinity was also evident in the responses of two boys whose fathers are policemen. "Brian" is 14 years old. His parents live separately and he stays with his grandmother. It is clear that his life is not materially very secure, but for a variety of reasons his masculinity is bound up with academic achievement and the respect of his elders. He shares with virtually all of his colleagues a love of soccer, but the physicality of this sport can lead in many directions. In his case it bolsters his ideas of being a man—being physically fit and healthy and having a future in the world of work.

> I play soccer at home, not at school. My mother doesn't work. My gran doesn't work, but my father gives her money. I go to church. Gangsters are bad people that do not want to go to church and to school. I want to be a pilot when I grow up. I am planning to finish Matric. School is good. You get information about life and have a better mind. You know how to write and to read. You can't work without going to school.

"Sihle," aged 13, is similar to Brian. "I want to be a doctor when I am finished school. You must be educated to get a good job, and make your own money. Gangsters think that school is a waste of time. They get arrested, some gangsters are scared, it is a bad way to live. You are not liked by the people in the community and you cannot trust your friends."

Although gangs are common, they are not the social bandits described by Eric Hobsbawm (1972) more than thirty years ago. They are generally reviled by the communities in which they live and on whom they prey. This is possibly the strongest reason why young men contemplate other styles of masculine performance. Community support and peer approval, which can still be obtained by playing soccer and performing well in school, are reasons to reject gang membership and the violent masculinities associated with it.

Girls and Relationships

It is probably more important to look for emergent, non-violent gender discourses amongst boys in the area of sexuality—its display and performance—than anywhere else. The incidence of rape, sexual assault, and harassment in South Africa is very high. Amongst the many reasons for this are patriarchal expectations of female submission and the need that young men feel to demonstrate their masculinity in heterosexual ways (Wood and Jewkes 2001).

The group discussions conducted by Ravani Chetty are both depressing and promising. They reflect high levels of acceptance of "might is right" and "man is right." They also contain, however, interesting contradictions reflecting the state of gender turmoil fuelled by gender equality policy.

In one group discussion among 14 to 16 year olds, the following conversation took place:

Student 1: My friend hit his girlfriend at his house because he caught her smoking, because he doesn't smoke.

Interviewer: ...Do you think it's correct for him to not allow her?

Student 1: No, she has her own rights.

Student 2: If she wants to smoke she can smoke.

Student 1: But at the same time the boy was correct.

Interviewer: How?

Student 1: He was stopping her from smoking.

Interviewer: Do you think that beating somebody up means that she is going to stop smoking?

Student 2: No. You are making it worse.

Interviewer: Why do you say that?

Student 2: In any case the girl gets more [angry] and she wants to make you more upset, so she continues smoking.

There is confusion about the responsibility a man has for his partner, his entitlement to obedience, and her rights. This was a theme in most of the interviews, with respondents divided on the issue. One of the reasons for this was made explicit. When Chetty asked about changes in the country, the boys responded that "women were taking over."

Interviewer: If the women are taking over, how does that make you feel?

Student 1: Like we are baboons, miss.

Student 2: I don't feel anything, miss.

Interviewer: Alright, why?

Student 3: Just that the person who works hard gets the thing that they want.

Student 4: They are best in everything.

Student 1: Because you work hard, you gonna get everything.

Interviewer: Anyone else want to say anything about the change in the country?

Student 5: Maybe you want a job, miss, and you go with a girl. She looks pretty and maybe the manager likes her. He won't give you the job even if you have good marks, he will take the girl.

Student 3: Men were in power before but they have to change, because if women work harder than men they have to take over. Because if men take over without them the country won't have success.

Interviewer: There are all these things on the TV and radio about the violence in this country, especially about the violence against women, what do you think about that?

Student 2: With this women's rights, miss, I am scared. They use their rights to bring the men down, miss.

Interviewer: Give me an example.

Student 2: They say "he was trying to rape me" or something like that miss. You know when you get like, you are well known, when you are famous.

Student 1: Ya, like Makhaya Mthini [Ntini—the first African cricketer to earn national colours, who was found guilty of rape but had the conviction overturned on appeal much to the outrage of feminist anti-rape groups].

Interviewer: Alright, what do you think about what happened to him?

Student 1: See, I don't know much about it. But I think that guy didn't rape.

Interviewer: Why?

Student 2: He looks innocent.

Interviewer: Okay, you say he looks innocent, what about him looks innocent?

Student 2: He is shy miss, he don't talk too much.

Interviewer: If you are saying that he looks innocent and the lady has been saying all along that he raped her, then you are saying that the lady is lying?

Student 2: Yes. But there is some confusion mixed in with the resentment.

Interviewer: Why do you think the girls are afraid of the boys?

Student 1: Because they are strong.

Student 2: The man is always strong, miss—even with Adam and Eve, the man was strong.

Laughter.

Interviewer: Who told you that?

Student 2: Miss, I read. Now we have women's rights, we didn't have that when we were working in the mines.

Laughter.

Student 3: The woman must cook, make everything, we the man. Now it's a new South Africa, we cannot do anything. They say "sexual harassment" if we do anything.

Interviewer: Why do you think that change is taking place in this country?

Student 5: Because they think that men and women are equal, miss.

Interviewer: Do you think that men and women are equal?

Yes. (*Chorus*)

Student 5: Women can work, they can get a good job, women can....

	Like you miss. (*An interrupting voice.*)
Interviewer:	You just said to me now that women must stay at home....
Student 1:	No, before.
Interviewer:	So how has that changed?
Student 2:	Because now we don't get any jobs, the women are taking over.

Laughter.

This is very much in the language of men's rights and locates men as the victims of advances in women's rights. It is likely to remain a powerful theme, particularly among the working class where jobs are hard to find, men still expect themselves to be breadwinners, and the advancement of women (even in fairly poorly paid jobs) will be keenly felt. It feeds into a strong misogynistic line of reasoning which locates women as alternatively parasitic or domineering.

Student 1:	We do get into fights, miss. Especially when you are in a relationship with a girl, miss. When you have any problems, you have to hit the girl. Because sometimes you have to pay your money to take the girl to whatever and the girl will make you a...will use you.
Interviewer:	You say she uses you...
Student 1:	Yes, miss...for money.
Student 2:	She sees a boy, she doesn't like...she wants him to have like expense clothes. Maybe, like lots of things, like a gold tooth. He must have money all the time.

But girls are also seen as very powerful.

Interviewer:	Will your girlfriend beat you up if you have another girlfriend?
	Laughter.
Student 1:	Miss, she doesn't have power to, miss.

Interviewer: Now that's very important that you said that. Why doesn't she have any power? What do you think?

Student 1: She has the power to dump me.

Interviewer: Does she?

Student 1: Yes, miss.

Interviewer: Will she get a beating after she dumps you.

Student 1: Yes, miss.

Student 2: Of course.

This is possibly the greatest challenge schools and learners face. Compulsory heterosexuality linked with high expectations on the part of boys and girls to be seen to be performing raises the stakes, promotes a competitive (and violent) attitude towards relationships, and raises the chances of HIV/AIDS transmission.

Homophobia has been identified in the British context as a major feature of school masculinities (Mac an Ghaill 1994a; Epstein and Johnson 1998). In the southern African context, its centrality is less clear. In South African schools, there is a prescriptive attitude towards heterosexuality and a biblically-based condemnation of homosexuality (Deacon, Morrell, and Prinsloo 1999). However, Pattman (2001) found, that in Zimbabwe, school masculinities were constructed more in relation to women (who were perceived as a threat) than to gays. The findings of this chapter echo this conclusion, though it has to be noted that homophobia is present and feeds a climate of intolerance.

Interviewer: Do you find that boys are fighting with boys?

Student 1: Yes, miss.

Interviewer: Over girls?

Student 2: Miss, but sometimes it's because of name calling.

Interviewer: And what brings about the name calling?

Student 3: Boys who act like girls.

Interviewer: What would you describe as a boy who acts like a girl?

Student 3:	Somebody who is gay.
Interviewer:	And how do you know if somebody is gay?
Student 3:	The way they talk, the way they look...
Student 1:	He talks to girls.
Interviewer:	So other boys that are looking at him, what is happening there?
Student 3:	They laugh at him.
Student 2:	They don't like him.
Interviewer:	And what do they do to the boy?
Student 3:	Mostly, they don't do nothing. They start bullying him.
Student 4:	Sometimes they go and hit him.
Interviewer:	So you are saying the boys that you think are gay get harassed by other boys?
Student 1:	Yes, miss.

These extracts suggest that high levels of intolerance still exist amongst boys—towards girls and boys who do not fit in. Yet, this is not the only story. Some boys recognize that violence is a problem and that peaceful and more harmonious ways of relating to others need to be found.

Interviewer:	Why do you think they (boys and girls) hit each other?
Student 1:	Because they think that it will solve the problem.
Interviewer:	Do you think the hitting solves the problem?
Student 1:	No.
Interviewer:	What do you think solves the problem?
Student 2:	Talking to the girl. Telling her to stop what she has done. Or if the girl hits the boy back, telling her to do it different.

Interviewer:	Do you find that people talk to one another?
Student 2:	No.
Student 3:	Sometimes, but it depends on what kind of boy it is.
Interviewer:	From your experience, from what you have seen here. Do you think that people talk to one another to solve a problem? Or do they resort to other means?
Student 1:	Maybe they don't talk, they just fight.
Interviewer:	And when they are fighting, is it physical or is it verbal?
Student 2:	Sometimes physical, sometimes verbal.
Interviewer:	When you are standing there watching two people fighting, how does that make you feel?
Student 1:	Maybe you feel like you want to help the person getting beaten. But you know that maybe the person has done something wrong....

Conclusion

Listening to schoolboys talk about gangs, crime, and girls, one might conclude that nothing has changed in the last decade and that schools are simply reproducing violent masculinities. In this chapter I have taken a different tack. A close examination of school discourses has revealed signs of change. Gender equity policy, school interventions, and the broader shifts in society towards redressing inequalities, particularly racial ones, have had an impact on the construction of masculinities. The effect can be seen not only in the language that boys use to make sense of their lives, but in the new political vocabulary about gender.

School masculinities reflect the changing national context. Changes are not automatic, linear, or necessarily progressive. But in schools where specific efforts are being made to promote democratic and peaceful schooling, there are signs that boys are becoming more receptive to the idea of gender equality. The process is far from complete. The content of hegemonic masculinity has not yet changed and there are still strong pressures to preserve the patriarchal dividend for boys. The shape and form of school masculinities hang in the balance, but so long as state policy and resources support gender equity programs in schools, the prospect that new masculinities will emerge lives on.

Acknowledgment: I would like to thank Fran O'Brien, specifically, and the CRISP project, in general, for their generous provision of research material for this chapter.

Chapter 4

Confronting Masculinity at the University of Zimbabwe

Marc Epprecht

Zimbabwe is the richly endowed, mid-sized nation in southern Africa formerly known as Rhodesia. Like much of the region, it has experienced severe health, environmental, political, and economic strains in recent years. Economic globalization and other external pressures bear an obvious responsibility for many of these problems. Feminists, however, have argued that the external pressures upon Zimbabwe have been significantly exacerbated by the hegemonic discourse of masculinity within Zimbabwe. Patriarchal African traditions, reactivity to imperialist violence and paternalism, and the influence of American consumer culture, notably, have all been implicated in the catastrophic spread of HIV/AIDS and other sexually transmitted diseases. Hegemonic masculinity is also seen to be behind rising levels of criminal, domestic, and sexual violence—including a climate of increasingly overt hostility against gays and lesbians. African ecofeminists have linked the masculinist values of much of Africa's post-colonial leadership to the widespread corruption that corrodes civil society, contributes to the devastation of the natural environment, and frustrates efforts to develop.[1]

Many African governments today accept the fundamentals of this critique. Indeed, Zimbabwe positively embraced the principle of education toward gender equity as a key developmental strategy since independence in 1980. Yet, pursuing that principle in actual classroom practice remains fraught with difficulties. I encountered some of these during three years in the History Department of the University of Zimbabwe (UZ). In this chapter I reflect on that experience. I consider some of the main obstacles to anti-masculinist pedagogy, as well as specific methods that I (and colleagues) used to confront hegemonic masculinity. I conclude by proposing ways to enrich anti-masculinist teaching in both African and non-African contexts.

Academic Culture

The University of Rhodesia and Nyasaland was founded in 1957 during a brief flowering of colonial liberalism. Intellectual standards were set to Oxbridge traditions. In the context of colonial rule, these standards effectively excluded all but a smattering of mostly expatriate African faculty members and elite, mission-educated, male African students. Nonetheless, the university made active efforts to cultivate that elite and was opposed, in principle, to racially discriminatory practices. This inevitably drew it into conflict with the government as a crackdown on African nationalism intensified in the mid-1960s. Faculty members were deported from the country for supporting African nationalism, or even for questioning racist fantasies such as the non-African origins of Zimbabwe's ancient ruins.

Independence in 1980 ushered in radical changes, including the return of exiles and the rapid expansion of African faculty members. The student body doubled in the first six years of independence and was transformed to the point where it is now overwhelmingly black Zimbabwean. The background of these students is much less elite than before. The huge expansion of the secondary school system in the rural areas and the provision of scholarships by the state have given the sons and daughters of African peasants educational opportunities for the first time. The new secondary system also involved radically revised curricula at the lower levels. The first cohort graduated in 1984, having imbibed the muscular Marxist-Leninist, anti-imperialist interpretation of world history then espoused by the new government.

Notwithstanding these changes, two fundamentals of academic culture remained the same as in Rhodesian days. First, the university basically adhered to its Oxbridge standards and structures. Indeed, the secondary school system did as well, despite (some argue, because of) the new curricula and expansion. Whatever revolutionary jargon they picked up in Forms 1 and 2, for example, students understood very clearly that they needed to pass three Cambridge "A" level exams to get into university. Having demonstrated their mastery of "real" knowledge, they then enjoyed relatively small classes at the UZ structured around seminars and tutorials. The bulk of assessment continued, as before, to rest upon final examinations. In the History Department these and, indeed, the little term work that there was, consisted entirely of essays. They were largely memorized by rote by the students in small groups in the final three weeks of term.

Second, the administration continued to define its social role in classically liberal terms. Student leaders also promoted social transformation, often in the inflated Leninist jargon of their Form 2 days. As long as the government pursued moderately socialist policies and rhetoric, this produced a fairly harmonious relationship. In the early 1990s, however, the government embraced structural adjustment policies that have squeezed the university financially and deeply alienated faculty and students. The latter, in particular, have resumed much the same adversarial culture as existed two decades earlier. Indeed, during the time that I taught there (1995–98), scarcely a term passed without almost ritualized, violent confrontations between students and riot police that sometimes culminated in prolonged closure of the campus.

Official policy is supportive of gender equity. In 1995 the university administration introduced affirmative action to boost the number of female students. Women in African History had also recently been introduced as a mandatory first-year course for history majors. Although none of my male colleagues actually wanted or was able to teach it, all of them appeared at least to accept women and gender as legitimate areas of historical investigation. This fit the agenda of the major international donors. Ironically, as wear and tear and government cutbacks rapidly eroded traditional library holdings, donor funds sometimes made quite radical feminist literature more readily available to students and faculty than the conventional canon.

Notwithstanding official and donor policy or the goodwill of individual teachers and administrators, hegemonic masculinity remains profoundly entrenched in the academic culture. Both the faculty and student bodies at the UZ are still overwhelmingly male. During my sojourn the Department of History had one junior female lecturer. My course on North American history had three female students out of sixty. All of the students in my graduate course on historiography were male, and so on. The confrontational, militaristic student politics of recent years both reflected and exacerbated this male dominance. Yet hegemonic masculinity also appeared in the form of hierarchical, authoritarian, gender-blind and other patriarchal discourses, including sexual harassment of female students by their male colleagues, and alleged "A's for lays" by some professors. More subtly, the physical infrastructure of the university itself reinforced the patriarchal aura of authority around teachers, with imposing lecterns and desks to remind students of their passive, subordinate role in the learning process. The heavy emphasis on final exams rewarded students for the passive collection and regurgitation of apparently authoritative facts, abetted student fear of intellectual risk, and discriminated against students (especially young women) who had not been socialized to perform well under intensely stressful conditions. Examinations scheduled for November had to be submitted by instructors in May, scarcely weeks after classes began, to accommodate the external examiner, effectively imposing a pedagogical straightjacket on the teachers. Technology that could potentially liberate teachers or empower disadvantaged students, such as the Internet, was simply not available.

The role of the state in promoting gender equity, however, was deeply contradictory. On the one hand it made regular professions of allegiance to the ideal. Yet its structural adjustment program eroded faculty compensation and compelled many lecturers to moonlight just to make ends meet. Incentives to try new approaches to teaching (or to continue teaching at all!) were reduced. Structural adjustment also undermined affirmative action for both female students and the children of peasant families as user fees at the primary and secondary levels began to winnow them from the system. The structural adjustment program has curtailed employment opportunities for graduates, removed key aspects of the social safety net, intensified gender and ethnic rivalry over diminishing resources, and is widely believed to explain burgeoning levels of prostitution. The state's shrill campaign of vilification of gays and lesbians, the erasure of key legal rights for women, and the closing down of Harare's Feminist Studies Centre made the ruling party's anti-feminism quite explicit.

Students in this context felt intense pressure from their families to succeed at university according to traditional expectations. Not surprisingly, they were often highly resistant to challenges to Oxbridge standards of knowledge. They also were wary of perceived deviation from "correct" learning paths as defined by course title and description: if the course were called Women in African History, then why "waste" time discussing gender or masculinity? Some of my confrontations with student conservatism in this regard were almost wryly comical: a young White man from North America pointing out racist words and imagery in African students' essays, or male chauvinist assumptions in the work of female students, or undue deference to male European scholars in student debates, for example. Yet who could blame them when they received such contradictory messages from authority figures, the state above all? Even students who showed sympathy to ideals of women's or gay emancipation knew what side of the ideological bread was ultimately buttered. Passing those finals and getting a job understandably counted more to them than experimenting with potentially dangerous ideas.

Classroom Approaches

My approaches to confronting masculinism in this context built upon the official policy that sanctioned gender equity and the expansion of human rights. My ultimate goal was the Freirian one of "humanizing" the students, *and* my colleagues *and* myself, in a continuous dialectic. This, I hoped, would attract a small number of converts who, in turn, would pass the joy of gender analysis on to their future students. In moments of heady idealism, I believed such an approach could contribute to Zimbabwe's liberation from both oppressive neo-traditions and dehumanizing global economic structures. The strategy included equal parts of learning (hitherto hidden histories of women, gender, and sexuality) and unlearning (the subtle ways we reproduce masculinist values in our lives).[2] In pursuit of these goals, I adhered to six basic, mutually reinforcing guidelines:

- to draw attention to the anti-imperialist, anti-racist, and indigenous nature of feminist and queer scholarship and activism in Africa
- to define gender as an analytic concept that holds at least equal importance to class and race
- to demonstrate the power of the dominant discourse to "invisibilize" or diminish women and gender, and to counter that discourse with subaltern perspectives on historical events and personalities
- to historicize the process of production of knowledge about history by foregrounding debate, controversy, and struggle or setback (as opposed to the masculinist paradigm of history-as-progress)
- to challenge masculinist structures in the teacher/student relationship by "empowering" the students to be creative, responsible to each other, and socially engaged
- to challenge the manifold lines between "us" (teachers, authorities, knowers, moderns, real people) and "them" (students, neophytes, recipients, primitives, others).

These guidelines were undoubtedly idealistic and in no way consistently achievable; there were days when I could not rely on the chalkboard, let alone the electricity, to work in one of my lecture halls. Nonetheless, certain fairly simple techniques helped in challenging masculinism in the academic culture.

Drawing Attention to African Queer Scholarship and Activism

It was quite easy to ground feminist theory in broader revolutionary and anti-imperialist political struggles, including references to men the students knew and respected, such as Marx, Lenin, Samora Machel, and Nelson Mandela. Discussing the historical "pedigree" of feminisms among African nationalists and using African rather than European or American authors also went a long way toward opening minds closed by anti-feminist prejudices. The same may be said for queer theory. African nationalists who have supported its political goals are admittedly thin in their ranks, but they are nonetheless persuasive. Employing Desmond Tutu and the 1997 ANC policy platform was far more effective than spouting the often more polished but alien-sounding, and alienating, queer theory out of the West. Making the effort to ensure that each topic contained as much African scholarship as possible, including African perspectives on North American and world history (for example, Mobonda 1992), mitigated enormously the students' suspicions that gender and feminism were simply another Western missionary enterprise to undermine African dignity and independence.

Another effective gambit in overcoming anti-feminist suspicions was to take time to expose the implicit or structural racism in conventional syllabi, maps, and texts. The Mercator projection of the world, for example, was once the map of preference in high school texts and is still widely used in authoritative sources, for example, behind television news desks. Although this map portrays the shape of continents accurately, it distorts relative sizes. Africa appears to be roughly the size of Greenland. The Peters projection, by contrast, portrays slightly distorted shapes but accurate relative areas. The result is quite startling. Not only does Greenland fit into a single African nation such as Sudan or Algeria, but seeing a superimposed image of Europe (pop. 650 million) fit snugly into southern Africa alone, or seeing Congo swallow up the whole of the United States east of the Mississippi, prodded students into questioning the objectivity of "science." Other maps have even challenged the orientation of the world that places Africa beneath Europe. There is indeed no "up" in space, so why do we cling to this image of super- and subordination?

A quick deconstruction of *National Geographic* did the same for ostensibly scientific discourses on geography, anthropology, and linguistics. Why, for instance, does one recent atlas dignify San Marino (population 24,000) with its own language ("Sanmarinese") whereas Congo (population 38 million) merits only unspecified "African languages"?[3] Why do the Letts, scarcely a million in number, comprise a "nation" whereas the Yoruba (25 or more million) are a "tribe"? The inescapable conclusion is that scholarship that purports to be objective often devalues Black people. This insight provides an easy jumping-off point into an appreciation of androcentrism or heterosexism in a similar light.

Defining Gender As An Analytic Concept

My second guideline—defining gender as an analytic concept equally as important as race and class—meant insinuating gender consciousness into every aspect of the course, rather than treating it as a distinct unit. I urged students, and mentored them by example, to reject masculinist universals such as "mankind" or "man-made" in favour of gender-neutral terms such as "humanity" or "manufactured." As much as possible we avoided gendered European translations of African terms (such as "king," "chief," or "brideprice" for *oba, morena,* or *lobola*). Dualistic concepts and categories that imply a gendered hierarchy (men are farmers, women are gardeners; men are workers, women are dependents; men in the city are migrant labourers, women are prostitutes, and so on) were also easily demolished and discarded. The absurdity of the notion that African women are "dependents" simply because men—often unreliably and insufficiently—give them cash, for example, could often be illustrated from students' own personal experiences. And what is a prostitute anyway? According to whose definition? Getting students to look closely at the gendered value judgments hidden in apparently gender-blind descriptions often surprised them and appealed directly to their desire for powerful analytic tools.

Gender consciousness at this level also requires an effort to differentiate between women's and men's historical experiences and to periodize according to major changes in gender relations rather than men's activities in the public sphere. This would tend to blur the lines dividing pre-colonial, colonial, and post-colonial eras while drawing out the continuities across them. Rather than emphasizing symbolic achievements, the new dates would focus attention on more meaningful events in people's daily lives; for instance, for many Zimbabweans, women especially, the transition to independence in 1980 was less significant than the imposition of the Economic Structural Adjustment Program in 1990. Defining and historicizing gender can also show that the concept includes heterosexual men and that it is not simply another way of saying women's or gay studies. A growing literature demonstrates that heterosexual men are gendered beings whose sexuality is constructed over time in social contexts.[4] Simply making this point invited the men in the course to relate to the readings; otherwise, they felt alienated from what they viewed simply as women's issues.

Countering Invisibilizing and Diminishing Discourse

To enrich the students' understanding of discourse, I emphasized that the implicit meanings of words are often more important than what the words say explicitly. An ongoing project for students was to bring to class examples of diminutives, euphemisms, and linguistic demotions of women that they encountered in their readings: "chieftainess" compared to "chief," "Native female" compared to "Native," "wife" (or mother or daughter) instead of a proper name, and so on. I also tried to foster consciousness of the concept of "unsaying" by resolutely challenging an extremely common tendency in the students themselves—the use of the passive tense. Many students, and indeed many established scholars, appear to think that the passive tense makes their writing sound more objective or scholarly. However, the passive tense unsays or erases agency and relations of power and constitutes one of the principal discursive tricks by which masculinist scholars evade responsibility for their prejudice and invisibilize the systemic violence perpetrated by men against women. Hence we hear that "women were left behind in the rural areas," instead of "men compelled women to remain in the impoverished countryside and used violence against those who tried to go to the cities," or that "women were left to fend for themselves," instead of "men abandoned their wives and daughters to starve," and so on. Taking a hard line against the passive voice forced students to get into the habit of identifying power in relationships—who has it and who does not. Rather than calling this consciousness of discourse "political correctness," or language fascism, as some American reactionaries have called it, I invited students to embrace it by calling it "respect" or simply "accuracy."

To help counter the invisibilization of women and gender, I also tried to include at least one example of women's history or feminist analysis in every topic. These examples included African women's critical responses to Western scholarship, as well as novels, autobiographies, dance, poetry, journalism, and film.[5] Systematically including women's history was important to counter the inference that some male students took from expansive definitions of gender, that is, that they could now get by without having to know any women's history or that male alienation is equivalent to female oppression. It also called attention to the contradictions in women's roles and status and the existence of class, ethnic, age, or other conflicts among female-bodied people. The fact that all African women were not the same quickly became self-evident from the readings. The *signares* of Gorée, the rulers of empires or commanders of armies, the *MamaBenzi* and *shebeen* queens of contemporary urban life—all patently undermine stereotypes of either a uniformly downtrodden or a heroic African womanhood. They illustrate the type of day-to-day issues and concerns which Africans encounter but which academic texts commonly neglect.

Listening to African women's voices directly also gave insight into the mitigating features of life for those women who were objectively oppressed, exploited, or victimized. This is an important pedagogical goal since women's collusion in patriarchal structures or customs can otherwise appear quite irrational and frustrating from the dominant perspective. Why would women perform and vigorously defend female genital cutting? Why would women insist upon *lobola* that "sells" them into a man's family and allows them to be "inherited" by a brother-in-law? Why have women often enthusiastically embraced patriarchal religions like Islam and Christianity? Why do poor women not practise birth control or follow other seemingly sensible advice from Western experts and feminists? Unless the positive aspects of these behaviours and choices are brought out, African women appear to be passive victims of the weight of tradition or the dupes of honey-tongued patriarchs.[6]

Historicizing the Process of Production of Knowledge About History

My fourth guideline was to destabilize the masculinist conception of history-as-progress. For this I sought to develop an awareness of the sometimes bitter political struggles by which new facts and interpretations emerge into the public domain. I tried to achieve this by explaining the process of knowledge production through research grants, peer review, patron/client relationships, and so on, and illustrating it with select passages from different historiographic or ethnographic schools. We treated these as primary documents whose value lay not so much in the facts they recorded but in how they shed light on the times of recording. For example, reviewing the changing ways in which Africa, and African women in particular, have been understood and portrayed by scholars over the past century fostered awareness of the precariousness of "truth" at any given historical moment. In groups, students had fun—but sometimes got cross—picking out the political ideals and the racist or sexist assumptions which appear in these works, often transparently cloaked as objective or scientific commentary.

Racism and androcentrism are obviously easiest to discern in the literature from the heyday of imperialism. Their remarkable durability over time can also be illustrated by using selections from *National Geographic* from the 1930s to the 1960s or cuts from sundry Hollywood films (see Davis and Riesenfeld 1993). Having cut their teeth on these crude representations of Africa, students were then able to move to the masculinist articulations of African nationalism and Marxism that continue to be the main anti-imperialist discourses. Graduate students were able to make the further analytic leap of differentiating between feminist positions and learning to discern the structural racism, heterosexism, and even androcentrism built into some feminist scholarship. Why, for example, do so many anthologies cite Van Allen's famous "Sitting on a Man" article (1972) but not Ifeka-Moller's erudite critique (1973)? Why allow Ifi Amadiume to stand for all African feminism when she is so effectively demolished by her colleague Nkiri Nzegwu (1998)? How many African names (actually count them) are there in the bibliography or text compared to European names?[7]

Encountering African women across the full range of issues rather than in domestic or sexual ghettoes will also facilitate students' questioning of the dominant paradigm. Notably, the empirical data show that the struggle for women's emancipation and human dignity is neither as new nor as Western, nor even as exclusively female-driven, as people commonly assume. Selections from Ibn Battuta's journey through medieval West Africa (see Gibb 1983, especially 320–30), for example, provide a striking testimony to the relatively emancipated behaviour of African women hundreds of years ago. Excerpts from the memoirs or diaries of European women in the early colonial period can also disabuse students of any notions they may have that European women were necessarily more advanced than Africans in their conceptions about gender roles and sexual propriety. Documents that discuss the detrimental effects of colonial development policies and prejudices on women and children from the 1930s, to give another powerful example, thoroughly discredit the hubris of contemporary aid agencies that claim, for example, to have discovered the need to include women in the development process (Blacklock 1936). Close scrutiny of Victorian-era scholarship can also undermine uncritical faith in progress by illustrating how stale or retrograde much recent scholarship actually is. The Victorians, for all their shortcomings, at least noticed African women, which cannot be said of many contemporary scholars. They even talked about people who did not conform to heterosexual norms. Colonial ethnographies that frankly relate homosexual practices among Africans in pre-modern settings demolish the post-colonial stereotype of an exclusively heterosexual African nature (Murray and Roscoe 1998).

Challenging Masculinist Structures by Empowering Students

A substantial body of literature provides ideas on how to empower students, and classroom strategies necessarily vary according to the objective limitations of every course and classroom context. As noted above, the limitations at the UZ were daunting and I would hesitate to say that my efforts were successful. Nonetheless, some specific empowering ideas that I tried included giving students the opportunity for meaningful input into the syllabus; debating, rather than dictating, answers to historical controversies; and developing alternatives to the most disempowering traditions or structures in the teaching and assessment process, above all, exam orientation. Once courses got underway (past historiography, definitions, and so on), I invited students to choose from a menu of discussion topics according to prior or developing interests. The content of survey courses is so vast that there was plenty of scope for flexibility. Students also helped to define some of the term tests by generating lists of concepts that they judged essential to their understanding of the course, rather than simply having the learned professor impose his personal preferences. In the same vein, students defined questions and paths of research interest for their essays, rather than my simply dictating set topics and research parameters. I encouraged students to approach local community leaders to ask if there were topics that the community would like to know more about or if they had specialized local knowledge that they were proud of and would like to share. Responding to external requests that may potentially filter into the public domain helped foster a sense of ownership of and responsibility to the process of learning, rather than dependency upon or appeasement of the teacher's views.

Debating, Not Dictating, Answers to Historical Controversies

Debate gives practice in translating privately held ideas into coherent publicly argued statements. It can also lead students to a consciousness of how difficult it can be to make historical assessments from often wildly contradictory evidence. The implications are important to feminist scholarship: you will not win converts by merely asserting your strongly held beliefs but must present them in a way that accounts for, and effectively disarms, opposing opinion. To that end, I provided provocative statements or broad thematic questions that set the parameters for research: "Traditional culture oppressed and exploited African women," "IMF/World Bank support for the 'empowerment of women' is a ruse," and so on. By validating the students' right to air their educated opinions, debates more actively engaged them in the course than straight lectures ever could.

Developing Alternatives to Disempowering Teaching and Assessment Traditions and Structures

Introducing a variety of term assignments helped cultivate the different types of skills and critical thinking that good scholarship demands. Although I am a historian, I always included map work and book or film reviews in my courses. Continuous assessment also increased recognition of students who did not perform well under exam conditions.

In the end, I was not able to put in place many of the alternative exercises that feminist teachers have used successfully in North American universities. The following are some I would have liked to adopt, and have adopted in Canadian contexts: have students keep on-going journals that comment on readings, lectures, and other classroom experiences; have students deconstruct contemporary media for evidence of bias; have students perform their research as theatre; have students prepare a "counter-lecture" to one of yours, which, point by point, deploys alternative sources, evidence, and explanations. Assessment in these exercises is not according to empirical correctness. Rather, good marks are achieved by evidence of effort to grapple with new, contentious ideas and by effectiveness of communication to the other students.

Blurring the Us/Them Dichotomy
The final guideline—blurring the dichotomy of Us/Them—took place at several levels. Being a White male, I felt it important to begin by surrendering some of the Otherness, which traditions and the physical milieu tended to bestow upon me. I first tackled the hierarchical layout of the classrooms, literally bringing myself down from the pedestal upon which professors have historically been placed. I stood in front of the dais rather than behind it, and re-arranged class seats and office furniture so that the students were not walled off from or placed in opposition to each other and me by desks. As much as possible, I invited students' input and encouraged them to look to and respect each other's expertise or personal experiences in addition to mine. I tried to mitigate the isolating effects of ivory-tower life by participating in anti-masculinist activism outside academe, visible to students in the form of letters to the editor in local media. Student appreciation of these efforts was evident.

Relinquishing the trappings of authoritarianism in the classroom, particularly the teacher's traditional aura of objectivity and omniscience, can redound to the disadvantage of the teacher in the case of some students. On the whole, however, I would argue that it sends a powerful, anti-masculinist message to the majority: they should respect ideas and practices rather than titles and uniforms or the possession of an apparently virile phallus.

The psychological chasm between Us (of the present) and Them (of the past) can also be partially bridged by an exercise in oral history. Colonial and nationalist tropes tumble quickly as grandmothers and grandfathers put a human face on the past. For instance, many of my students found to their surprise that men did not migrate to labour in South Africa simply because they were forced to do so by poverty and landlessness, as their earlier education had drilled. Oral informants admitted that they had migrated out of a desire for adventure and fun or to escape from the nagging of wives and mothers or mothers-in-law.

Blurring the lines between Us/Them has been taken to extremes in some American colleges which, from the UZ perspective, appear to endanger even the minimal goal of preparing students to be competent, self-confident scholars and citizens. Examples of such blurring are the "dumbing down" of standards and even linguistic ability, "Ebonics," and talk of love affairs between teachers and students. Moreover, some disparity of power between students and teachers is necessary in order to maintain a classroom atmosphere that is conducive to learning. In the case of female teachers or those from other historically disadvantaged groups, the conventional trappings of classroom power can be salutary in that they provide students with a counter-example to stereotypes of the powerlessness of women "Others." The social barriers that signify differential power can also protect the teacher from unwanted and inappropriate behaviour from students just learning about their sexuality (and vice versa). It would be wrong to underestimate the importance of the latter, given the *frisson* that discussing gender and sexuality can generate in societies where open talk about such matters remains a fairly strict taboo.

Challenging masculinism, including racism, therefore should not mean the abdication of standards of intellectual rigour or exposing oneself as a teacher to potentially improper or abusive situations. On the contrary, a condescending, kid-glove, or "buddy-buddy" approach undermines the feminist goal of inclusiveness almost as much as more blatant exclusiveness. Admittedly, this is a fine line to walk. True respect for "minority" work, however, requires using the same level of rigorous academic critique that one applies to the masculinist canon. Respect also requires pushing historically disadvantaged students to acquire the skill sets that will serve them well in the real, competitive, racist, and sexist world.

On the Bright Side

Who can say whether my attempts to challenge masculinism at the UZ had the effect that I intended? As often as not, I seemed to shoot myself in the foot with masculinist choices of words, demeanour, and bad jokes that unintentionally contradicted the gender-sensitive lesson plan. Some structures also proved insurmountable, notably the preponderance of final exams. The deteriorating political, economic, and health climate was frustrating, as was the inundation of Zimbabwean media with misogynistic and homophobic values and images from the West. Teaching of *any* sort, let alone gender-sensitive pedagogy, often seemed futile when I considered that as many as half of the students I addressed at any given time were HIV-positive.

However impossible it sometimes seemed, three years of confronting masculinity at the UZ was nonetheless hugely rewarding. Above all, I gained global insights into hegemonic masculinity, which continue to help me challenge masculinism in non-African contexts. Perhaps the most important of these insights is that the major obstacle to anti-masculinist pedagogy in Africa is *not* some vague Third-World primitivism. On the contrary, most of my African students and colleagues were basically open-minded to feminist political objectives, research priorities, and teaching principles. Students did the readings I assigned and we discussed supposedly embarrassing topics with fewer titters and giggles than I typically encounter in Canadian schools. In some cases students offered sophisticated understandings of the interrelationship between identities or the expressions of sexuality that made my own North American conceptions seem crude. In short, there is no reason to assume that gender, as a concept, is alien and threatening to Africans. African perspectives on gender are in fact clearly important to the project of deconstructing oppressive gender relations worldwide.

Conversely, the rare overt expressions of opposition to exploring issues around gender tended to come from either Christian fundamentalists quoting scripture from US Bible-Belt translations, or cool-pose would-be gangstas modelling American ghetto fashion.

The biggest obstacles to feminist pedagogy in Africa are thus not indigenous to Africa at all, but can be linked directly to the role of the supposedly progressive West. Western nations have collectively refused to meaningfully address the legacies of colonial rule, have imposed structural adjustment regimes and other unhealthy and destructive developmental models, have propped up or otherwise apologized for some of the most odious tyrants in the world, and have exported noxious consumer cultures and patriarchal religions. Western scholars have played a role in this as well by refusing to acknowledge the pain of racism and imperialism, and to make concrete gestures that show a commitment to challenge their more subtle forms. The dominant discourse of masculinity in Zimbabwe, in other words, cannot be understood or effectively challenged without understanding and challenging racism and imperialism. The key, therefore, to unravelling unhealthy and destructive masculinities in Zimbabwe and elsewhere in the so-called developing world is to confront the hegemonic masculinity in the West.

The main specific lesson I drew from teaching at the UZ that may be helpful in developing anti-masculinist curricula and strategies in non-African contexts is, therefore, that anti-racism and anti-imperialism need to be built systematically into one's course material and one's demeanour as a teacher. In the contemporary context, where structural racism is so profoundly woven into the global political economy, this is virtually synonymous to anti-capitalism. Self-identified Marxists have historically been among those most guilty of macho, heterosexist analysis and politics. The fact remains, however, that the anti-masculinist teacher who neglects her or his Marx and the Marxist critique of capitalism will be at a disadvantage in explaining the persistence of sexism and homophobia in the world today. Well, no one said it would be easy.

Notes

1. On African feminisms, see, for example, Meena (1992), Nnaemeka (1998), and Green (1999), and on panAfrican men's profeminism, Zeleza (1993). Bozzoli's 1983 critique of structuralist (that is, masculinist) tendencies in Marxist analysis still deserves revisiting. In Zimbabwe, rich debates unfold on the pages of *Southern Africa Political Economy Monthly* (SAPEM), *Southern African Feminist Review* (SAFERE), and *Zimbabwe Women's Network and Research Collective Newsletter*, as well as in the popular media. Dominant, or hegemonic masculinity, of course suggests alternatives or dissidence, of which I encountered an encouraging variety among Zimbabwean men. I would particularly like to express my gratitude to Boniface Chikorwa and Charles Nyaradzo for sharing with me (and allowing me to share with them) concerns about our behaviour as male teachers. I would like as well to acknowledge the courage of the counselors (for example, Romeo Tshumo and Keith Goddard) at Gays and Lesbians of Zimbabwe, who are at the forefront of critical, practical thinking about Zimbabwean masculinities.
2. Radical pedagogy had a brief flowering among Zimbabwean intellectuals in the post-independence era (for example, Moyana 1988), but almost without exception it was gender-blind. Overviews of feminist pedagogy that I found helpful (and available at the UZ) were Culley and Portuges (1985); hooks (1989); *Women's Studies Quarterly* (1993); McLaren and Lankshear (1994); and Redman (1996). Anti-homophobia as a classroom goal is discussed in Chan (1996) and Mager and Sulek (1997), whereas the topic of feminist pedagogy and male students is addressed in Sethna (1993) and Orr (1993). For suggestions for democratizing teaching in and about Africa, see Maylam (1995), Bastian and Parpart (1999), Bloch, Beoku-Betts, and Tabachnick (1998), and Hay (2000). The most vibrant fora for these discussions, and invaluable teaching resources, can be found on the Internet, above all H-Afrteach (www.h-net.org/~afrteach/)
3. Here I am picking on Dickinson (1993, 117 and 216 respectively).
4. Pioneering deconstructions of masculinity in Africa are Morrell (1998a, 1998c; 2001b), Murray and Roscoe (1998), and Lindsay and Miescher (2003). For one particularly effective video that broaches the topic of Black African masculinities from Black gay men's perspectives, see Alberton and Reid (2000).
5. A recent helpful bibliography is Snyder (2000), but see also Berger and White (1999), Nfah-Abbenyi (1997) and the website of the African Gender Institute (www.uct.ac.za/org/agi).

6. I would argue that bringing in subaltern perspectives can pay off in gender consciousness even when the subaltern has apparently nothing to do with gender. Thus, I disproportionately emphasized Canadian content in my History of North America course, plus a range of ethnic "losers" (like the Palestinians and Kurds) in Historiography. Such "losers" alert us to the triumphalism typically hidden in the dominant discourse, the detection of which is an easily transferable skill.
7. See also Zeleza (1997) for his analysis of Western feminists' failure to include African women in their debates.
8. Empowerment in this sense cannot succeed unless students are assured that they will not be penalized for the risks that you ask of them. Transparent processes must be available for them to appeal what they perceive as unfair assessments. Achieving that degree of political empowerment is a whole other issue.

Chapter 5

Men's Violence Against Women:
An Urgent Issue for Education

Jeff Hearn and Hans Wessels

Introduction

The persistence of men's violence against women is a well-established problem throughout the world. This presents a further problem for the education of boys and men. There is now a large literature of official records and statistics, social science and policy surveys, and victim/survivor studies that chronicles the extent and pervasiveness of men's violence against known women and children worldwide. A World Health Organization report on violence (Krug et al. 2002) summarized forty-eight population-based surveys of women and found that between 10 and 69 percent of the respondents had been assaulted by an intimate male partner at some time in their lives.[1] However, such estimates should be treated with caution because they may not take full account of rape, sexual harassment, coercive sex, and emotional, psychological, and other abuse.[2]

At the same time there has been a substantial development of policies against such violence—internationally, nationally, and locally. Much of this has quite rightly focused on the provision of women-centred services in the state, community, and voluntary sectors. Key initiatives have included criminal justice system reforms; the support of victims/survivors; the establishment of the women's refuge and rape crisis movements; the provision of safer housing alternatives for women and children; and the attempt to create safer public spaces. These and similar developments have important implications for the education of both boys and men about and against violence. There has also been a recent increase in the development of a critical focus on men and masculinities. The inspiration for this has come from feminist work, gay and queer work, men's responses to feminism, and a variety of other critical perspectives.

The last thirty years have seen major advances in bringing the problem of men's violence to women into public-domain debate, primarily as a result of feminist theory and practice. This period has also witnessed the problematicization of men and masculinities. Yet, although many aspects of men and masculinities have been put under the spotlight, the problem of men's violence against women has not generally been the main focus in this problematization. The need to focus critically on men and men's power and the problem of men's violence against women has been made apparent by feminist theory and practice; yet, not surprisingly, this work has not made its main priority the giving of support to women, the hearing of women's voices, and the improvement of women's lives. Accordingly, much remains to be done in spelling out the implications of feminist and critical studies on men for analyzing the problem of men's violence against women; critically deconstructing men's violence and violent men; changing men to reduce, stop, and abolish their violence against women; and, specifically, educating boys and men against violence to women. Educating boys and men about violence and getting them to change their ways are steps that need to be taken alongside political, policy, and practical initiatives for women.

A basic educational task for boys and men is for them to understand more fully the nature of men's violence against women. Many men have a very limited understanding of what counts as violence. Violence is not only physical violence; nor is it only physical violence that is visibly damaging or that leads to police intervention. It includes pushing, shoving, blocking, pinning, holding, and throwing—all forms of physical violence excluded by some men from the definition of violence. It is also sexual violence and abuse; violence against and abuse of children and threats thereof; and the control of money, time, friends, and potentially the whole social life of a woman (Hanmer 1996; Hearn 1998b). Violence is that which the woman experiences as violence from the man: a sense of the situation being out of control (Hanmer and Saunders 1984). Men do not have to use physical violence in order to be experienced as violent. Boys, young men, and men have to understand this broader definition of violence in order to work against violence. This is important in schools, youth work, and agency work more generally.

In this chapter we discuss some of the major arenas in which men and boys can be educated to counteract men's violence against women. These arenas are self-education and the education of the self; men in groups; men's programs; schools and educational institutions; and campaigns and public politics. Within each arena, education—the education of men against violence to women—has a rather different significance and place. There are two other very important arenas that, because of the limitations of space, we will not directly address in this chapter: education through policy development in agencies,[3] and the education of boys and young men in families. Families can be places where violence is encouraged or discouraged, and sometimes treated inconsistently or unpredictably.[4]

Self-Education and the Education of the Self: The Personal is Political

The self, the male self, has a double significance in the education of men against violence to women: men can educate themselves through what may be termed self-education; and the self can be educated by others. Men's violence against women, though a structural phenomenon, is enacted by individuals; the responsibility for violence lies with individual men. Educating and changing men to be against violence is always a personal and political matter. In keeping with the slogan "the personal is political," a prime site for educating men is the male self. Whatever the social arena, the education of boys and men against violence to women involves the education and changing of the male self. This is not to say that the individual boy or man is necessarily or naturally violent; however, the dominant social constructions of the male psyche or male subjectivity are themselves intimately bound up with violence. Violence is at least a reference point for the social construction of dominant male subjectivity.

The most obvious place to begin the education of boys and men against violence to women is within men's relationships with girls and women. Indeed, many girls and women may be engaged in a shorter or longer process of trying to educate men on how not to be violent, even though it is quite probable that neither party will define the process as education. This form of education may involve a boy's or man's need to recognize the experience of girls or women, to listen to the girl or woman with whom he has a relationship, to end violence completely (where it has occurred), and, if necessary, to end the relationship. It is thus likely to entail change in the private and the domestic spheres, the form of arrangements and relationships for living with and relating to others. Change in relationships is among the most difficult areas of personal practice to face and effect, not least because the domestic sphere is itself constituted as "private," and beyond the concerns, interest, and interference of others, in the first place (Hearn 1987, 168).

Men in Groups: Educating Men for More or Less Violence

Much of men's information about how to be a man comes from being with other men in groups. A number of previous studies of men who have been violent to known women have emphasized the importance of men's support for each other in perpetuating this violence (DeKeseredy 1990; DeKeseredy and Schwartz 1993; Boswell and Spade 1996; Godenzi et al. 2001; Schwartz et al. 2001). In particular, Walter DeKeseredy and his colleagues have shown how "male peer support" reproduces men's violence, through providing attachments and resources in the form of social integration, information support, and esteem support. They cite a number of studies that have found a strong relationship between the frequency of abusers' contacts with friends and female victimization. It is not so much the quantity but the quality of those social contacts that is important. Social support from friends that is anti-violence is likely to have very different effects from that which is pro-violence. Many men prefer to keep a strict separation between public and private life, so that what happens within men's relationships with women is seen as the men's private business; accordingly, men are often unwilling to challenge each other's violence to women (Hearn 1998a, 1998b).

In contrast, this separation of public and private spheres has been questioned by men's profeminist, anti-sexist politics (Hearn 1987, 174–6). Educating and changing men to be against men's violence to women are addressed in such politics. Anti-sexist men's groups provide one obvious place for the mutual education of men against violence, personally and politically. However, although such opposition to men's violence has been present in anti-sexist men's politics since the 1970s and 1980s, it has often not been the central defining principle of action. An early 1980s statement of "ten commitments" produced by a men's anti-sexist collective proposed the following areas for commitment: commitment to the (anti-sexist men's) group; consciousness-raising done rigorously; support for the Women's Liberation Movement; support for Gay Liberation; sharing child care; learning from gay and feminist culture; action on their own behalf; propaganda and outreach programs (linked to action); link-ups with other Men Against Sexism groups; renunciation of violence (physical, emotional, verbal) (Commitments Collective 1980). Changing men and educating the male self can occur in any social situation, not just those labelled "anti-sexist" or "profeminist." It can be just as possible among neighbours, friends, lovers, relatives, and workmates as it can be in more formally organized men's groups. However, men's support for men needs to be viewed with caution because there are pervasive tendencies and pressures for men to shift away from more progressive, even profeminist, stances towards stances that are ambiguous or even anti-feminist (Hearn 1987, 1993; Pease 2000).

Men's Programs: Specific Education Against Violence

During the 1980s there was a growth in the development of group-based educational programs specifically designed for men who have been violent to women. There are major variations in the philosophy, theoretical orientations, and practical methods of different men's programs, including psychoanalytic, cognitive-behavioural, systemic, and profeminist approaches (Gondolf 1985; Dankwort 1992-93). Each program type places a different emphasis on education. Peer support among men in men's programs is one way for some men to change their behaviour through a process of mutual re-education (Gondolf 1984; Saunders 1989). The focus on education is clearest in profeminist models (Holmes and Lundy 1990), where the task is to educate men, sometimes didactically, on the inaccuracy and oppressiveness of their beliefs and actions—what has been called "profeminist resocialization" (Goffman 1993). Gondolf (1989) has argued that "those batterers in deep denial and resistance may be more likely to respond to the didactic confrontation of the feminist approach" (xi). Particular problems have been identified with programs focusing on anger control as the central intervention. For instance, anger control "implies that the victim provokes the anger and precipitates the abuse"; "fails to account for the premeditated controlling behaviours associated with abuse"; "tends to diffuse responsibility...and prolong the batterer's denial"; and "is often misrepresented as a 'quick fix' that may endanger battered women" (Gondolf and Russell 1986, 3-4).

Typical methods used in programs include having the men describe and analyze their violence, abuse, and controlling behaviour, and then move away from that power and control towards more equal relationships (Pence and Paymar 1990). More specific techniques include cost-benefit analysis (of the gains and consequences of violent and abusive behaviour), safety plans (strategies for avoiding violence and abuse), and control logs (diary records of attempts to control partners) (Gondolf 1993). Some programs are fixed-length, say twenty-five weeks; others, particularly those that are voluntary or self-help, are more open-ended.

There has been much interest in the evaluation of the effectiveness of men's programs (for example, Pirog-Good and Stets-Kealey 1985; Edleson 1990; Edleson and Syers 1990). Evaluation of different curricula and approaches amongst programs have shown uneven results. The longest evaluative research, planned over four years, by Gondolf (1998) found that nearly half (47 percent) of the men (both completers and non-completers) used violence during the first thirty months. Only 21 percent of the men were reported by their partners to have been neither verbally nor physically abusive during the period. Tolman and Bennett (1990) found that 60 percent of men who completed programs were not physically assaultive of women after six months. However, with the wide variation in methods and approaches used, the international evidence on the programs' effectiveness is such that they cannot be evaluated or recommended in general.

A recent meta-study summarized the international evaluation research on the programs:

> Early evaluations...consistently found small program effects; when more methodologically rigorous evaluations were undertaken, the results were inconsistent and disappointing....Most of the later studies found that treatment effects were limited to a small reduction in reoffending..., although evidence indicates that for most participants (perhaps those already motivated to change), BIPs [batterer intervention programs] may end the most violent and threatening behaviors.... (Jackson 2003, 3)

In their own research, the authors of the study found, in one case, no significant differences between men who battered in the men's program and the control. In the other case, more complex findings indicated that men completing the 8-week program showed no differences from the control group, but men completing the 26-week program had significantly fewer official complaints lodged against them than the control group, but they also had no significant change in their attitudes towards domestic violence (Jackson et al. 2003).

Accordingly, clear priority measures that need to be addressed in developing programs include

- Ensuring, as the highest priority, the safety of women and children victims through contact between the program staff and the women and staff working with them;
- Not avoiding or diluting the legal consequences of criminal behaviour;
- Working in co-operation and co-ordination with programs dealing with the protection of women and children;
- Working with clear principles in programs, including the recognition that men's violence to women is largely about power and control, in contexts of men's dominance;

❖ Recognizing that men are responsible for their violence within a gender power analysis (Respect 2000; Edwards and Hearn 2005).

Schools and Other Educational Institutions

Schools and other educational institutions are very obvious arenas in which the education of boys (and thus men) against violence to girls and women may be developed. As Jeffrey Edleson and Richard Tolman (1992) observe, "One of the most logical avenues to influencing future behavior is through contact with children and adolescents in the educational system" (109).

A real-life example of gender relations in an early-years school helps speak to the problem of gendered violence and abuse. This scenario shows how, even from a young age, girls may modify their behaviour to avoid potential violence and abuse.[5]

At lunchtime, K. (7 years old) came to me and complained that she was scared to go outside during recess. She explained that 8-year-old W. had told her he would hit her in the face in the playground. Surprised, I asked K. whether she knew why W. would make such a threat. She explained that it was because she had decided to sit next to him while eating. It turned out that another boy had threatened her in the same manner. When I asked another girl whether this had happened to her as well, she told me, "No, but I don't sit next to the boys."

It is quite common for teachers to think that this is simply normal behaviour for young boys. But this scenario serves as an example of how boys often deal with situations of conflict, resorting to violent solutions rather than compromise. It shows how negative masculine values of strength and power can be well established in the behaviour of young boys and reproduced through their actions, and how the acquisition of a shared male identity through the distancing from what is perceived as "the girl group" can occur for young boys in the early grades of schooling.

By identifying themselves with what is perceived as a masculine identity, many young boys tend to become very violent (verbally and physically) towards girls in the classroom. Especially when it comes to activities that they see as male-orientated (sports, science, mathematics), boys can show a disturbing hostility towards the participation of girls, and strong anxiety about having to be part of a "girl group." The boy in the example was angry not just because someone wanted to sit next to him. His anger was provoked because it was a girl who wanted to share the dinnertime with him. Somehow, sitting next to the girl would reflect negatively on his boy identity and threaten his status as a boy within the group. Regarding this as "normal" behaviour for boys denies the violent nature of the separation, especially the act of violence towards the girl in question.

When talking about boys' violence there is a tendency to refer mostly to the behaviour of boys in the higher school grades. This might suggest a notion of innocence when it comes to early-age education. The example shows, however, that gendered violence is very much an early-age education issue as well. Pre-school and the lower grades in primary school are exactly the places where intervention against male violence against women should begin. An obvious problem in working with young boys is that it can be very difficult to refer to the issue in a concrete and direct manner. This means that it is up to the teachers and the school to create an environment that challenges traditional ideas of gender and masculinity.

Non-Violent Educational Environments

One focus of attention in addressing the problem of violence should be attempts to create non-violent educational environments. A particularly significant issue is the abolition of corporal punishment. Teachers and school administrators should also assess their methods of maintaining authority and discipline in general. Too many male teachers still apply violent, hard-line methods of keeping authority. Loud voices directed at particular children, as opposed to getting the attention of the group, are sometimes used to maintain a regime of fear and intimidation. Male teachers should also be aware of the messages contained in their gestures and postures towards their students.

Many teachers seem to perceive their authority as non-negotiable. It is important for teachers to reflect on their methods of punishment and the impact they have on students. For many children, being sent out of the classroom or receiving detention can be a traumatic experience of embarrassment and confusion, especially if the reasons for the punishment are not entirely clear to them. The implementation of certain forms of punishment without the possibility of appeal can mean that authority is misused and constitutes a form of violence on the part of the teacher. Methods of and reasons for punishment should be transparent, and the teacher should create possibilities for the children to be involved in maintaining discipline in the classroom and school. Power issues are very likely to take on a prominent role in the development of young boys; the teacher thus has the responsibility to bring her or his own power position up for debate. This may help to show that maintaining authority does not necessarily rely on assertion of power, and can, in itself, be an educational experience.

In maintaining a non-violent environment teachers should take an active interest in the influences of the extra-school environment on boys. Boys are constantly confronted with violent themes through different channels, including peer groups, sports, TV, magazines, and video games. These various influences on boys should be taken seriously and, although critically challenged, not immediately dismissed as inappropriate. As Buckingham and Sefton-Green (1994) demonstrate in their excellent analysis of a story written by a young boy, the attraction to violence can also be a expression of young boys' adolescent masculinity and experiences of powerlessness in relation to an authoritative adult society.

There is also the problem of what is usually labelled "bullying" in schools. This topic has attracted a good deal of attention in recent years (Tattum and Lane 1993). Clear connections may be made between bullying, sexual harassment, and violence in general. There is even a danger of seeing bullying as somehow childish or normal for boys and thus not part of the general question of male violence. Bullying among boys can be understood as comprising particular versions of boyhood enacted by boys on other boys (Salisbury and Jackson 1996), which in turn eventually encourage or discourage violence in adulthood. Thus anti-bullying policies and practices can be part and parcel of an educational environment in which men's violence against women is not tolerated. They can re-examine the whole educational ethos of the school, the style of management, the relationship between bullying and student learning, and so on.

Local school districts and other educational authorities have also been prominent in producing their own studies of bullying and guidelines for dealing with bullying in the context of the local community (see, for example, Bradford Educational Social Work Service 1994). For instance, issues around racialized bullying may be very important in many localities. In some schools, particularly in the United States, there has been considerable interest in peer mediation as a means of conflict resolution (Schrumpf, Crawford, and Bodine 1997). Such mediation methods, however, need to be used with caution because they can obscure social divisions (such as by gender or race) in the guise of equality (Quill et al. 1993).

Focusing only on boys, however, is not enough. Violent behaviour against girls is also often accepted by girls themselves as "boys will be boys." Making a fuss about the behaviour of boys can lead to very negative reactions from other girls in the class. Certain types of boys' behaviours are sometimes simply tolerated as normal, and therefore accepted, regardless of their violent nature. This can turn the classroom into an environment in which the behaviour of boys dominates the girls and is rarely challenged by them. It is crucial that the education of girls encourages them to speak out against violent behaviour, whether it is inside or outside the school. This is not a matter of seeking to further frighten or victimize girls, but of ensuring that they have a voice with which they can speak out against behaviour that they perceive as negative. Most of all, this is to ensure that they are aware that it is they who can decide which behaviour is appropriate and which is not. It is very important to establish a way for girls to report violent behaviour, confidentially if they wish. Finally, there is the question of responding to violence against school staff, including violence by boys, especially older boys, against women teachers (see, for example, Education Service Advisory Committee 1990).

Gendered and Sexual Power Relations in Schools

There has been increasing concern worldwide over the operation of gender and sexual dynamics in schools, and how they may include violence, abuse, and harassment. This perspective often emphasizes the ways in which the social production and reproduction of boys and young men in and around schools are a major part of the production and reproduction of adult men and masculinities, and men's violence against women. To reduce that violence it is thus necessary to challenge and change the ways in which boys are brought up and educated in schools and elsewhere (Mahoney 1985; Askew and Ross 1988; Whyld, Pickersgill, and Jackson 1990; Mac an Ghaill 1994a; Connell 1996; Frank and Davison 2000).

Schools do not just reflect dominant forms of masculinity, but actively participate in their articulation. Therefore it follows that education against men's violence should not just be an addition to the curriculum but rather be integrated within the curriculum and the teaching methods of schools. An excellent review of theory and practice for working with adolescent boys around these issues is provided by Salisbury and Jackson (1996) in their book, *Challenging Macho Values*. In such broad approaches to the challenging of boys' sexist behaviour there is a huge range of possible interventions, exercises, and practices that may be relevant to reducing boys' violence in the present and men's violence in the future. Salisbury and Jackson consider a range of pertinent questions, such as the school as a gendered institution, boys' sexualities, media education, language, the body, sport, learning to provide care for others, life stories, and fathers and sons. In each case they suggest practical exercises for raising awareness and challenging sexism, usually by drawing on boys' own experiences. Though these exercises may not be directly focused on violence, they are designed to produce a general change in boys', and thus men's, behaviours, which should contribute to a reduction in violence.[6]

The importance of works such as Salisbury and Jackson's book lies in their emphasis on the school as the institution where boys shape their masculine identities. The school is not only the institution where boys' violences can be either ignored or countered; it is also the institution where violence can actually be "taught" to boys. It is not enough to counter violence in boys without discussing and confronting the gendered power relations within which they develop. In this sense it is crucial to examine how schools function in gendered ways as part of a gendered society. These issues of gendered power are not just general or abstract but recur in the everyday life of schools. As the following example shows, an awareness of them, and practical action towards them, are crucial.

> T. (age 11) *walked into the classroom making thrusting movements with his hips and simulating masturbation. He started bragging openly about how he had touched a girl classmate's behind. His gestures and language were of an extremely sexual nature and, when confronted with the seriousness of the act, he responded that all the boys had been doing the same. The idea that the girl might have felt uncomfortable didn't enter the boy's mind at all, and even when first told off about it, he didn't fully understand what the fuss was all about.*

Even though this would be easily recognized by most schools as extremely inappropriate behaviour, it would not necessarily be recognized as male violence. Again, it is important to approach the problem not only as a specific form of inappropriate behaviour but also as a symptom of structural power relations. Whitelaw, Hills, and De Rosa (1999) make the important point that the response of the individual teacher to situations such as this is crucial and that ignoring this kind of behaviour can be regarded by students as "tacitly approving" (207). The boy in the example did understand that he was doing something inappropriate within the context of the school's code of conduct and rules. Indeed he made the conscious decision to brag about his actions to improve his status in relation to other boys and to challenge the male teacher. He understood his behaviour to be inappropriate in the sense that it would be considered rude or dirty. From his perspective, however, the indiscretion was committed against the school rules, not the girl. Also from his perspective, the girl was merely an instrument in his rebellion against the authority of the teacher and the reinforcement of his male status among the other boys. The example shows clearly why male violence against girls and women in schools should be dealt with on the structural level. To treat his behaviour simply as "inappropriate" does not challenge the fact that he was in the position to treat the girl the way he did in the first place. Simply telling the boy off for inappropriate behaviour would probably only improve his status amongst the other boys and therefore encourage him to feel good about his actions. Thus, schools should actively reassess the ways in which they reinforce dominant discourses and practices on gender relations and gendered power structures.

Are There Gender Divisions Within the School Itself?
In many schools one still finds a distinction between female and male staff in terms of the grades they teach (higher grades are taught by men and lower grades by women). This division will also often be found in subject teaching and characteristically corresponds with the increased importance placed on higher grade levels and certain subjects.

How Are Masculinity and Femininity Represented Within the Curriculum?
A subject like history is an obvious example of how ideas of dominant masculinity and male violence can be glorified through imperialistic and nationalistic male heroes and other "great men." However, it is also important to look at other subjects. Fox Keller (1982), for example, has written a compelling critique of the masculine language of science and the objectification of nature.

In Which Ways Are Male Ideals of Strength, Power, Competition, and Individualism Promoted in Sport and Physical Education Activities?
Salisbury and Jackson (1996) observe that "as the erosion of traditional masculine values goes on, sport has become one of the sites where boys and men can establish and validate their manhood" (209). For many boys, sports and physical education are the most crucial elements of school life, even though there has been a reduction in the amount of formal school time given to these activities in some countries. Schools should examine why this is the case, and determine how to emphasize elements such as cooperation, non-competition, and non-violent behaviour. There should also be a focus on the relationship between male identity, the body, and sexuality within the physical education curriculum and activities. Many boys develop very distinct and well-protected body boundaries and, therefore, often a fear of intimacy. Activities in physical education and other subjects should be geared towards overcoming these boundaries and validating care and intimacy amongst boys.

Does the School Normalize Heterosexuality?
Many boys appear to display strong anxiety and hostility towards homosexuality. Even at a very young age being "not gay" is a very important aspect in acquiring a

"normal" boy identity within the group. We have heard boys calling each other "gay" at the age of 7, without knowing what the word means beyond its being a derogatory term for them. Unfortunately it is very difficult to make this an issue in the education of boys when their school environment presents them with a picture of society, culture, and social relationships determined by a heterosexual standard. Teachers and schools therefore should become conscious of how they may normalize heterosexuality and be active in providing pupils with alternatives in sexual identities.

Focused Education Against Men's Violence
More concrete attempts to introduce education on men's violence against women into the curriculum may be made as part of general education on peace and conflict resolution, personal and social development classes, or specific teaching on violence, gender equality, and equal opportunity. Edleson and Tolman (1992) have reported on several such initiatives. For example, *Skills for Violence-Free Relationships* was a curriculum developed jointly with the Southern California Coalition on Battered Women and the Junior League of Los Angeles for students 13 to 18 years of age (Levy 1984). Four major areas are covered: defining abuse; understanding the myths and facts of domestic violence; comprehending the social and psychological contributors to abuse; and developing skills that provide alternatives to abuse, such as stress management, conflict resolution, and assertion skills.

These areas are explored through a variety of brainstorming, discussion, role-play, and experiential activities. The sessions in the curriculum have no fixed length or number. Rather, educators may tailor the materials and activities to the particular needs of the learners. However,

> an evaluation comparing students in classes where the curriculum was delivered with those in classes where it was not delivered reveals that knowledge about woman abuse and community resources increased significantly. Student attitudes about male and female roles in intimate relationships did not, however, change significantly (Jones 1991). (Edleson and Tolman 1992, 110)

Another initiative has come from the White Ribbon Campaign (n.d.) in the form of the *Education & Action Kit*, which is a very useful package in helping teachers to educate boys about violence against women and to raise their awareness of the issue.

Curricular innovation can range from the attempt to introduce this kind of material on men's violence across an entire education jurisdiction (province, state, or school district) to individual talks and workshops by representatives of women's refuge organizations and criminal justice agencies. Furthermore, all of these educational possibilities in schools are equally relevant for the preservice and continuing education of teachers and other educational personnel (Jones 1991). Educating men teachers about gender awareness should include attention to issues of sexuality, violence, and their interrelationship.

Special attention needs to be given in sex education and other related curriculum and activities in schools to the interconnections of sexuality and violence. This is partly because of the generally sexualized nature of men's violence to women (MacKinnon 1983). It is also because of the increasing understanding that much sexual abuse of children and young people is enacted by young male adults and male youth (Kandylaki 1996). Sex education must address these issues for students in schools and other educational institutions. At the same time, the educational arena is one in which the past and present perpetrators and victims of abuse may become apparent. Teachers and other educational personnel thus need their own education, training, and support.

All of the attempts to re-examine schools in the manner discussed in this section have been threatened, however, by a growing concern in recent years about the so-called underachievement of boys. As both Reed (1998) and Mahoney (1998) observe in the context of the schooling system in the United Kingdom, there is a growing tendency to "remasculinize" the educational system because boys no longer necessarily perform better at school than girls. There is a serious risk that the growing concern about the achievement of boys at school could counter the need for structural changes in the manner in which schools reproduce violent forms of masculinities (See also Whitelaw, Hill, and De Rosa 1999).

Campaigns and Public Politics: Broad Education Against Violence

Broadly educating boys and men against violence to women involves campaigns and public politics. Campaigns are usually, by definition, partly educational; they can be promoted by state, third-sector, and even occasionally private-sector, organizations, or by voluntary efforts. They may be the outgrowth of men's anti-sexist activity, such as various Men Against Pornography campaigns; they can accompany men's programs, such as the *Männer Gegen Männer Gewalt* public poster campaign in Hamburg in the 1980s; they can be sponsored by local government, such as Edinburgh City Council's "Zero Tolerance" campaign against men's violence, which used posters, stickers, T-shirts, displays and other forms of publicity that were circulated widely in the United Kingdom and elsewhere (Gillan and Samson 2000). The modern custom of designating special days, weeks, or years to highlight men's violence to women has now been established in many towns, cities, and countries.

In Canada, two particularly interesting campaigns have been promoted by men as part of anti-sexist politics. First, the White Ribbon Campaign was organized in 1991 to urge men to wear or display a white ribbon on the anniversary of the 1989 "Montreal massacre." "Their idea was to create a symbol which any man...could easily display and thereby begin to foster a climate in which violence against women would become increasingly unacceptable" (Luxton 1993, 362). This campaign has now spread to many other countries. Second, following two deeply shocking murders of women in Toronto, a small group of men walked from Windsor to Toronto in the spring of 1992, and then to Ottawa in the autumn, as a way of speaking out against men's violence and making contacts with communities along the way.

There remains a need for large-scale, state-funded advertising and poster campaigns (of the car safety-belt type) that say simply and directly "don't do it, don't think it." Such campaigns can be created, and can be effective, when governments and other powerful lobbies want them to be. It would do no harm for all agencies to begin by making it part of their public statements of policy that they oppose men's violence to women, in all of its forms. Men's violence against women is itself linked to men's violence against other men, men's violence against the self (Kaufman 1987), men's violence against children (Hearn 1990), and militarism and global violence more generally (Strange 1983). These connections are being increasingly recognized on a global scale, not least through declarations of the United Nations, the Council of Europe, the European Union, and other international bodies—notably CEDAW (Convention on the Elimination of All Forms of Discrimination Against Women) and the United Nations Platform of Action from the Fourth World Conference on Women held in Beijing in 1995. In June 2000, the "Beijing Plus Five" Conference was held in New York and, in February/March 2005, the Review and Appraisal of the Beijing Declaration and Platform for Action and the Outcome Document of the Twenty-Third Special Session of the General Assembly was issued.

Circles: Vicious and Virtuous

All the initiatives we have discussed interconnect. Self-education and the education of the self connect with the education of boys and men in relationships and in groups. Education of boys and men in relationships and groups in turn connects with the education that may take place in men's programs, agencies, schools or other educational institutions. And these institutional programs and initiatives connect with the development of education through public campaigns and politics.

Our discussion of schooling reaffirms that changing boys and men relies not only on the goodwill of individuals and groups but also on restructuring the social context in which the boys are transformed into men. This restructuring has many implications for policy and practice in schools, for both the general educational and school environments and the curricula covered, including education focused on men's violence against women. In addition, schools, in cooperation with other agencies, are possible agents for intervention in the wider problem of men's violence against women, for example, by providing trained teachers or other professional advisers to young people who experience or witness violence at school or at home.

Educating men and boys about violence against women involves more than just bringing up the issue and talking about it. It should aim to develop understanding and to change dominant forms of masculinity. Educational interventions that are designed to work with boys and men, against violence and for non-violence, therefore involve rethinking how these forms are reproduced through and influence educational institutions. Broader social change requires and suggests change of the male self and of boys' and men's individual and collective practices. Just as thoughts and actions can become vicious circles of more and more violence, so too can they become virtuous circles against violence and its reproduction. Schooling is clearly one central part of such circles, vicious or virtuous.

All of these arenas are bound together by further forms of education—research, writing, and other scholarly representations. These activities (including this chapter, we hope) are part of, and a means of, educating men and boys against violence to women. Our motivation for researching and writing on this problem has been to try to move from a generalized opposition to men's violence to women toward practical initiatives against such violence. Similarly, other forms of media can be used to either encourage or discourage violence, and to educate for more or less violence. The representation of violence, through written, visual, and other media, is a fundamental feature of education for or against violence (Hearn 1996a). This is equally as important in fictional writing, journalism, photography, film, video, television, music, computer representations, advertising and other media as it is in academic research and writing.

Notes

1. There are also now a number of national surveys of such violence—some coordinated with the International Violence Against Women Survey—which use women's own responses rather than the much lower official figures.
2. A British survey (Stanko et al. 1997) of women in Hackney, London reported the following:

   ❖ More than one in two women had been in psychologically abusive relationships during their lives;
   ❖ One in four women had been in psychologically abusive relationships in the past year;
   ❖ One in three women had suffered during their lifetime physical and sexual abuse requiring medical attention; and
   ❖ One in nine women had suffered physical and sexual abuse requiring medical attention in the past year.

   A national survey of 4,955 women in Finland (Heiskanen and Piispa 1998) reported that "22% of all married and cohabiting women have been victims of physical or sexual violence or threats of violence by their present partner, 9% in the course of the past year"; and "violence or threats by their ex-partner had been experienced by 50% of all women who had lived in a relationship which had already terminated" (3). Broadly similar figures have been reported from elsewhere in the world. Researchers in the United States have generally found that between 25 and 30 percent of women report physical abuse by a partner (Stark and Flitcraft 1996), and that about 20 percent report sexual abuse (Council on Scientific Affairs 1992), though individual surveys have found even higher figures for such forms of violence.
3. For further discussion on agency policy development, see Hanmer et al. (1995) and Hearn (1996b). This and some of the other educational arenas examined in this chapter are discussed further in Hearn (1999).
4. A very useful discussion about bringing up boys, and the links between dominant forms of masculinity and violence, can be found in Miedzian (1992).
5. This and the following example are drawn from the teaching experience of Hans Wessels with children aged 7 to 13.
6. Rather similar approaches have been used in other institutional contexts; for example, David Potts (1996) has described possible methods for "focusing on masculinity in a prison group."

Chapter 6

High School Masculinities:
Unheard Voices Among "the Boys"

Michael D. Kehler

> *There's definitely sexism in school. I'm sure it's been there as long as school has been around...you know, the guys that tell jokes about keeping the women barefoot and pregnant in the kitchen. And a lot of guys joke about that kind of stuff but they don't actually believe that women should be kept in that kind of position. They kind of act that way around their friends. They kind of, try to impress their friends.*
> (Philip, in Kehler 2000)

Introduction

At the dawn of a new millenium the reports of girls and young women in education were not promising. For the most part, reports and mainstream accounts in the 1990s reflected a persistent concern that girls continued to be shortchanged during their public school education (see AAUW 1992; Sadker and Sadker 1994). Boys and young men, on the other hand, remained favoured and privileged heirs to an education. According to the American Association of University Women (AAUW 1992), young women were underserved and disadvantaged. As Philip[1], the young man quoted above, attests, there is little doubt that sexism has long been a taken-for-granted part of the school lives of many students. Absent from much of the research in gender and education, however, is any consideration of young men who are unlike the rest of "the boys."[2]

Philip's remarks reflect a depth and complexity that bespeak how fundamentally complicated it is to be a young man in high school. His comments highlight a tension between the ways of being a young man and the beliefs or views that inform the social practices and conversations that define high school masculinities. It is insufficient to assume that *all* of "the boys" act and interact similarly or with a sense of shared or common experience in the long history of sexism witnessed and experienced by students, both young men and young women. On the contrary, what is increasingly evident is that speaking of "the boys" as a coherent whole falls far short of the complex realities of school life for many high school young men (see Kehler 2004; Frank et al. 2003; Martino 2000; Imms 2000; Kaufman 1994; Mac an Ghaill 1994a; Connell 1993; Weis 1990).

Helping the Girls or Re-examining "the Boys"?

The tenor of much of the debate in mainstream gender and education studies remains grounded in a staid and unidimensional conceptual framework for examining both masculinity and femininity. The attention thus has been narrowly focused on the performance gap between young men and young women. Schools, administrators, and teachers have been left to implement and revise programs that "help" young women. The emphasis consequently has largely centred on the education of girls and young women and issues of femininity (Connell 1995). Very little has been suggested for promoting social change among boys and young men. To a large extent "the boys" have been left unquestioned. As such, high school young men have been "shown but not said [sic], visible but not questioned" (Hearn and Collinson 1994).

Until recently the actions and definitions of masculinity framed within a school context have remained intact and unexamined. Mainstream studies and reports have assumed that all boys adhere and subscribe to a common set of beliefs about gender. As such, according to Sadker and Sadker (1994), they willingly accept scripted roles. However, men's studies (see Martino and Meyenn 2001; Connell 1998; Kimmel 1994; Messner 1997; Hearn and Collinson 1994) and cultural studies (Weis 1990; Mac an Ghaill 1994a; MacLeod 1987) research has challenged the underlying assumption that there exist a coherent set of beliefs about and common ways for being a high school young man. Building on this research, then, the study discussed in this chapter reveals how and when high school young men construct masculinities through a process of negotiation. In both practical and theoretical terms, masculinity is fluid and changing in relation to a set of conditions that are highlighted in the following account of the daily interaction of two high school young men.

This chapter examines a practical and theoretical gap that moves beyond "the boys" as a coherent group and instead identifies how and when young men actively differentiate themselves according to competing versions of masculinities and gender politics. These differences, grounded in what Connell (1995) has described as "countersexist politics," are intricately connected and expressed in the daily lives of students. The following discussion reveals how and when two high school young men displayed versions of masculinity that competed with prevailing mainstream norms and social practices. Their daily school experiences shed light on both the fluidity of masculinity as well as a connection to what Connell (1995) and Messner (1997) have referred to as progressive or alliance politics.

Description of the Study

The experiences, conversations, and interview data that follow come from a study conducted during the final semester of the 1998 academic year at a mid-western high school in the United States. This chapter examines the interactions and comments of two of the four young men who participated during the six months of this study. The participants, David, Philip, Thurston, and Hunter, were White, middle-class high school seniors who were actively involved in various facets of school life, including hockey, theatre, school publications, and school government, respectively. The vignettes of these students' school lives emerged from the daily observations I recorded as a participant observer. The conversations comprised both informal dialogues and more formal, structured audio-taped interviews.

I attempted to capture routine moments when masculinities and gender politics were negotiated in different contexts and between people differently related to each of the participants. Informal interactions thus became a starting point for seeing and hearing how and when different sets of beliefs or gender politics were woven into competing and overlapping models of masculinities. Daily observations and records of conversations between these young men and their peers form the core data in this study. For the purposes of this chapter I will focus on a subset of the data based on the conversations and vignettes of David and Philip.

As Barrie Thorne (1993) has argued, researchers need to move past categorical claims about boys and girls and young men and young women and instead develop "an emphasis on social context [which] shifts analysis from fixing abstract and binary differences to examining the social relations in which multiple differences are constructed and given meaning"

(109). School experiences thus provide a window to a more textured analysis of the polyphony of voices and exchanges that colour the lives of many students. This shift in analysis allows gender to be seen both conceptually and practically as a process that "is not fixed in advance of social interaction, but...constructed in interaction" (Connell 1995, 38 and see also Skelton 2001; Canaan 1991; West and Zimmerman 1991; Butler 1990; Thorne 1990; Messner 1988; and Anyon 1984).

High School Masculinity: A Complicated and Contested Terrain

Mainstream media has left little doubt about the polar differences, or "gender gap," that divide young men and young women. Images of the young men dominating, alienating, and silencing the young women prevail (AAUW 1992; Sadker and Sadker 1994, 1986). The question unanswered and unasked is whether all "the boys" share the same views and beliefs that inform their daily interaction in schools. This tack in men's research raises a compelling set of questions: What about high school young men who reject the sexist attitudes and silencing practices of their male counterparts? Where are the voices of high school young men who refuse to degrade women and joke about them being "barefoot and pregnant" to impress their friends? To what extent can high school young men be agents for social change?

Men's and cultural studies research has extended the gender and education debate. The unidimensional conceptualization of "the boys," when traced to theories of socialization and a passive acceptance of sex roles, denies human agency (Connell 1985; Messner 1998). Students, both young women and young men, have been relegated to being social pawns. By moving beyond arguments that complacently accept sex roles assigned or ascribed to women and men, recent research has shown the complicated series of decisions and choices high school young men make during both formal and informal interaction in school (Kehler and Martino in press; Kehler and Greig 2005; Martino and Pallotta-Chiarolli 2003; Gilbert and Gilbert 1998; Messner 1998; and Mac an Ghaill 1994a).

High schools are home to multiple masculinities. The fact that gender and education research is often narrowly focused on a hegemonic masculinity does not deny the complexity of the relations among men (Kehler, Davison, and Frank 2005; Imms 2000; Kaufman 1994; Hearn and Collinson 1994; Mac an Ghaill 1994a). Identifying and responding to competing masculinities involve recogniz[ing] the relations between the different kinds of masculinity: relations of alliance, dominance and subordination. These relationships are constructed through practices that exclude and include, that intimidate, exploit, and so on. (Connell 1995, 37)

High school masculinity thus need not be framed by conceptual boxes that simplify and codify men's behaviour. Assumptions, for example, that men and women internalize beliefs and polar ways of being through daily interaction rely on a general social consensus to guide the process (Gilbert and Gilbert 1998). Theories such as these oversimplify competitive and even contradictory models of masculinities and femininities. Various ethnographies have revealed that young men and young women have agency in the daily negotiation of their gendered identities (Anyon 1984; Willis 1977; Weis and Fine 1993). Until recently, however, this has gone largely unexamined.

The cultural landscape of any one school is comprised of a hierarchy of masculinities. Willis's (1977) "lads" and "earoles" depict competing forms of masculinity within a British school setting. Each group of young men routinely expressed and subscribed to different sets of beliefs about education. At the same time their daily expressions or displays of masculinity reflected what Kessler et al. (1985) later described as a typology of masculinities. Young men and young women can be seen routinely and intentionally making choices that reflect a set of views of masculinity and femininity that are both individually and collectively understood among students.

In his study of high school students' aspirations, MacLeod (1987, 1995) further highlights the need to acknowledge how and when young men intentionally make decisions that are not always borne out by theoretical explanations. "We must appreciate both the importance and the relative autonomy of the cultural level at which individuals, alone or in concert with others, wrest meaning out of the flux of their lives" (MacLeod 1987, 139). In his research, two groups of young high school men—"The Brothers" and "Hallway Hangers"—formed opinions and made choices that reflected competing experiences and views revolving around an achievement ideology.

There is no single consensual model of masculinity but rather competing and co-existing models that are contextually and historically situated. Young men routinely choose how and when to express various elements of their masculinity (see Renold 2004; Redman et al. 2002; Nayak and Kehily 1996, 1997; Martino 1997; Kaufman 1994; Messner 1991;

Walker 1989). At any given time, then, classrooms and high school hallways are better seen as sites in which a "variety of styles of masculinity are waxing and waning and combining and dividing as ways of being male change over time and place" (Gilbert and Gilbert 1998, 49). The following section examines the terrain of masculinities and gender politics as witnessed in the school lives of both David and Philip.

Expressions of Masculinity:
"Touchy Feely" and "Hattrick Hugs"

Social practices such as daily greetings and varying forms of interaction among high school young men lead to distinctions and differences that delineate and further cement into place a hierarchy of masculinities. During an interview, David identified a tension between standard masculinized forms of physical interaction and a physically affectionate form of interaction less accepted among high school young men.

> *For some people like Rick, you just don't encourage them in that way [putting a hand on another man's shoulder] just because, you know, they don't take it as an encouragement type thing. It's like I never, I don't really touch Rick at all.*

For the most part, the physically affectionate closeness described above was taboo among high school young men like Rick and many of his male counterparts. At one point in class when David rested his hand on Rick's shoulder, Rick responded, "You're just a touchy feely type of guy." David did not identify himself as different. Rick made the distinction. In this situation, Rick named David as "touchy feely" in an effort to explain, if not excuse, his behaviour as unmanly.

David's repertoire of ways of expressing himself and displaying his masculinity contrasted significantly with mainstream versions of masculinity. His daily interaction with his peers was a powerful arena for the gradual if not subtle destabilization of typically masculinized social practices. In the following vignette, David's interaction with his male peer is contextualized by a strikingly familiar athleticized frame of reference that operated to legitimize some types of physicality among high school young men.

> *As David approaches math class he hears his name called out. "David, David, stop!" David turns to see Ross approaching him. He reaches out to David and fully embraces him saying, "Hattrick hug!" They smile and part, going in different directions.*

On another occasion the following physical exchange occurred.

> *While walking down the hall David notices Tom, a friend of his, leaning against the wall. He walks toward him. As he approaches, Tom raises his hand gesturing for a "high five" while David simultaneously extends his hands and places them around Tom's waist.*

David and his male counterparts clumsily negotiated their interactions amidst a familiar set of norms and rules of masculinity. Masculinity itself was being defined and redefined as their understandings of male-male interaction shifted. Though subtly, David expressed himself among his male peers in ways that suggested alternate possibilities of engagement among high school young men. The physical bumbling and mixed signs of socially acceptable norms of engagement between these young men are telling. The polarity dividing how men and women interact powerfully illustrates the boundaries that high school young men such as David cross by challenging what Kimmel (1994) described as the "rules of masculinity."

The informal interaction described above reveals the ways young men interpret and define masculinities in a high school. David was mindful of the rules of interaction standard within a hegemonic, heterosexualized masculinity. At the same time, he challenged these rules. David sensed his classmate's reaction to close physical contact. This "reading" of one's gender politics and receptivity or openness, as Philip later explained, was common practice but certainly not a perfect science for these young men. David explicitly defines the gender politics that underscored his routine expressions of masculinity among his friends.

> *Sometimes...being reassuring and hugging them [guys] that way can mean so much more than what I can ever say. I am saying "I am here for you" and it's just, like, that [a hug] helps them feel that.*

David's repertoire of interaction with his male counterparts was much broader than typically demonstrated by his male peers. He believed physically affectionate contact was a valuable form of communication that was particularly useful when words did not sufficiently express his feelings. Hemmed in by the expectations, first, that men did not share feelings and, second, that they did not have close intimate contact, David displayed a viable alternative form of masculinity that is largely undervalued in schools.

Hugging, or the physically affectionate closeness exhibited by these high school young men, was but one of several ways they challenged norms of masculinity. How often did David and Philip hug another peer, particularly another man? Could they hug some peers but not others? Questions such as these speak to the messiness involved in forming norms for non-conventional masculinities. These young men saw patterns and routines emerging out of their daily school lives that supported some masculinities while denying others. The significance of hugging is in the messages they convey as men and is not necessarily to be found in the frequency with which they hugged their male counterparts. The following section looks at the process of negotiating masculinities and, most important, an approach for destabilizing mainstream assumptions about high school masculinities.

Men Among Men:
The Challenges to "Avoid that Male Stereotype"

High school masculinities are partially displays of confidence and partially evidence of insecurity. In the following interview, Philip reminds us of the intense friction that separates masculinities. His daily interactions carry forth a theme: men define masculinities most potently among other men. Kaufman (1994) points out that it is in these male-dominated contexts, in particular, that "uncontested assumptions about what it means to be a man, combined with the deep-set securities about making the masculine grade" further support and maintain prevailing definitions of masculinity (158).

> We greet each other with a hug a lot of the time. We have a really close relationship like that where I am not afraid to hug him or pat him on the back or you know, give him a little back rub or something. And it's that kind of physical closeness, I mean, that is part of our relationship....I just think it's good that as guys we are able to avoid that male stereotype of "Hey, he's hugging that guy. He must be gay." You know, that kind of attitude.

These young men demonstrated a shift in the rigidity of boundaries that defined their high school masculinities. As Philip pointed out, drawing on a broader set of understandings and definitions of masculinity involved breaking down the traditional stereotypes that confined his male counterparts. Of the four participants in this study, three routinely displayed their affection for male peers in a public and unabashed manner. At the same time these men trod carefully when opposing traditional conventions of masculinity.

The actions and interactions of David and Philip were grounded in their sets of beliefs about masculinity. Just as many mainstream high school young men are guided by a set of beliefs about traditional norms and conventions of masculinity, so too were these young men. Their beliefs, however, were differently informed and variously enacted. For them, daily actions and conversations with their peers highlighted a plurality of masculinities. Their ways of being young men were challenges because they contravened the norms of masculinity. David and Philip enacted their gender politics because they saw the opportunities to do so but, most important, because they were allowed to do so. That is to say, both of these young men had peers and contexts in which, as Philip explained, they could "be themselves." There were places in which and people with whom they could not be themselves; instead, they had to abide by the prevailing rules of masculinity. However these young men saw and seized opportunities to fill the silences created by dominant images of masculinity that threatened to keep competing images of masculinity on the fringes.

The process of challenging gender stereotypes of masculinity among men involves knowing when and with whom it can be done. In the current context, it was increasingly clear that rejecting standard masculinized norms was risky. Philip described his emerging sense of masculinities at Central High as well as his apprehensions.

> *I think I read these people pretty well. And I guess it's just a matter of...sensing it....I mean, I don't always know. Sometimes I misread it. There are times when I go to shake their hands and they want a hug or I go to hug somebody and they walk away. I know there have been times when I have gone to slap him high five and he's gone, "Come here." I guess there are times when I just know. He looks like he needs a hug.*

At the same time, Philip was mindful of the competing definitions of high school masculinity:

> *There are a lot of backward thinking people in this school. A lot of people that I know take a hug as a homosexual gesture. There are some people I know that I would go to hug and they'd be, like, "What the hell are you doing? Get away from me you freak!"*

Rejecting gender stereotypes through this convention of interaction usually occurred among small groups of no more than two to three people and often with people the participants generally described as "close friends."

High school relationships among these young men rested on their expectations and understandings of masculinity. A pervasive frame of reference formed and informed how each of these young men displayed his masculinities as well as his gender politics. As Philip explained above, some young men abided by traditional norms—these were the young men who reacted negatively and often "walked away." Thus, although Philip, like the other participants, modelled alternate versions of masculinity, a dominant model remained, one which Gilbert and Gilbert (1998) described as "culturally exalted." This form of masculinity, with which David, Philip, and the other participants were aligned, was "a pervasive and powerful form of masculinity...exalted and practiced across discourses and social contexts, which regulate thought and action" (51).

There emerges in schools a set of competing stories or lived experiences among young men and women, in which masculinities and femininities are defined in relation to each other. Out of the experiences of young men arises a potential threat grounded in the differences among high school masculinities. The challenge for these participants was in adhering to sets of beliefs that ran counter to a stronger and often better supported set of beliefs about what it meant to be a man.

Voices of High School Men: When Are They Heard?

Differentiated masculinities often surfaced in the context of the conversations the young men had at Central High. Philip was on the outside of many conversations that echoed among his peer group. He explained at one point that the conversations he had with some of his male counterparts were not meaningful to him. His lack of investment and participation in these conversations reflected how he became an interloper, a young man finding his place among other young men. He elaborated:

> *They [conversations about cars and sports] are conversations that I guess are short, kind of like, not important conversations, just kind of like small talk....The first one was about junky cars and the third one is just about sports that I played for a while but I don't really play anymore and I don't have much interest in. And I guess they're about conversations that I was kind of listening in on. I was trying to maybe think of something to say but not really having anything to say...in some of these I wanted to say something but I [didn't] know what to say or how to say it.*

His struggle to become a part of the conversation, even though he was not invested in it, was a powerful indictment of the degree to which casual conversations were a point of entry or membership among his peers.

Philip's struggle to say something was an effort to be accepted and acknowledged as one of "the boys." Daily conversations such as these provided opportunities to demonstrate what these young men knew about a variety of subjects. In a sense, the conversations became a public arena for displaying certain aspects of masculinity that were valued at Central High. By focusing on topics considered male-centred, such as cars and contact sports, these young men demonstrated, as men, a very specific type of knowledge. Philip did not have the same interest or investment in these topics but eavesdropped, almost with anticipation that he might have something to say. The fact of the matter was, in Philip's words, he "wanted to say something but [didn't] know what to say or how."

Philip's efforts to be a part of these conversations illustrated the way in which "small talk," though substantively not terribly important, nonetheless operated in an exclusionary manner among these young men. Casual conversations became grounds for playing out their masculinities. The topics, some of which emerged in later conversations, included cars, engines, football, junior varsity soccer, and driving around with the guys. The content was typically "masculine," primarily about traditionally male-centred activities. The young men's investment in and contribution to the conversations were a display of what they knew and how they were connected to the events at hand.

Contrast the above topics with those that Philip found more meaningful and the subtle boundaries and means of differentiating masculinities become clear. Philip described the conversations to which he freely contributed with his other friends:

> We talk about the play. Just, you know, chatting about college. He asked me if I got into Michigan....We talk about English. I like talking to them [my friends] about religion because I like to question my beliefs...and so we talk about religion and choir...and about school, you know, the stuff in class and that typical stuff....We have good discussions about how everything's going and sometimes we carry over our English discussions into the play or about philosophy.

The conversations Philip described present a striking contrast to the daily "small talk" that he heard among his classmates. The list of topics included college, English, religion, choir, the school play, and philosophy. It is not surprising, then, that the typical male conversations seemed somewhat foreign to Philip. He struggled to say something but, as he later explained, he was "reluctant" to speak because talking meant asking himself, "Should I risk being wrong or what should I do?".

Facades of Masculinity:
Hiding "The Things That Are Wrong"

Particular voices among these high school young men were more highly valued and prevalent than others. As described above, Philip attempted to include his voice in different male-male conversations. David explained what he believed prompted some young men to make certain contributions to conversations.

> *I think it is easier for guys to communicate like that...especially with things that are wrong. Or, like, when girls walk by and guys are, like, "David, I would really like to have sex with that girl." So they kind of...say it as a joke and other guys go [changing his voice to a deeper, gruffer sound], "Yeah, yeah! I can relate to that!"*

His insight reveals the importance that specific impressions and images of masculinity carry among these young men. As David pointed out above, a particularly significant way of defining one's masculinity was by emphasizing one's heterosexuality. Similarly, young men tended to hide things that were wrong rather than show their vulnerability or weaknesses. David elaborated by describing one of his peer's efforts to hide his true emotions:

> *Rick cracks me up because no matter what's wrong, he would never tell you anything's wrong. He's that kind of person.*

High school masculinities are often constructed based on facades that protect and deflect the potential threat of being seen as anything less than a man. Rather than share openly or honestly with his peer, Rick in this case kept up a front grounded in a mainstream conception of masculinity.

High school masculinity can be better seen as a carefully constructed and orchestrated set of conversations and exchanges. Posturing and vying for space in which to talk and, in a sense, flex one's masculinity, were common among these young men. There was a process of valuing among these young men that occurred in the ways that some voices carried more weight and ultimately social value than others.

The struggle for power over conversations between men adds to the distances between masculinities. Access and membership thus become features that separate young men (Kaufman 1994; Kimmel 1994). The topics of conversation, such as sports, cars, and fights, contributed in a subtle way to isolating and differentiating these young men. Not only did they talk about different topics, but their experiences and relation to them further demarcated the boundaries between competing versions of masculinities. The exclusion from specific topics of conversation experienced by Philip is witnessed repeatedly. Young men intentionally and thoughtfully organize their interaction in ways that secure and affirm various elements of a high school masculinity.

Straddling Two Worlds: Curricular Choices Among Men

From academic success to athletic prowess, young men make choices about the type of masculinity that eventually defines them. Students, young men in particular, see these activities in terms of social power (Keddie 2005; Connell 1998, 1993; Messner 1991, 1989). The most striking contrast evident in many high schools is the differentiation between young men who pursue an academic path and are often seen as effeminate, and the "cool guys" who ultimately define masculinity (see Robinson 2005; Foley 1990; and Messner 1998). Both types of curricular and extracurricular pursuits reflect and maintain dominant conceptions of masculinity and femininity.

Philip negotiated between rival versions of masculinity. He was active as a football player in the athletic arena but felt conflicted because, as he explained, he was "not being [him]self." His interests remained elsewhere, namely, in theatre. During choir class his teacher commented about the rich experiences offered in the arts program. Philip reflected on that moment:

> *You know when he says "you can't get this kind of experience in sports," he's right. I'm not dissing sports because I was a football player and we had some good experiences but a lot of sports is competition. A lot of sports play up the macho angle of things. They play up this thing that (making his voice more gruff sounding) "You have to be tougher than the other guy is. Raggggghhhh!"*

Philip confirmed his own feelings about the differences between the arts and sports arenas at Central High. His differentiation, however, was more pointedly about the type of masculinities that were presented and represented by each of these curricular programs. And, although he began by delineating the different experiences each activity offered, he quickly narrowed his definition to the individual as a context. He spoke less about the collective experiences involved in each activity and referred instead to the emphasis on toughness and competition between young men.

Philip made an important observation about the differentiated types of experiences young men chose at Central High. In broad terms his comment illustrated the degree to which young men like Philip not only choose between venues for participation in school but also make significant choices between different versions of masculinity.

> *And the arts...you don't get the macho aspects in the arts. You can be who you are. You don't have to feel like you have to portray this image in front of people. Like, sometimes when I played football I felt like I had to project this image of myself, at least while I was on the field. But in the arts I can be who I am. I can do what I want to do and not feel like I have to answer to anybody.*

As a football player, Philip struggled to project a specific image. He contrasted his involvement on the field with his arts experience in which he was able to be who he was, not an image of something else more valued. The tension Philip described pointedly affirms a polarity that exists between competing masculinities that have become entrenched and sustained via school activities.

Expectations and the "Problem [of] Being Myself"

High school masculinities are partly constructed through a process of image management. In David's case, his peers were often surprised at the physical prowess he demonstrated as co-captain of the school hockey team. Their expectations of David, based on what they knew about him off the ice, were often exceeded. He explained: "A lot of people are surprised I can play hockey....People like Kevin, they want to hear, like, did I hurt anybody?" The emphasis was not so much on his ability as a player but on his ability to be aggressive—his ability to be a man. David later described the importance of physicality and brute strength as factors that defined one type of masculinity highly valued among his male peers.

> *Not be[ing] huge but to be bigger would be encouraged, just by what's attractive maybe. I think it is just the way guys compare one another against each other. It's like how much they can bench press....It's different ways of sizing people up.*

Again, David suggested the need to present or represent a certain type of masculinity, an aggressive and forceful one. Elements of competition and physical attraction were central components supporting prevailing definitions of masculinity in this case. David and Philip expressed little doubt about what aspects of masculinity were most valued. Being a young man meant identifying these aspects and invariably supporting or rejecting them.

In the school sports program, Philip operated under a traditional set of definitions of masculinity. He identified several distinctions between the types of masculinities produced and supported in each of the programs. In particular, he made the distinction that in the athletics arena he had a specific image to portray, whereas the arts allowed him to be himself. As a football player he acted in ways that were expected of him. He added that these expectations extended to more informal settings as well.

> *Some girls I have a problem being myself in front of because I feel like I have to live up to some expectations. I kind of feel I, like, have to act in a certain way....Part of it might be the expectation of how they think we [guys] are going to act and part of it is just some girls.*

The expectations to which he referred were narrowly about what it meant to be a man within a sports context but, more broadly, they were about competing definitions of masculinity within his peer group. The difficulties he experienced being himself were exacerbated when he was not only dealing with the formal structures of curricular and extracurricular activities but also feeling compelled to behave in certain ways in daily school interaction on the basis of his peers' assumptions about how "guys are going to act." Philip's experiences draw attention to the "effects of what girls may say or do on boys as a context for the production of certain kinds of discursively constituted masculine behaviour" (Nilan 2000, 56).

Making Choices To Be Unlike "The Boys"

In this chapter's opening quotation, Philip alluded to the history of sexism in education. He followed up perceptively by acknowledging the role high school young men played in maintaining and perpetuating sexism. Putting down women to impress one another was described as common practice among young men. However, as Philip also pointed out, the belief systems or gender politics behind these actions were often in conflict. One is left wondering, then, why some young men remain tied to particular definitions of high school masculinity that degrade and belittle others, particularly women. At the same time, one is struck by the realization of what it can mean to be unlike the rest of "the boys." Being accepted as a young man in high school need not be tied to impressing other young men or "being tougher than the other guy." These young men have expressed the depth and complexity of high school masculinity in both theoretical and practical terms.

Plural high school masculinities force one to see the competing and contradictory lives of young men. Scripts are not simply handed down, one for the young men and one for the young women. As the young men in this study have shown, they shared a similar gender politics that underscored their masculinity. At the same time, they responded to sexism differently within the context of different types of relationships. Their expressions of masculinity were fluid and partial, depending on specific contexts. Certain aspects of masculinity were more fully displayed in different places and with different people within a school context. More broadly, then, it is understandable how competing versions of masculinities are either rejected or accepted within a school. It is also understandable how the approaches of these young men might be overlooked, and their ways of being young men unnoticed and overshadowed by "the boys" or consumed by the clamour of others.

The young men in this study demonstrated that masculinity is fluid, not static. The terms for defining oneself within a high school context are negotiable. Masculinities thus are not restrained or constricted by scripts seemingly thrust into the naïve hands of willing participants. Instead these young men have shown that there are choices to be made as men. High school masculinity is a process. Rather than being blinded by the prevailing images of masculinities embraced and hailed by muscle magazines and touted in routine conversations at school, David and Philip saw the possibilities beyond these images. They listened, observed, and eventually acted upon what they knew as young men about the context of high school masculinities and about what they wanted to present and represent. David and Philip intentionally acted and reacted to their peers and the situations that framed competing high school masculinities. They made choices about when and with whom they would resist traditional definitions of masculinity. In doing so they challenged the boundaries of masculinity that too often restricted the actions of their male peers.

In an effort to eradicate sexism or at least to begin to interrupt the dailiness of sexist remarks among students, particularly men, more attention needs to be given to seeing and hearing young men who are unlike the rest of "the boys." These are the young men who have the potential to be the social allies of women in the pursuit of a progressive gender politics.

David and Philip demonstrated that the plurality of high school masculinities can also reflect possibilities for change from among "the boys." Their school experiences suggest that high school masculinities are connected to differing sets of beliefs that frequently go unquestioned. As Philip pointed out, there are without question

> *a lot of typical guys that will say "oh, he's gay, if he's acting a certain way." That's a big thing. I don't quite understand it. I don't think it's a big deal if someone is gay. I think it [a person's response] is just (pause) ignorance and comes out of society.*

Competing masculinities and gender politics among students are fertile ground for nurturing and supporting greater acceptance. This tempering and shifting of views among high school young men will not occur, however, unless young men see, hear, and eventually begin to accept these differences. By stepping away from the definitions or images of "the boys," with which teachers are most familiar, a more complicated and richly textured conversation emerges. Out from the shadows of "the boys" come the voices of young men who have chosen to be unlike their male counterparts, to be young men invested in social justice.

Notes
1. All of the student names are pseudonyms.
2. The use of the quotation marks around "the boys" in the title and throughout the chapter is meant to draw attention to the underlying essentialism in a term that assumes that boys comprise a coherent category. Rather than employing the term "the boys" liberally, as is done in the media and elsewhere, I am acknowledging the complexities and rejecting the simplicity of a category that flattens and unidimensionally conceptualizes the boys.

Chapter 7

Boys on the Road:
Masculinities, Car Culture, and Road Safety Education

Linley Walker, Dianne Butland, and Raewyn Connell

This chapter[1] draws upon the results of two research projects: a large-scale ethnographic research project entitled *Masculinity, Motor Vehicles and Government Intervention* (Walker 1999a) and conducted in western Sydney between 1991 and 1994, which we will describe in more detail later; and a search and analysis of the road safety literature entitled *Gender Issues in Communicating Road Safety Messages to Boys: An Examination of Research Literature and Current Educational Approaches* (Connell et al. 1997).

The Problem

"Essentially the problem of young drivers is a problem confined to young males" (Henderson 1972, 2). It has long been recognized that young men are involved in relatively more motor vehicle crashes than any other group. This has been a constant feature of road use in Western societies, and one that is evidenced by a large body of road safety research. For instance, in New South Wales, Australia, young male drivers between the ages of 17 and 25 are involved in four times as many serious speed-related casualty crashes as young women and are "over-represented in nearly all types of road related crashes" (Connell et al. 1997, 1).

It is surprising, then, to find many road safety policies and educational approaches that are gender-unaware. For instance, the European

Conference of Ministers of Transport (OECD, 1994) made a number of key recommendations regarding road safety education for young children and teenagers. These included that road safety should not be taught in isolation but should be incorporated into more general approaches, that road safety should be ongoing, that young people should be given a larger role in the designing of road safety curricula and activities, and that parents need to be involved in the education process. These are admirable principles, but their formulation ignored the gender dimension, as well as the class and ethnic dimensions, of road safety and road use. Similarly, the 1996 OECD study on the effectiveness of road safety education programs failed to list among its criteria for effectiveness any consideration of gender issues.

This paradoxical situation, where massive gender differences were recognized in road casualty statistics but ignored in much policy and education, is increasingly recognized as a serious problem for road safety strategy. One of the underlying sources of this problem has been a limited understanding of gender, even in the road safety research that acknowledges gender difference. Very commonly, the gender categories have been taken for granted as fixed "natural" differences between males and females, or gendered behaviour is assigned relatively superficial causes (e.g., sex differences in "attitudes"). The research literature shows more interest in the effects of young men's driving than in its causes.

Discussions of road safety education are located in, and draw on, a broader literature on road safety. The treatment of gender in road safety education cannot be divorced from the way gender appears in this wider discourse.

Road safety research was originally conducted in engineering and the physical sciences, fields that place a high value on quantification and formal cause-effect models—characteristics of the general intellectual style known as positivism. Increasing recognition of the importance of drivers in the causation of motor vehicle crashes did not lead to a change of framework. Rather, "human factors" were incorporated into positivist accident research models on much the same terms as vehicle design factors and physical environment factors.

Research of this kind often fails to recognize gender at all. But when gender is acknowledged, positivist research has a simple way of dealing with it. Gender is included in quantitative models as "sex difference," one of a range of independent variables to be correlated with the outcomes being examined. This is, technically, easy to do in multivariate statistical procedures. Accordingly, the dominant way of talking about gender, in the road safety literature as a whole, is in the form of *sex differences*. There are well-known statistics on sex differences in fatalities and injuries, on sex differences in "exposure" to risk and in driving skill (or lack of skill), and on sex differences in types of casualty crashes.

In this approach, the sex categories are taken for granted, not thought to be in need of any further examination or explanation. Because these categories are widely believed in our culture to be "natural," the result is that an implicit biological determinism is smuggled into the whole discussion—often signaled by the use of the terms "male" and "female" rather than "man" and "woman." For instance, the literature on why men and boys have a higher number of road casualties discusses their greater "exposure" to the chance of sustaining injury or death on the road. In most of this discussion of sex difference, it seems as if this "exposure" on the roads were a natural consequence of being male, like the risk of baldness or prostate cancer. Such language erases the active social practices that constitute men's presence on the roads and their agency in producing casualty crashes.

As the road safety literature matured, it drew in more psychologists and gave increasing attention to "human factors" as aspects of individual psychology. One example was the idea of dangerous driving being produced by a high level of aggression or thrill seeking in the driver. In this perspective, gender could be understood as the psychological difference between women and men, and road safety research could be linked to the very large literature attempting to measure sex differences.

This opened space for an important departure. In the 1970s, in the wake of the new feminism, "sex differences" were widely reinterpreted in the language of "sex roles" and seen as the consequence of social learning, not biology. The sex-role framework entered health and accident research as a way of explaining sex differences in mortality and morbidity (e.g., Waldron 1976) and in due course entered road safety research along the same lines.

Because the sex-role framework emphasized the role of social expectations and social learning, it assigned greater importance to education, which was thought to have the power to change social norms. Thus was launched a range of educational enterprises, targeted especially at girls, in a period of great optimism about gender change. But there were weaknesses in the sex-role framework, including a vital scientific weakness. An immense volume of psychological research has attempted to measure "sex differences," and the general finding of this research (compiled in Maccoby and Jacklin 1975) was that in many areas where psychological traits could be measured, there were no differences between the sexes at all; and in those areas where differences (on average) *between* sexes were well documented, they were very small, compared to the range of differences *within* each sex. The idea of sex-differences-as-internalized roles is inadequate to explain (just as biological determinism was inadequate to explain) the very large differences that are found between men and women (as groups) in important aspects of social life, such as wealth, political authority, home ownership, gun ownership, car ownership, and traffic crashes (Connell 1987).

A different approach developed in the area of road safety research was concerned with alcohol and other drug use. As drunk driving became more recognized as a social problem, it was interpreted in terms familiar from the sociology of "deviance." The notion that social problems are due to a deviant minority is of course a widely popular one, in the media and political discussion. In itself the concept is not gendered, but it is one path toward a new conception of gender.

Discussions about deviant individuals, while recognizing the importance of their environments, have often led to a discussion of the cultural background of behaviour. This may take the form of research on "subcultures," some classic examples of which have been subcultures of self-consciously masculine road users such as motorbike riders (e.g., Chambers 1983; Cunneen et al. 1985; Willis 1978), or it may take the form of analyses of mainstream culture, such as Sheehan's (1994) discussion of the culture of "mateship" as a background cause of drunk driving in Australia. In a striking piece of research on young drivers in Canada, Rothe (1986) consciously broke with the positivistic traditions of road casualty research to explore young people's own understandings of cars, roads, and traffic crashes and produced a wealth of information on the social processes (including the gender processes) leading to traffic crashes. In contrast to deviance research, Rothe emphasized the *normality* of car use and the social practices leading to crashes.

In these approaches, in contrast to "role" notions, there is recognition of the agency of the group in creating gender. For instance, social drinking enacts mateship, drunk driving is an actively chosen way of displaying one's masculinity, and cars are used, for example, for dating or for peer-group outings. This approach is consistent with the conclusion reached in the intensive study of young drivers in Britain by Rolls, Hall, and McDonald (1991) that found that the social situation in driving (e.g., the presence of peers in the car, peer approval for driving dangerously) is important in understanding the higher error and casualty crash rates of young men.

In the subcultural research, there is a further important recognition of *cultural difference* in definitions and enactment of gender. This is an extremely important issue when thinking about gender in multicultural societies. It is important to acknowledge the varying subcultures of youth, and the particular social circumstances in which masculinities are being constructed, at the stage in the life-cycle (late adolescence and early adulthood) when young men are most likely to be causing death and injury on the roads.

The idea that definitions of gender are contained in cultural codes, which are played out in road use, seems to be the state-of-the-art treatment of gender in current road safety discussions. Sometimes this takes the form of recognizing "lifestyle" elements in road use; sometimes it acknowledges the issues of culture that arise in educating specific groups of men (e.g., non-English-speaking or Aboriginal men). We think this conception is merely the *beginning* of an adequate treatment of gender issues in road safety research and road safety education.

With a certain lag, the changing conceptions of gender in road safety research parallel the development of ideas in other fields. The broad view of gender as a simple pair of categories (often presumed to reflect biology directly) has been replaced by a relational view of gender. This view emphasizes that the experience and practice of gender are social constructions, involving both intimate relationships and large-scale structures. The structures involved are complex, including a social division of labour, relations of power and authority, emotional attachment and antagonism, and discourses and symbolic systems. Out of this structure emerge categories that are much more complex than simple dichotomies (Connell 1987; Lorber 1994).

The relational approach to gender is the intellectual key to the emergence of a new generation of research about men and masculinity. Masculinity, like other forms of gender, is a social construction. There is no one masculinity that is found in all times and all places; rather, there is great cultural diversity in meanings and practices of masculinity (Cornwall and Lindisfarne 1994). Further, masculinities vary even within the same time and place. In particular, there is an important difference between "hegemonic masculinity," the pattern that is most honoured or dominant in a given setting, and other masculinities that are marginalized or subordinated. The masculinities constructed in working-class settings are shaped differently than the masculinities constructed in a milieu of privilege, and relations between dominant and marginalized ethnic groups are also woven into the making of different masculinities (Connell 1995). As discussed below, the recognition of different masculinities and their varying claims to power is most important in understanding road safety issues.

Problems in Road Safety Education

As we noted above, the literature on road safety has long had difficulty in understanding, and sometimes even recognizing, gender issues. This difficulty extends to the educational literature. For instance, in their extensive study of road safety curricula in Australian schools and education systems, Marsh and Hyde (1990) made no significant mention of gender issues. Their data indicates that the available programs and resources displayed little awareness of gender as an issue. However, newer teaching materials on road safety indicate a greater awareness of gender issues. Kits such as *Driving with Attitude* and *The Driving Experience* (R.T.A. 1994, 1996) recognize sex differences in their target audience and provide materials for classroom discussion of the ways males and females relate to driving and to drug and alcohol use. The notion of boys and girls as different "target groups" is merely a first step that may embody only a very limited understanding of gender. Serious educational problems remain, as documented in our discussions with road safety educators.

First, there is the problem of even-handedness. A primary concern with reducing road crashes, injury, and death among young people would lead to a focus on boys as the group most needing to change. Such a focus, in the context of a coeducational school, is open to criticism for neglecting girls—an all too familiar criticism levelled at both education and transport policy. On the other hand, a focus on changing boys might leave the boys feeling that they were unfairly targeted. Teachers are, rightly, wary of having to criticize the group they are trying to teach.

Second, there is the problem of stereotyping. Defining boys and girls as distinct target groups is likely to lead to a "categorical" approach to gender (Connell 1987) that treats each group as distinct and homogeneous. Boys are like *this*, girls are like *that*, and curriculum is then constructed around the presumed character of one or the other. Some elementary school road safety education materials we have seen are distinctly stereotyped in this sense. What happens is that a familiar image of hegemonic masculinity is taken to be the character of all boys, ignoring the diversity of masculinities and the contradictions within masculinity. In this way, the recognition of "gender", paradoxically, may make the problem worse by reinforcing stereotyped images of masculinity in relation to vehicles and road use.

Third, there is the problem of diversity. Even where wide consultation with teachers occurs in the development of material, there is an evident middle-class and Anglo bias in the video material designed to stimulate student interest. We think it particularly important that the unfashionable topic of "class" should be central in thinking about masculinity and road safety, given that the rates of road injury are worst among working-class youth, and the grip of car culture is strongest in working-class milieus. It is particularly important to recognize this, because it is precisely working-class boys who are least attached to the formal school system in which most road safety education occurs—or, to put it another way, are worst served by the current patterns of curriculum and pedagogy.

Beneath all of this there is a basic problem about road safety education and masculinity, a problem that is also found in anti-violence work, HIV-AIDS prevention, and other fields where change is needed. That which creates great danger is also that which is greatly desired.

Boys, Young Men, and Car Culture

The ethnographic project described here had been preceded by a pilot study in 1991 with juvenile offenders in a detention centre for motor vehicle-related crime (Walker 1998a). For the pilot study, the researcher and two young women student assistants interviewed ten men between 16 and 19 years of age on their life histories, focusing especially on the reasons for their interest in motor vehicles: the origins of their passion for motor vehicles, the collective practices that were centred on cars, and the ways in which motor vehicle use had led to criminalization. If the detainee had been convicted of crimes but did not have a love of cars then the researchers did not proceed with the interviews. For ethical reasons these interviews could not be tape-recorded, but they were written up immediately.

The large study of subcultural groups was conducted between 1992 and 1994. The research team was led by one of the authors (Walker) and included two research assistants, one of whom was a young woman who had gone to school with many of the participants in the study and who shared their interest in motor vehicles. The other research assistant was a mature man. All researchers partook in the ethnographic project of observations, informal discussions, and semi-structured interviewing. The majority of the formal interviews were recorded in the interviewees' homes.

The participants, aged 16 to 21, were of Turkish, Greek, Lebanese, Italian, Serbian, Croatian, Macedonian, Cypriot, Vietnamese, and Anglo-Celtic backgrounds and were from two distinct groups. All of the members of the first group were of non-English-speaking backgrounds and referred to themselves as "Wogs and Slopes,"[2] counterpoised to Anglo-Celtic "Skippies," named after the famous television series *Skippy* about a boy's love of a kangaroo (see Walker 1999b for a discussion of the prevalence of racism in car culture). The second group, predominantly Anglo-Celtic, was known to the researcher through one of her University of Western Sydney students who was a car culture adherent, and she came to know the rest through a "snowball effect." This group referred to themselves as "petrol heads" or "rev heads." Although most were employed in motor vehicle-related industries, some were still at school. A minority of both groups was unemployed, although more of the NESB (non-English speaking background) subjects were unemployed.

Eighteen tape-recorded, semi-structured interviews were conducted with the Anglo-Celtic group and twenty-two with the NESB group. The interviews were not commenced until the researcher was confident that rapport had been established. There was an eight-month period of fieldwork before the first interviews were conducted. Clarification was sometimes sought after the analyses of transcripts.

The fieldwork included interaction and discussion with hundreds of others: immediate family (older and younger siblings and parents), other relatives, friends, girlfriends, teachers, youth health and community workers, local government officers, police, and road safety personnel. However, because young men were the subjects of the study, all but two of the recorded interviews were with them. At least one member of the research team was consistently in the field to maintain continuity. The tape-recorded individual and group interviews were done mostly in the evening in the participants' homes.

The fieldwork involved attending motor races, rallies, and motor shows. Regularly on weeknights and weekends the researchers accompanied the subjects in their cars to their entertainment venues. Streets near favourite beaches and back streets in industrial areas were popular sites for drag racing and demonstrating their driving skills and the prowess of their motor vehicles. McDonald's restaurant car parks, service stations that provided takeaway food, and streets around local parks were used for social gatherings of friends and acquaintances to show off and discuss their motor vehicles. For the young working-class men who become involved in car culture, the practices of road use allowed the building of a masculine identity, and thus a sense of dignity and self-worth, in a context where the culturally approved source of masculine dignity—holding down a job and being a breadwinner—is no longer generally available because of high youth unemployment.

More generally, motor vehicles and their use offer boys and youth engaged in the construction of masculinity a number of experiences that many of them very much want: a sense of technical mastery, a realm that is symbolically masculine, a forum for friendship and peer recognition, thrills, laughter, and a certain amount of danger. Conceptually we may argue that motor vehicle use has become an arena of domination—of both hegemonic masculinity over other masculinities, and men over women—in which many young men are able to assert (at least until the police catch up) a degree of power and authority that is denied them in most other realms.

In nearly all cases an interest in motor vehicles was passed on from father to son, or, occasionally from another male relative to the young man. This applied to almost all of the young men in the study. Of the forty young men who participated, all but three had fathers who either currently or in the past had worked in motor vehicle-related industries. Two young men had grown up in single-mother households and had been encouraged into car culture by uncles, brothers, and other older male relatives. The remaining participant had been raised as a state ward and had constructed his own fantasy world based on motor vehicles. Men's domination of automobile technology has its origins in childhood. Generally, fathers teach car culture to their sons. An analysis of this form of gender-based, familial cultural reproduction from father to son is found in Walker (1998b). The mass media reinforce the father's message.

The cultural ubiquity of motor vehicle toys is obvious enough, but a "serious" interest, according to the respondents, often begins with the gift of a bicycle between the ages of 4 and 6 years. The memory of their first bicycle was evoked for many of the respondents when we asked when their interest in cars began (Walker 1998a, 1998b). The responses to questioning about how their interest in cars was first engendered were very similar. Daney's reply was typical of nearly all of the respondents in the study:

Daney: I did a lot of cycling to start with, I mean not pro-
(Turkish fessional cycling, but when you're a kid you've got a
Australian) bike, and you're riding your bike around everywhere and it was easy to get places, you were free, and, you know, you'd work on your bike.

Interviewer: What do you mean "work"?

Daney: It was like, you know, working on a car when you grow up. You know, you work on your bike when you're a kid. It's a fantasy type of thing, you know, chrome wheels, chrome body on it, all these things. You know, you want to be better than the rest.

Interviewer: What age did you get your first bike?

Daney: I was about 6 when Dad actually got me my first bike. It was good. It was good knowing that you've got your own things and that. You could go wherever you want.

Interviewer: So what did you do to your bike?

Daney: I always liked to put stuff on then, like make stripes on it, put little chrome bits here and there, put tufts onto it, which are the rims of the bike, which are... you know, just look better, stood out.

Interviewer: Did your friends do that as well?

Daney: Yeah, they surely did. There was a guy nicknamed Senior. He actually started off, you know, he was always, you know, "I've got better things than everybody else, and mine stands out more." I suppose that got everybody else going. It was sort of competition. Yes, or jealousy if you want to call it.

Interviewer: And was he older?

Daney: Yeah, about 2 years older. That's why he was called Senior and because he was bigger than everyone else in the sense that he was chubbier than everyone and taller than everybody, so Senior was a big name.

The learning of car culture is a collective endeavour. The peer group and older boys at school and play also reinforce what fathers inculcated from infancy. Although pleasurable and fulfilling in itself, an interest in bicycles is often a fantasy substituting for the "real" toy, the car or motorcycle. Nonetheless, the main components of adult forms of car culture—competitiveness, freedom, mateship, display, technical skill and agility, speed, and performance—are present in peer-group bicycle culture.

By Year 10 in high school (when boys are approximately 16 years old, the age at which they may gain a driver's licence), boys' interest is strongly focused on cars. Schools are a site for sharing and developing this interest:

Interviewer: When did the bike phase end?

Daney: In about Year 10 in high school. Year 10, you know, at that stage you're all going for your L's or learner's [license], and you know then you move up onto something upper class. At that age you can call it upper class even though you know you haven't got one, which are the cars. I just got really stuck into cars at that age, you know I'd had enough of school in Year 12, and my mates had all these machines, had stuff sticking out of the bonnets and, you know, that put a lot of interest in us. I mean the background that I come from, Dad used to deal with a lot of cars, used to buy them and fix them up and sell them, [and I] used to help him out a lot so that got me going in cars. I got one, too.

Interviewer: Can you describe your first car?

Daney: First car was a beaten up old Ford that I had. It was a '74 model Fairmont. I mean it wasn't anything fancy, but it did the job, it got me to school and back. It was green in colour, which I didn't really like. But I mean I couldn't do anything about it, I didn't have the money for it. That's when I started working and had to earn the money to get the car I wanted.

Interviewer: So is that why you went to work?

Daney: Basically yes, basically it was to build my own car up.

The boys' interest in cars increases at the same time that their attachment to the formal curriculum decreases. Retention rates at Australian schools in working-class catchment areas have increased over the past quarter century with the loss of manufacturing jobs. The development of a suitable curriculum for working-class children has not kept pace with the changing composition and needs of all students. The hegemonic curriculum disables and disempowers the working class (Connell et al. 1982; Walker 1993).

Children who are alienated from the formal curriculum and whose relationships with teachers cause class and race injury, and consequently low self-esteem, create their own space within the school environment outside of institutional authority. Extracurricular activities relating to boys have been described in detail by a large number of sociologists of education. Paul Willis's (1977) *Learning to Labour* is the most well known study. Typically, working-class boys create cultures of *protest masculinity* that allow them a substantial measure of self-respect. Recent literature analyzes modern formations of identity where there is very little labour to learn (Jackson 1992; Mac an Ghaill 1994a; White 1993). For working-class boys and young men, car and motorbike cultures are constituted as protest masculinities. The possession of a motor vehicle is a rite of passage to "manhood," which is denied them by their exclusion from both the labour market and the academic curriculum.

In school, teenage boys and young men are subjected to the infantilizing, demeaning, and often racist insults of teachers (Poynting, Noble, and Tabar 1999). As well as having a functional use, motor vehicles provide a cultural medium in which young men, whether or not they are physically small, labelled "dumb" by others, or are from a vilified ethnic or racial group, can demonstrate masculine strength, virility, and prowess: their technical ability to control a "performance" motor vehicle at high speed and their courage and daring through risk-taking. The young men involved in car culture believe this is egalitarian, that any man can be empowered in this way (though many do not participate, and some cannot). Car and bike culture prevent to some extent isolation and anomie and engender a sense of freedom and equality, a sense of pride through the admiration of significant others (their fathers, peers, girls and young women, and sometimes their teachers), and a feeling of importance through standing out as an individual because of their cars and belonging to a special group.

> John: We're born equal, we're all the same unless you're
> (Lebanese born rich or something, like you're a jock, but they
> Australian) don't count, and cars, well, they're all the same too—like mass-produced production cars. So you have to make yourself different, so you customize your car, make it individual so you stand out and people will say, "There goes that Holden, that's John Terse." Like they know the car so they know you. And the people that know their cars, well, you get their respect. They're just like me.

The aim of car culture is to be noticed, and to this end young men spend a great deal of time and money on making their vehicles stand out from the rest. Cars are created as art objects and painted in unusual, often brilliant, iridescent colours. Car stereo systems are essential, and loud music is used to attract the attention of others—often the police! The sound of the engine is also of key importance.

> Mark: When they drive around the block past the milk bar
> (Anglo or the movie cinema in Bankstown they can give
> Australian) it a bit of a tap on the throttle and spin the wheels, and they think that it is going to impress the crowd of onlookers....You get all these guys that build all these cars that operate in racing specifications, and you're driving around town and you're more likely to be in the low rev range. So you get these guys driving around the streets in these cars that go du, du, du, du, du, you know these little Mazda rotaries. They are modified so that they can hardly even idle but that's like part of the image. They get noticed.

Girls in school are less likely than boys to take a confrontationist approach when they are placed in the situation of having to accept a humiliated, subservient role in relation to teachers and academically "bright" pupils, but some young women do, and the educational results for girls are equally as disastrous (Walker 1993). Young women who have been alienated by the school often turn to the culture of femininity for social acceptance (McRobbie 1978; Walker 1989). The young men turn to display and performance to enact masculinity. They conceive the road to be an egalitarian space where all men, regardless of race and ethnicity, "brains," or social class can demonstrate their superior masculinity and self-worth, unfettered by what they perceive to be illegitimate social structures and "bullying" teachers. In their eyes, it is only women who should be excluded. They believe that women are naturally inferior and therefore cannot and should not compete with men on the road (Walker 1998b).

> Interviewer: So you went for your L's [Learner's Licence] in Year 10 and you always had your interest in cars, because of your father and also the kids around you?
>
> Oswald: Yeah, also kids, and kids at school, guys older than
> (Turkish you, I mean when you're at school you always look
> Australian) up on your seniors or you look at people that's got something better than you have, and you get motivated. You want what they've got or something sim-

ilar to it or something better than they have, and that's what gets a lot of people going because they know they can be there up at the top with the best. We used to go up to Kingsford, hang around Kingsford, park the cars and hang around. It was like a little meeting place. We used to go after school there. People from other schools would come down, like a social gathering. That was all we did, a social gathering, talk, [and] play games.

Interviewer: Do girls go to these places, too?

Oswald: Yeah, yeah, they do with their boyfriends. But girls don't drive—like really drive. It's not a natural thing for girls.

Interviewer: Why?

Oswald: They don't have the body, the strength. You need fast reflexes for serious driving. [He dismisses the obviously silly question by shaking his head and continues.] I got the Fairmont when I was 16. I was no good at school. The teachers called us "wogs," hoods, and hoodlums, and most of the other people into cars, the teachers hated them, too, called us all hoodlums.

Interviewer: Were you [hoodlums]?

Oswald: Yes and no. We didn't make school boring, you know! [Laughter] Sometimes you got blamed, and you didn't do anything. Because you'd been in trouble before so many times, and they think it was you automatically, but it wasn't, it was somebody else. But the people get caught for silly things, and the teachers, they're not interested in you anymore if you get into trouble, step out of line.

The domain of car culture provides an arena for the satisfaction of many of the emotional needs of young men. It provides them with a group of friends, to feel that they are "making it as a man" and thus achieving an identity that commands others' respect. They feel that they are not insignificant and that they are part of a worldwide club of young men who share their interests. Additionally and importantly, there is the exhilaration of driving at high speed, the great pleasure in out-accelerating a rival vehicle when the traffic lights turn to green, of overtaking "every vehicle on the road," and of having a beautiful girl sitting in the front passenger seat.

For some young men the use of alcohol and a variety of other drugs—marijuana, cocaine, LSD, ecstasy, heroin, and amphetamines—enhances the driving pleasure. Alcohol and marijuana are the most used but because of the high risk of detection of alcohol by police, other drugs are used to heighten the effect of alcohol. These are often used in combinations. The effects of this kind of drug use on driving and road use are sometimes lethal, both directly and indirectly. Greater "courage" in risk taking is one such result of drug use. We heard many stories of drug-induced bravery in outrunning police in a chase or of hit-and-run incidents and of abandoning crashed vehicles and reporting them as stolen. The element of competition in car culture is strong, and the most desired victory for many is beating their archrival, the police.

Dangerous forms of road use are not just expressions of masculinity, as "sex role" approaches would suggest. Rather, they are means for *producing* hegemonic masculinity and establishing its dominance. This is the process visible when groups of upper primary boys race each other on bicycles, or swerve in and out of traffic; or when groups of post-adolescent youth egg each other on to feats of dangerous driving, or jeer at "wimps" who will not drive after drinking. Less spectacular, more routine, constructions of gender are also involved. It is important to stress that not all young men involved in motor vehicle cultures drink or use drugs and drive and flout the law. For instance, in a gendered car culture the mere fact of being the driver, in a family or other mixed group, is a way of "doing masculinity."

Prospects of Road Safety Education

For these reasons, coming up with a strategy to handle the gender issues in road safety education cannot be easy. Yet we have some new starting points: recognition of the masculinization of car culture, the complex structure of masculinity, and the dynamic character of gender. These suggest the possibility of new pedagogies in this area, and we will close with some suggestions about their foci.

The complexity of masculinities is now recognized as an important resource in anti-violence education. Denborough (1995), for instance, emphasizes the "counternarratives" arising from disparate masculinities in his work with boys around issues of gendered violence. Connell (1997) suggests the diversity of masculinities as an important resource in peace education. Road safety education can undermine the hegemony of a competitive and dominating style of vehicle use by exploring the diverse and often contradictory ways boys and young men interact with the transport system.

The dynamic character of masculinity is a theme of Martino's (1996) work on boys and the study of English. Martino uses literature to explore with boys the ways they are actively constructing their notions of masculinity. Davies (1993) is remarkably successful in getting elementary schoolchildren to move beyond fixed gender identities in reading and telling stories. This work, which in effect opens up the construction of gender to inspection and debate by the pupils, suggests many possibilities for road safety education, because the whole process of gendering the transport system can be opened up the same way.

Road safety education, even at its best, is but one of the messages that young people receive about roads and road use. Advertisements by the motor car industry, alcohol distributors, and other advertisers, and film and television programs all convey messages about cars, car use, and masculinity and femininity. These messages are so powerful, attractive, and well resourced that the limited resources of road safety education cannot hope to beat them in a head-on propaganda contest. But road safety education can address, and build up, the pupils' capacities to deconstruct and re-interpret the media messages for themselves. This is a technique well developed in media and gender studies at the university level, but less often done—though quite feasible—in schools. Because of the attention most children and youth give to the media, learning how the media work, and exerting their own power over the messages, can in fact be a task of absorbing interest.

Though schools are an important arena of gender formation (Connell 1996; Delamont 1990), teachers are well aware that they are not sealed off. Schools operate in constant interplay with families, communities, and larger institutions. It is now a familiar feature of gender policy in schools that parents should be included in discussions of gender issues. Parents, of course, have a major interest in road safety for their children, and may find this an easier issue on which to connect with the school than many others.

Of course, road-related education does not occur only in schools; as we have argued, families themselves are important educators in this area.

There is research evidence of the importance of parents, especially fathers, in learning to drive (Fletcher, Hamilton, and Hewitson 1997; Walker 1999a). Creative thinking about road safety education should consider ways of resourcing the process of education in peer groups, families, ethnic communities, and neighbourhoods.

The complexity and interactive character of gender point to another important group for these issues: girls and young women. "Masculinity" is not simply to be equated with boys, and motor vehicle use is one of the arenas in which girls may acquire masculine practices. Some road safety educators think that young women's approach to driving may be changing and converging with that of young men. Some research studies, though not all, support this idea (Fletcher, Hamilton, and Hewitson 1997; Ginpil and Attewell 1994).

Even if there is no convergence, girls are a key part of the social field in which boys learn masculine conduct and a key audience for masculine display. Girls as passengers have an interest in learning how to deal with reckless drivers, and the gender dimension of that interaction is crucial. Expanding girls' gender repertoires may be a crucial tactic in the safety education of boys.

Finally, in developing a response to this set of problems, it is important to think about the workforce: the teachers who are entrusted with the job. Teachers are not socially neuter instruction machines; they are social beings like other adults, and that means they, too, participate in gender relations. Indeed, the school as a whole institution is in many ways bound up with the gender order of society (Connell 1996). There is no way that teachers can escape this—though they may or may not choose to do something about it educationally. Some teachers, especially men, participate intensively in car culture; others are more distant from it. The gender division of labour among teachers generally makes men responsible for areas like science and technology, and women responsible for the humanities. These facts will affect the way road safety education is delivered, and they imply that gender issues among teachers need to be considered when designing and delivering teacher education in road safety. We have seen no research on this issue at all.

Teachers need the road safety and driver education materials that have long been supplied to them by conventional safety programs; but they also need skills, knowledge, and materials for work on gender. This need is well recognized in modern gender equity policy, in which teacher education has become an important focus, and both pre-service and in-service courses are now quite widely available. What has not been so well recognized in teacher education programs is the need for training in cultural awareness and social class sensitivity. A great deal of literature in the sociology of education has noted that the traditional pedagogy with its top-down method of teaching children and of treating them as akin to "empty vessels," that is, the deficit model of education, is especially ineffective with working-class children (see, for example, Connell et al. 1982). This model disempowers working-class children and children of colour. Because, as we have already observed, working-class young men have higher rates of traffic casualties, a more effective style of teaching, one that empowers working-class children and children of colour, is particularly important in road safety education. As well as developing in teachers the skills and knowledge necessary to cope with the diversity that divisions of class, gender, ethnicity, and race bring into the classroom, along with pre-service and in-service courses, we need to develop appropriate teaching materials and to connect all of these with the arena of road safety education. Making that connection at the level of policy and programs is vital if educational efforts around boys, masculinity, and motor vehicles are to have a large and lasting impact.

Notes

1. This chapter is an edited and updated version of an article by the authors in *The Journal of Men's Studies*, 8 (Winter 2000). Copyright © 2000 by the Men's Studies Press, LLC. Reprinted by permission.
2. "Wogs" is a racist term used mainly against non-White people of Mediterranean origin. "Slopes" is likewise racist and used to describe people of Indo-Chinese origin.

Chapter 8

The Thin Line Between Pleasure and Pain:
Implications for Educating Young Males Involved in Sport

Lindsay J. Fitzclarence, Christopher Hickey, and Bruce Nyland

Introduction

In this chapter we set out to analyze and explore the dynamics of the relationship between personal narratives from participation in sport and military myths, including the stories of bravery in battle and devotion to a cause. We explore this link within the context of what we identify as "boy culture," that is, the peer associations that are important to young males within sport. We conclude the chapter by considering the lessons for coaches and educators that are derived from such an analysis.

We need to declare a specific standpoint, a position that points us in a particular direction. The focus on "bravery" in dealing with pain and injury to overcome adversity is only one part of the equation leading to a better understanding of the enduring popularity of sport in the lives of young males. The myths and stories about sport and its participants tend to dominate commonsensical understandings of the social processes involved. However, beneath the surface representations of sport, there are complex micro-issues that involve the active identity making of individual participants. Within this equation there is a dark side to participation in sport that is often overlooked. Our thesis in this chapter is that there is a very fine line between the narratives of bravery, valour, devotion to a cause, and unquestioned loyalty to one's companions—narratives represented in many of the grand myths of military campaigns and sporting achievement—and between the abusive and damaging behaviour that is often presented as a masculine prerogative around sport and that often characterizes the culture of masculinist entitlement associated with sport.

This chapter explores relational politics and the need for a form of sports education which fosters a code of personal responsibility. As such, we assume that sports such as "football"[1] involve complex processes of personal decision making. In our opinion, this is an area where opportunities for active coaching and teaching exist. This view is endorsed by Kevin Sheedy, one of the most experienced senior coaches in Australian Rules football. Sheedy's observations in this vein are reported by Kerley (2000):

> In my time as a coach, I've always found that if a player is not responding, or if he is performing below standard, you can normally put it down to three things: problems on the home front or with relationships, problems with work or career direction, or financial problems. (26)

It is significant that Sheedy put family and relationships at the head of his list. In other words, from the players' perspectives, what matters most are social factors. We intend to build on this insight in this chapter. Our line of inquiry explores the world of young males in terms of their relationships with their immediate peers. Our central proposal is that young males actively seek the positive and pleasurable inducements of participating with their "affinity groups" in games such as football. Our analysis is framed by the following questions:

- ❖ What social narratives invite young men into competitive and combative sports such as football?
- ❖ What meanings do young males ascribe to their painful and pleasurable experiences in football?
- ❖ How do the subjective accounts of participants compare to the mainstream analyses of involvement in sport?
- ❖ What are the implications for education of an understanding of the narratives of pain and pleasure in sport?

The methodology that we have used to answer these questions combines several approaches. We begin with a historical review, which involves textual analysis. Section One links themes from myths of war with accounts of contemporary Australian football.

Section Two relates a narrative which we have called "Bruce's story." This section documents one of the authors' experiences as an Australian footballer who played at the elite level of football in the 1960s and 1970s. In this section, we utilize some of the ideas developed through use of "memory work." This method, developed by Frigga Haug and her associates (1987), is one which activates memories, then systematically records and analyzes them. Within this narrative we continue to build on links from military discourses, particularly excerpts from work by Joanna Bourke (1999). Her study involved an analysis of the letters and diaries of soldiers who fought in three different military campaigns. This work challenges the popular view that the experience of war involves unimaginable horror. Although this is doubtless accurate in many cases, Bourke's work uncovered a counternarrative. Bourke

> suggests that the structure of war encourages pleasures in killing and that perfectly ordinary, gentle human beings in civilian life can become enthusiastic killers without becoming "brutalized," as one pervasive cliché would have us believe. People find ways of creating meaning out of the chaos of war, and one way is to find great satisfaction in it....Violent and sadistic men are not the best killers; men motivated by emotions like love and empathy, rather than those of hatred and bloodlust, become the most lethal individuals on the battlefield. (dust cover)

This is the insight on which we build. Although we are not interested in Bourke's focus on the capacity to kill, we are interested in the experiences that produce powerful feelings of belonging to a particular group of companions. Indeed, it appears that it is this social context that fostered the reactions that Bourke discovered in letters from the frontline. One way of reading the information that Bourke compiled is to acknowledge that the motivations to perform in the arena of battle were generated by the close bonding of "brothers (and sisters) in arms." We assume that it is the experience of "groupness" which provides feelings and experiences similar to those which occur within sport. In both contexts, issues of identity reach far beyond the colour of a uniform to affect the construction of particular values, morals, and ethics. It is from within these constructs that many soldiers and footballers learn, albeit subconsciously, what is and is not expected of them and what they can and cannot do if they want to be part of the group. Indeed, it is from within these group knowledges and practices that many young men will interpret their masculinity.

Section Three, Clint's story, brings our account into contemporary times and into the sports world of teenage males. This account demonstrates how many of the themes that appear in other contexts and other times live on in the life of a talented and highly motivated young footballer. Clint endured considerable pain to play football, the game about which he was passionate. Our discussions with him also provided the opportunity to record his transition into senior football with its various inducements, rewards, and pressures. Preliminary discussions framed the issues and were followed by Clint's recorded response to a series of central questions. The transcript of his responses was then discussed several times to clarify and extend the answers. Clint's account helps demonstrate the thin line that separates pleasure and pain.

Section Four of the chapter provides an interpretation and discussion that cross-references the issues raised and explored with a selection of appropriate academic literature. Here we examine the origins of emotions associated with belonging to an affinity group—one's peers. We examine a study by Rotundo (1998) that documents the features of "boy culture." Rotundo's work helps acknowledge the formation of identity for young males through peer-group interactions. Specifically, Rotundo examines how young males are readily recruited or seduced into the dominant masculine culture. This culture is often built around the identification of a particular group's tribal values and myths. There is a strong desire to understand the self as something distinct from others. Rotundo points out that the process of "othering" can be based on differences, albeit unperceived, along territorial, class, or ethnic lines. Within the meta-discourses that describe hegemonic masculinity, there are clearly contextual applications according to cultural demands, definitions, or mythologies. Rotundo's work enables us to contextualize Bruce's and Clint's stories.

We conclude by considering what our analysis means for educators who work with young men in sporting situations. Mindful of the consequences of "throwing the baby out with the bath water," we are eager to explore new ways to ensure that sporting participation is a valuable and constructive experience for young males. Throughout Bruce's and Clint's stories we invite readers to keep in mind that, as footballers, both of these young men gained a great deal of personal satisfaction and social respect. However, we are acutely aware that, like so many before and since, they walked the thin line between success and failure, aggression and abuse, pride and arrogance, and pleasure and pain. For those who view sport as a medium for the potential development of socially responsible young males, the challenge is to instill all of the positive qualities instead of the negative ones.

The methodology that we used unites our different experiences as participants in and students of sport. As "intellectually trained" (Sharp and White

1968) professional educators we share a motivation to better understand the wider implications of the personal sporting experiences of youth. Furthermore, we recognize the importance of education, including the work of teachers, coaches, and administrators, in reframing the personal experiences of males involved in intensely competitive activities such as football.

Section One: Background

On April 25, 2000, at the Melbourne Cricket Ground (MCG) a crowd of 88,390 people assembled to witness an annual football game between Collingwood and Essendon, two of Melbourne's oldest teams. This is more than a game of sport. The annual event also commemorates the deeds of soldiers during a famous battle in Turkey during the First World War. On April 25, 1915, volunteer soldiers from Australia and conscripts from New Zealand were part of a force numbering between 55,000 and 60,000. They attempted to secure the strategic Gallipoli Peninsula in a battle for the Dardanelles waterway. The attempt failed: 8,700 allied soldiers were killed, and another 25,600 were injured during months of bitter fighting. In the process, however, a legend of great cultural and political significance for Australians was born.

This battle occurred just fourteen years after the federation in 1901 of distinct colonial states into the new nation-state of Australia. April 25, 1915 therefore became a defining moment in the development of Australia's nationhood. The war correspondent C. E. W. Bean, who later became Australia's official World War I historian, coined the term ANZAC (Australian and New Zealand Army Corps) and reported the immense bravery and struggle against overwhelming odds displayed during this conflict. According to stories recounted by Bean and others, the Australian and New Zealand troops displayed unique characteristics of mateship, resilience, and unflinching courage in the face of overwhelming opposition.

The stories of April 25, 1915 were quickly absorbed into the official discourse of nation building and found their way into school curricula and also into many different forms of popular culture. In the process of mythologizing the deeds of the soldiers at Gallipoli, "ANZAC Day," as it is now known, has become an official holiday on the national calendar. Each year on April 25th, solemn memorial services are conducted around the nation to honour those who have served and died in wars and peacekeeping campaigns since the birth of the nation.

Sport soon found a home in the process of remaking and extending the ANZAC myths. This link was fostered by the media. One sports historian noted this symbiotic relationship in commenting on the revival of football after the First World War:

> This new interest in football coincided with the popularisation of the Anzac myth. Sports journalists began to construct more elaborate metaphors of football, especially around the theme of battle. The widespread Anzac values percolated through this coverage: individual players became heroes of battle, just as the common foot-soldier was seen to have won the day through particular acts of courage and tenacity. (Pascoe 1996, 92)

In 1995, eighty years after the landing at Gallipoli, Essendon (popularly known as the "Bombers") and Collingwood (the "Magpies") played a commemorative ANZAC Day game at the MCG in front of a massive crowd of 94,825 spectators. The game finished in a draw and, in the short time since, it has been mythologized alongside the heroes of ANZAC Day. The football game played in 2000 continued the tradition.[2] Media headlines the day after this game, which Essendon won, included "Bombers march on," "Invincible bombers," "A day for heroes," and "Brave Hird rekindles the Anzac spirit." The last caption is particularly significant for our analysis.

James Hird, the captain of Essendon, was awarded a medal as best player on the ground in the 2000 game. This medal, struck by the Australian Football League, was "for the player who best personified the 'Anzac Day' spirit, skill, courage in adversity, self-sacrifice, team work and fair play" (Pearce 2000, 1). The media subsequently praised Hird as a most worthy winner of the best player medal.

Hird had missed the three previous ANZAC Day games because of severe injury. Stress fractures of the feet had limited his participation in football to a mere handful of games in three seasons. Despite the pain, frustration, and loss of confidence, Hird was reported to have worked hard to overcome the limitations of his serious injury. Matthews (2000) recorded that, on ANZAC Day, 2000, Hird "led by example when the battle was at its most fierce" (84). This report suggests a distinct cultural politics. We find here the union of sport, the development of national identity, and the glorification of certain forms of masculinity. James Hird, the footballer, is seen to embody the characteristics and capacities of the soldiers of Gallipoli. It can be seen how the mythologies of wartime heroes—a strategic aspect of nation building—have carried over into the world of sport and the lives and identities of particular individuals. A newspaper photograph which shows Hird with the ANZAC game medal draped around his neck is a concrete expression of these cultural politics. The media indeed plays an important role in this process of recirculating and reinventing the ANZAC mythologies.

Section Two: Bruce's Story

I was born in the heart of Port Adelaide during the post-war baby boom. It wasn't a place for faint hearts or weak bladders then but it was a place that could explain the genesis of justifiable agoraphobia. To venture outside you needed eyes in the back of your head and a slingshot in your pocket. Dominating the local terrain was the Alberton oval, home of the most famous Australian football club, Port Adelaide.[3] For young males in the area with any football talent it was an irresistible magnet. All roads led to its sacred turf. It was our Mecca.

It is clear that fantasies of combat drawn from books and films also dominated many men's daytime and night-time dreams, encouraging them to volunteer in anticipation of being given an opportunity to emulate heroes that they had read about since infancy. (Bourke 1999, 20)

Within these precincts lurked the menace of the Riley brothers. They were gargantuan predators who handed out hidings like they were mandatory lessons for disobedient peasants or social heretics intent on destroying the existing order. The Rileys were at the top of the food chain. They gave you a thrashing for simply being there. No warnings, no rules, no foreplay, and no escape. Occasionally there were pre-quake indicators, such as, "What are you looking at?", "Gimme that," and the worst, "What did you say?" Any of these statements meant that very soon you were going to lose your physical integrity or quite literally some of your teeth. You had to cop a hiding. Otherwise evidence of your cowardice would be posted in every village for all to see. God forbid if this sort of news reached your girlfriend because it would be the end as she would definitely not compromise her pride by going steady with a wimp. I received one beating at the end of a Riley bike chain, which resulted in my being hospitalized. When my father saw me, he just said, "I thought you could fight." He was genuinely depressed and shamed in front of his mates. Meanwhile, I was a now toothless victim of peer-group abuse, with a paternal caregiver oblivious to the fact that the Riley boys were not only several years older than me, but much bigger. Such is life.

Picture this. I was a skinny, pimpled adolescent of 16, built like a basal ganglion with Barney Google eyes when I was selected in the reserve team at Port Adelaide. I had played a few games in the junior grades and now I was on my way to unpredictable fame and glory. I borrowed a friend's Standard 8[4] and headed off to Richmond oval, a distance of no more than of 10 kilometres, without having a clue where it was. Somehow, despite deliberately fraudulent directions from locals, I arrived—albeit late. I was a boy on a man's errand, minus a driver's licence.

Sheepishly I entered the players' change rooms. A bony finger pointed me in the direction of Jock, playing coach of the seconds team. His biceps were like tree trunks, his thighs like stobie poles[5] and his head was like a robber's dog with five o'clock shadow. Frightened of nothing and no-one, Jock took no prisoners, including me. "You Nyland?" he demanded. I think I answered in the affirmative. "You're late." His handshake squeezed the blood from my fingers and destroyed the integrity of my knuckles as he delivered his tour de force for beginners. "Fuck up son and it will be on your headstone. Got it?"

Then followed the pre-match address. What did it mean? What did I have to do? The theme, as I remember it, included clearly "FUCKEN," interpolated with this and that, mainly incantations to inspire acts of heroism. Everyone seemed to get the message except me. An unrestrained chorus of "FUCKEN" rose from the team every time Jock's body language required a sympathetic affirmation of his life position in this matter. I "FUCKENED" along, sounding like Minnie Ripperton[6] in a herd of elephants.

The siren went. Time to go. I tell you, I did not want to, but a tide of large sweaty bodies swept me up from my childish inertia and carried me legless into the concrete race whereupon I promptly slipped and smashed my head against the wall.

In a mental haze I scanned for an opponent. He found me. Why does every Australian Rules football team have a player nicknamed "Blackstick"? Well they do, and in this particular setting he was my avowed enemy for the day, much to my chagrin. He was too slow for first-grade-level football and built like an eighteen gallon keg on wharf-pylons with a reputation for capricious violence and hatred for young upstarts. Like me. His cordial greeting was "Hey, sissy lips, get in my way and I'll plant your pretty arse in outer space." A place no doubt he was from. I needed help. It came in the form of "Cowboy."

The "Cowboy" could do everything. Despite a diet of beer and cigarettes he was a fine athlete and a brilliant footballer on a good day. He noticed my distress after I was poleaxed behind the play by "Blackstick" simply because I had the audacity to be in the vicinity of the ball, and he decided to even things up on my behalf. "Ignore the prick, son, he is about to disappear up his own arse."

At the time, it was tradition that everyone was expected to have a drink after the game even if they did not drink. I didn't drink so I'm not sure how the schooner of beer reached my lips and got into my brain cells. Through the mist produced by several drinks I saw how two working-class teams bonded easily in the afterglow of battle. I was right into the players' snappy verbal exchanges of reverse snobbery, which belittled the educated and wealthy as an underclass of self-indulgent parasites with soft hands.

The "Cowboy" ambled up to where I was perched and took the glass from my hand and said, " Ease up, son, plenty of time for this later. Anyway if you listen to this shit much longer you will start to believe it." What was he saying? "Cowboy" a turncoat? An apologist? A revisionist?

"Cowboy" was living proof that the human race can stand equally condemned and venerated at the same time. The bloke had a will of iron and a heart of gold. He was a bloke who would give you the shirt off his back, a shirt of course which had been lifted off the back of someone else who was completely unaware of their indirect generosity.

༺༻

These myths of honour in combat were clearly diverse and contradictory, and there was intense rivalry between men adhering to different traditions… combatants who thought of themselves as warriors placed similar emphasis on chivalry, intimacy and skill. (Bourke 1999, 51)

༺༻

Milton got it right when he said, "They also serve who only stand and wait." I played my first league game on ANZAC day 1962. It was an ordinary event in the stream of human achievement, but not for one who has fulfilled a dream. With disbelieving eyes, I saw my name in the team line-up alongside a galaxy of stars, the heroes of my boyhood. I was a giant, to my mates, to my girlfriend, bigger than Elvis, to my mother, a god, and to my brother, a complete mystery.

I reached Adelaide oval without my feet touching the ground, my heart pounding and bursting with pride. It seemed to me that the supporters formed a guard of honour all the way to the change rooms, generously welcoming me to that inner sanctum. I felt a spiritual continuity with souls I had never met or would ever break bread with. Urban solidarity at Port Adelaide was, and still is, a tangible reality which carries with it a heavy price for those who stand and wait.

Before I had dropped my bag, two hands landed firmly on my shoulders. "Bro" and "Bones," both captains and keepers-of-the-gate, were at the end of the grip. Together they formed an awesome prospect for any impressionable young lad entering this world. Mixed with the players' jabber were other unmistakeable messages of heartfelt significance, not only for "Bones" and "Bro," but for all the faithful:

You're you but not you….You have inherited greatness but you are not great….The tradition you are now part of made you great, and now you will make it great….You are not a ghost but you will become one….Your importance is temporary but history is seamless……welcome to the family.

As a working class kid, I was indoctrinated to feel nothing, say nothing, and remain indifferent to everything but I still remember how the hair stood up on the back of my head and pride saturated every part of my being as I heard the words.

The senior coach at that time was as tough a human being as ever walked the earth. One of the training routines he used to love involved getting us to line up opposite each other in four queues. He would stand in the middle of us with the ball, and then demand that we charge head-on at one another. Whoever arrived first got crunched. The last to arrive incurred his wrath, which was much worse.

> Group solidarity lead [sic] to a return to primitive forms of behaviour, including reliance on the leader as father-substitute. Crowd psychology also promoted automatic movements: group drills, with emphasis on monotony and everyone doing the same thing together, enabled men to carry out the required movements almost without conscious thought, all the time feeling supported by the formidableness of the group. (Bourke 1999, 98)

ANZAC Day for the coach was no ordinary occasion because it evoked visions of slaughter, bravery, ultimate sacrifice, and loyalty. As he spoke images from hell arose, enveloping the living (us), the half dead ("Bones" and "Bro") and the dead (ex-Port players who had died in war). His pre-match address was so inspirational it would have made Charlton Heston weep.

> Do not come back unless you are a shell....Remember all that has gone before....Look into my eyes and see what I see....I ask nothing more than I would give.

Was it motivation? Incantation? Jockery? I don't know for sure. I do know that the feeling of euphoria I had then stays with me today, not so much as a living memory but more as a sense of shared dignity with friends when what was required were trust and interdependence.

I still see those faces and feel those moments with a smile and a grimace. Their heartbeat is mine, mine is theirs. Corny but true.

> The army itself acted as a crowd and, as such, was governed by the same laws which governed a crowd. Like the individual, crowds were ruled by voices from the past. (Bourke 1999, 85–6)

My return to football after injury was farcical. I had to convince the coach and medical staff that I was ready to play, which of course I wasn't. The truth was I could not handle the ball with two hands and could barely walk. Nevertheless, a fitness test was required. The test was designed and undertaken by the coach, a man whose tolerance for equivocation was zero. In front of the medical staff, he ordered me to grip his hand with my fingers to see how much force I could exert. My grip was firm and the doctors were persuaded of my fitness.

My comeback, married to the shortest recovery of all time, was not blessed. After being struck in the chest by a ball which planed from the surface of a rain-soaked oval and wrestled headfirst into the mud by the "Enforcer," I spent the rest of the weekend in hospital with three broken ribs and a concussion. I had little time to reflect on the mystery of pain and pleasure as important guiding principles for human behaviour because within two weeks I was back at training, limping and heavily bandaged. On this occasion, the club doctor decided to take charge of the fitness assessment so he applied a simple but, alas, unscientific test. A bear hug. His grip was gentle, and the pain tolerable. The coach, head cocked, and eyes impatient with his familiar look of suspicion, was manifestly unimpressed. "Christ, Henry, he's not about to play netball! I need to know if he's ready. Get out of the way!" The coach then applied his version of the appropriate fitness test. A Hulk Hogan special, without the theatrical safety net. I wanted to pass out. I needed to pass out. My chest screamed with pain. My legs turned to jelly. The coach looked into my blood-drained eyes and said, "Can you get through this? I want you to get through this. You know I would not ask something of you that I would not ask of myself." I had seen him play when I was a kid so I knew that every moment of every game for him was a critical examination of his courage, manhood, and sacrifice, all of which he passed with distinction. Physical health was never a question with him. He wanted to know if I was made of strong stuff. Somehow, I got through the next two games without incident and went on to play in the 1965 grandfinal match, which we won. The prospect of glory and triumph had far greater appeal for me than spending the rest of my life labelled a worthless "gimcrack.?"

Foolish or not, I treasure the respect I secured in the hearts of others. Nothing is more certain than that injuries and setbacks are unwelcome visitors to the home of sport. Equally, nothing is more certain than that the exhilaration, excitements, and rewards of participation and success exorcise the demons of passing agony. Ask anyone.

Section Three: Clint's Story

Fast forward thirty years from the early 1960s. Although so many parts of society have changed beyond recognition, other features endure. For young footballers in the 1990s and 2000s the dreams, struggles, highs, and lows remain linked to the narratives of other times and other places.

Clint's first football memories involved learning to kick in the streets and parks and at the principal football oval in Geelong, a provincial city in the state of Victoria. Clint's family had moved to Geelong during a period of alternating employment and study.

In the early 1990s, Clint's dream and fantasy of life as a footballer started to become a reality.

> *When I started to play I enjoyed the whole rush because I was actually quite scared. It was a rush to play these bigger blokes but once I got over that I enjoyed the skills and sort of the roughness of the game. At this time my dad was coaching and my friends were playing and it was great fun.*

Clint made rapid progress in football as he got older. By the end of primary school, at 11 and 12 years of age, he was playing representative football at state championships.

> *School helped me a lot with competitive football because I got my first real look at the highest standard of football at the state carnival. I got to see how much better the game could be played in my age group.*

Because of these opportunities and aptitudes Clint's social world and horizons quickly expanded.

> *I've made friends through footy from Cairns in Queensland to Finley in New South Wales. Meeting friends and being able to travel has given me pleasure. The greatest pleasure involved being selected in the Under-fifteen state team for the first time to play in the national championships in Cairns in 1998. That was a pretty amazing feeling when I heard my name get called out. I'd finally achieved something I'd been working at for a pretty long time.*

A high status in one's peer group and an opportunity for extended social interaction are powerful motivators for many young people. Selection at the state level brings recognition and celebrity status, both of which are often generated by the local media. These were some of the spoils of competitive football, which Clint achieved at a relatively young age. However, success in this sport, especially at this age and in a provincial environment, often comes at a cost. Jealousy and innuendo sometimes consume those who are not selected for the high-status teams. Others simply find it hard to be mere observers as a teammate flies off to experience adventures and the glory attached to high status. Subsequently, Clint and his parents found themselves embroiled in a bitter dispute with some teammates and their parents. This development was the source of a great deal of distress and soul searching:

> *Having a big fight in my old team was bad because I was so involved in it and people get hurt. And you get hurt too. It causes a lot of pain.*

In 1999 Clint changed clubs and schools and began to play senior football. For Clint, this was a big step into the adult world. He was playing with and against men who were used to hard physical work as timber workers, farmers, and fishermen.

> *In the first game I was really scared. They were big blokes. My teammates helped me to settle down. I had to "man up" on their rover and every time I went for the ball he tried to hit me. Our blokes saw this and just laughed at him and this made me feel better.*

In the second game of the season, Clint suffered grade 1 ligament damage in his shoulder. The injury was not debilitating but it was serious enough to require treatment. Clint continued to play with his shoulder strapped, but successive bumps, falls, and constant hard contact continued to aggravate the damage. A mid-season diagnosis indicated possible widening of the AC (acromioclavicular) joint. During this period, and in spite of his injury, he was selected to play on the state team in the under-sixteen Australian football carnival, the most prestigious event in underage football. After this event, and despite his pain and discomfort, Clint returned to his home team with renewed enthusiasm.

> *I was really keen to play well so I trained hard and just put up with the shoulder. By now I knew that it was good to play footy with mates. We played for each other, not the coach.*

It is apparent that by mid season he had fitted into the routine of playing at the senior level and being a permanent member of the team. Carried along on the wave of team success, with encouragement and support from his older teammates, Clint nursed his damaged shoulder towards the end of the season. He kept to himself the truth about the full extent of his injury:

> *I played half of the season with it (serious injury) which was hard because you try to hide it from some people, like your coach and selectors.*

Meanwhile the team was building momentum and it steamrolled its way into the finals and then on to secure a place in the grandfinal. In the biggest game of the season, Clint and his teammates shared the ultimate prize. They won the premiership convincingly with a score line of ten goals and seventeen points (seventy-seven points) to five goals and eight points (thirty-eight points). Clint remembers the game and the final siren:

> *It was stressful but it was joyful too. At the end I felt relief. It was a strange feeling. Like a big "YES," which was relief at not getting hurt anymore. I had "popped" my shoulder in the game but kept playing.*

Clint had managed to achieve in his first season what many players never achieve in a lifetime, a place on a premiership team. More than this, he was subsequently awarded best first-year player by his club. He was 16 years old but still a schoolboy, and he knew that he had earned the admiration and respect of experienced sporting people both in his district and beyond. However, these achievements came at a price. A post-season assessment of his injury revealed a dislocated shoulder involving damage to the head of the humerus and associated tendons. One can only imagine the pain that he endured to keep playing through to the end of the season. In late 1999, Clint underwent a shoulder reconstruction operation. He spent the 2000 season rehabilitating the damaged joint and reflecting on his experiences and their cost:

> *It was worth having the experience of 1999 but somehow it all felt [like] it was out of my control. Now I'm paying for the significance of something that was so grand. It's hard on your head 'cause you're not...in the same ritual that you've been in for so long.*

Clint and Bruce do not know one another, and had not even heard of one other before this chapter was written. Their football worlds are separated by hundreds of kilometres and several decades. Their stories, however, are remarkably similar. The desire to play at the highest level was a long-held passion. Their local cultures generated intense interest in football and provided the initial impetus to participate. The lessons and attitudes developed in junior football paved the way for crossing the threshold into the adult world of sport. As a result, the motivation to perform well, under extreme duress, was strong. The enjoyment of fitting in with men, much older and more worldly, was seductive. The capacity to withhold vital information about injury and to endure extreme physical pain was pronounced. But, *why* are these narratives so similar?

Beyond the obvious connections between the two stories, there are other links to be explored. The stories of Clint and Bruce are connected to that of James Hird in that all three men struggled through the pain of injury to continue playing football. At the same time, each account is part of a richer discourse that stretches back through the lives of footballers, soldiers, and men of previous times. The letters of young soldiers, which Joanna Bourke has studied, remind us of this fact. Bourke's study has recognized that the dominant, critical narratives of war involve accounts of pain, damage, and destruction. Alongside this dominant narrative, however, is a secondary one. Here, too, there is evidence of quite different personal reactions and emotions, involving images of strong and pleasurable motivations. Although we are keen to not reinforce a glorification of war and violence, we are nevertheless interested in better understanding the social processes that produce strong pleasurable emotions. In the following sections we explore these links and their meanings for education and those who work with young males in the sporting context.

Section Four: Interpretation and Discussion

Around the globe, large numbers of young boys continue to participate in the different codes of football. In the southern states of Australia, literally thousands of young males are involved in Australian Rules football each week during the winter months.[8] James Hird, Bruce, and Clint are all products of the junior-football factory. The stories of these people, represented here as young participants in football, are linked by the common capacity to overcome pain and discomfort in order to experience the pleasures of participation and the rewards of belonging, acknowledgement, and recognition. The forces behind such capacity are not well understood. In our opinion, football and, by implication, footballers have been represented by two very different discourses. The first involves narratives developed within the mass media and thereby popularized. Against these are more critical narratives relating to the damage and danger involved in games such as football. We will highlight these two contrasting narratives before posing an alternative theory.

Many cultural forces combine to promote and maintain interest in football. In particular the mass media promotes the virtues of the sport. Books, cards, television and radio shows, magazines, and newspapers all promote different aspects of the game and its participants. According to Stoddart (1986),

> daily media outlets deluge Australians with results, articles, opinion and biographical sketches, as they have done for over a century. Specialist magazines continue the process as do numerous books that appear on a variety of sports. The point is, rather, that sport has been eulogised rather than criticised: there have been few attempts to stand off and analyse exactly what role sport plays in Australian society. (4–5)

Evidence is easily found to show that the media tends to portray a one-sided account of the virtues of sports such as football.

On the other hand, critical analyses of sport and physical activity have started to appear over the last three decades. In the 1970s and 1980s athletes were described as "prisoners of measured time" (Brohm 1978) and, as such, the puppets in social-class politics. Feminist works have also generated important insights into hegemonic masculinities (Segal 1990). This work, in turn, has generated new possibilities for critique by a generation of male academics who have reinterpreted sport and physical activity and questioned some of the dominant assumptions about the so-called virtues of sporting participation. The North American academics Messner and Sabo have been particularly important.

> The fact we both experienced more agony than ecstasy in doing what we loved most, playing sport, made us feel as though something was seriously deficient or wrong with us as individuals. Many years after the ends of our athletic careers, we learned from feminist women to examine our personal experiences and problems within the context of larger social realities. The idea the "personal is political" allowed us to see our bad experiences in sports not as manifestations of personal failure, but as normal consequences in a system that values victory over all else, including relationships with others and to reexamine, through a feminist lens, some of our youthful experiences as athletes. (Messner and Sabo 1990, 10)

This line of inquiry has opened the way for an examination of the physical and psychological damage experienced by many sports participants. In turn, though, it has fostered an analysis that sometimes leads to a damning critique of many sporting practices. This form of analysis tends to be blind to the power of the emotional pull of games such as football. There is little evidence here of the sort of inquiry that can help us better understand the forces that actively attract and hold young males within the subculture of football and similar sporting activities. Bruce and Clint both actively participated in their chosen sport. They both made active choices about what they needed to do if they were to continue playing. The type of critique provided by writers such as Messner and Sabo does little to register the agency expressed by participants like Bruce and Clint. Instead it uses a method that implies that athletes are not often passive and ignorant about the wider circumstances of their behaviour. We find that such a method renders athletes relatively mute about the social construction of their life experiences. The stories of Bruce and Clint demonstrate their sharp awareness of the different forces and factors in their experiences of football.

Thus there is a discourse about sport that is, on one hand, conservative and non-critical, and on the other hand, hypercritical and unable to offer much in the way of registering sport's positive qualities. The debate between these contrasting positions gives minimal consideration to the motives and stories of the actual participants. The narrative method that we employ recognizes that individuals live in interconnected cultural contexts. The commemoration of the events on the beaches of Gallipoli in 1915 becomes part of the cultural mosaic that defines acts of personal sacrifice as normal, even expected, within the world of young males. As such, the stories of the past from distant lands flow through us and, in part, make us who we are and who we hope to become. Such a cultural perspective also recognizes that young people live and learn together in distinct affinity groups.

Bruce and Clint came to senior football as very young participants, with skills and self-understandings that had been developed and honed within their peer contexts. Their stories have developed and been constructed within "boy culture" (Rotundo 1998). Rotundo coined this phrase within a study of nineteenth-century America that documents significant shifts in social relations. In this analysis, Rotundo demonstrates the impact of the movement from an agrarian to an industrial culture, which provided young males with the space and licence to develop an independent social sphere. Many young males lived separated from the domestic environment and the world of close and ongoing contact with adult males. Play, recreation, and sport provided opportunities to actively shape their own subcultures.

> These later generations of the 1800's spent more time in the peer world of school house and school yard. Middle-class boys were needed less to do the work of the family. They were increasingly isolated from males of the older generation. A growing proportion of them lived in large towns and cities, which brought them in contact with a denser mass of peers. And in a world where autonomy had become a male virtue, there were positive reasons to give boys time and space of their own. In sum, the conditions were ripe in the nineteenth century for a coherent, independent boy's world. (Rotundo 1998, 338)

We assume that "boy culture" has lived on into the twentieth and twenty-first centuries, albeit in a different form. The freedom and autonomy afforded to middle-class boys in the nineteenth century appear to have been extended to other classes throughout the last century and into the current one. Indeed Sharp (1985) points to the emergence of a general ideology of autonomy common to most social settings. One implication of this insight relates to the emergence of distinct social cohorts or subcultures. Thus class, ethnic, and geographic divisions become transected by age groupings which, in turn, are heavily influenced by the abstract forces of mass marketing and the media. In this sense "boy culture" becomes a far more generic term, applying generic patterns of identity making within specific locations. That is, although the world has changed almost beyond recognition since the nineteenth century, there are important clues here about the world that is shaped and regulated by groups of boys themselves.

What are the specific characteristics of "boy culture" that live on into the present? Rotundo's work suggests that the world of "boy culture" is constantly divided by geographic, ethnic, class, and age differences. Within this separated world, Rotundo notes, boys exercised and were engaged in hostile combat. Here they developed traits that valued friendships based on companionship and unshakeable fidelity (Rotundo 1998) and protected local turf against outsiders. Bruce's memories of the cultural boundaries of Port Adelaide, and within this space the territorial dominance of the "Riley brothers," resonate with this insight. It is also possible to see how territorial feelings can be re-ignited within the context of organized sport where regional and urban rivalries are played out in games such as football.

Within "boy culture," courage involving stoicism and daring was a primary value. "Stoicism involved the suppression of 'weak' or 'tender' feelings that were readily exposed in the feminine world of home feelings such as grief, fear, and pain." "Boy culture" also enabled the suppression of displays of fear and pain (Rotundo 1998, 346). If we are searching for explanations for Bruce's desire to hide the pain of broken ribs, a dislocated finger, and a broken toe, as well as Clint's capacity to internalize the pain of his damaged shoulder, the lessons of "boy culture" become relevant.

Rotundo notes that despite the regulating impulses of the dominant adult community, especially that of specific mothers and fathers, "boy culture" invested a great deal of energy into maintaining autonomy and independence. The act of shaming was one of the potent methods used to internally police "boy culture" (Rotundo 1998). Shame is a powerful emotional force and could partly explain Bruce's and Clint's efforts to remain members of their squads leading up to their respective Grand Finals. It is possible that anxieties around being shamed had been established well before these specific events. This suggests that the desire to be part of one's group can be so strong that fears, anxieties, and actual physical pain are pushed aside. What is it about belonging to a group that produces such a powerfully seductive feeling? And how do the forces within a group manage to produce compliance with and subservience to the dominant mores of the group? For an answer to these questions we need to seek out other sources.

Rotundo's observations are echoed in Judith Harris's (1998) examination of contemporary childhood and the importance of peer culture. Harris suggests that

> though childhood is a time of learning it is a mistake to think of children as empty vessels, passively accepting whatever the adults in their lives decide to fill them up with. It is almost as far off the mark to think of them as apprentices, struggling privately and individually to become fully-fledged members of adult society. Children are not incompetent members of adults' society: they are competent members of their own society, which has its own standards and its own culture. (199)

> ...In the long run it isn't the home environment that makes the difference. It is the environment shared by children who belong to the same peer group. It is the culture created by children. (216–7)

Though simple, Harris's thesis has powerful implications. She argues that, from an early age, children learn many lessons from each other through their efforts to be securely part of a group of their peers. Through a process of self-categorization, children work hard to be similar to their affinity group and dissimilar to those categorized as different from the group. In this sense, Harris's ideas are "constructivist" (Harris 1998, 210) in that they assume that active identity work is an ongoing aspect of growing and learning. On a larger social scale, according to Harris, children pick and choose values and patterns of behaviour from adult peer groups. This process does not require having direct contact because "today's children watch television. Television has become their window on society, their village square" (211). Within their groups, children actively create, recreate, and police the norms and behaviours that are, in the first instance, "read off" older peer and adult groups. This suggests that group members actively represent their interpretations, versions, and variations of the aspects of the wider culture with which they most closely identify.

So far we have been referring to Harris's work about children in general. This chapter, however, is specifically about young males, about whom Harris observes the following:

> Boys' groups tend to be hierarchical. There is a leader and he tells the others what to do. Boys vie with each other for status. They refrain from showing their weaknesses. They don't ask for directions because they don't want anyone to know they are lost. (232)

Her observation suggests that to better understand the desires and motivations apparent in the stories of Clint and Bruce, one should look first inside their affinity groups. We believe that there is enough evidence in both narratives to provide prima facie support for Harris's ideas.

What does this line of inquiry mean for educators and coaches? Harris believes that schools are important cultural sites for change and social influence because students are in the same space with the most important people in their worlds, their peers. It follows from this that teachers, and in sporting clubs, coaches, are in strategic locations to make a difference. Harris asserts that

> teachers have power and responsibility because they are in control of the entire group....And they exert this influence where it is likely to have long-term effects: in the world outside the home, the world where children will spend their adult lives. (241)

In this sense the messages are clear. In the spaces "where the boys are" (Hickey, Fitzclarence, and Matthews 2000), peers, teachers, and coaches make a difference.

Conclusion

There are logical implications that follow from the insights of Rotundo and Harris about "boy culture." In particular, we are concerned about the form of education that is appropriate to assist young males to move from the closed world of their peer groups to the wider world of more complex responsibilities and possibilities. These lessons are most significant for educators and coaches who work with young males, either in schools or in sporting contexts. In particular, there is a need for careful consideration of the most effective form of communication within and between the individuals in peer groups and between peer settings and the adult world. We can see in the two narratives and within Rotundo's analysis that there is intense pressure to withhold information from adults. Indeed there are powerful sanctions for the disclosure of information. This suggests that there is a need for forms of communication that foster open exchanges.

At the same time, our analysis suggests that there is a need to foster ways by which young males, within their peer groups, learn to self-manage effectively and prudently. In the intense fishbowl environment of "boy culture" there are clearly pleasures from the bonding often associated with sports such as football. But dangers lurk there as well. Rotundo's observations about the strong desires of young males to forge an in-group, involve a politics of "them and us." Taken to an extreme, this can produce intense hostilities against individuals and groups who are deemed to be different. Sometimes such feelings and loyalties get out of hand, and an outsider can be at risk. For example, there are times when group politics encourage members to actively harass other males who do not follow the same interests or who even look and move differently. Equally, within boys' groups, individuals have to learn to toe the line and stay within the dominant norms of their groups. Pity the individual who breaks ranks with his peers to stand alone on an issue. Under these circumstances the dominant members of a group are often quite unforgiving.

We thus reach a crucial issue in the education of young males through sport and recreation. Teachers and coaches are in key positions to challenge intolerance of differences. To do this they need to encourage young males to be able to make independent choices when they deem it necessary to do so. However, this is difficult emotional territory. Taking a stand against one's group can come at a high price. Isolation, even rejection, is what most young people fear most. By his own admission, Clint's conflict with his former teammates was "painful." Learning to understand such feelings and reactions thus becomes an important step in the process of developing emotional maturity.

On the other hand, the social resistances to confronting such issues are very strong. As noted in Rotundo's work, "boy culture" has a history of suppressing displays of certain emotions because they are seen to represent softness and therefore weakness. The suppression of emotions was not invented by young boys. It exists and develops in adult male culture and from there it is actively imported into the world of younger males. As is often the case (and as dramatized by Bruce's story), many coaches and teachers have a history of accepting this logic and have ended up reinforcing the dominant mores of hegemonic masculinity.

Times have changed and the stakes involved in changing the old "boys will be boys" ethos are now very high. For example, in 2004, police investigated the behaviour of players from at least three different football clubs who were accused of sexual violence (see, e.g., Jopson 2004; Kennedy and Tomas 2004; Prichard 2004; Wilkinson, G. 2004; Wilkinson, I. 2004; and Wilson 2004). These are far from isolated incidents. Over the years, there have been many documented cases of groups of males from sporting clubs being charged with sexual abuse of females. This is where "boy culture" has fused with what Jenkins (1990) labels "male entitlement"—the belief that males have the right to dominate and control females. A recently retired, elite-level, footballer describes this pattern of behaviour:

> The "gang bang" appears to be flavour of the month, and it's been that way for the past eighteen months or so....It's been mainly two on one, three on one. Most of the older blokes have the brains to ask the girl first, and a lot agree to do it. But kids have got shit for brains: they're eighteen and they're with younger girls, and sooner or later they cross the line. (Egan 2000, 29)

Coaches and teachers have a duty of care to make sure that the communities of practice that they preside over do not reinforce such views of entitlement. Put positively, coaches and teachers are in a strategic position to encourage socially and personally responsible practices of "boy culture."

In this chapter, we have examined the thin line that separates pleasure and pain, winning and losing, and responsibility and abuse. The common factor in this social equation is the relationship of a given individual to his peer group. Thus we come to a simple conclusion. There is a need for education about the social skills required to balance the desire to belong to a group with the capacity to do so but not to the excesses of group thought. Players need to be helped to discriminate between what is required to play physically combative games like football and what sort of behaviour is required to live a socially responsible and civilized life off the field. Increasingly, there is an expectation that the entitlements, which were once a part of games such as football, can no longer apply. These are issues that are not in coaching manuals or even in most school curricula.

Such complex and challenging issues are part of learning about emotional awareness and interpersonal relationships. Understanding one's own emotional reactions, within the context of peer and sport cultures, is a prerequisite for making appropriate personal and group decisions. Traditionally, such concerns have been seen to be beyond the jurisdiction of the football club or even the classroom. However, sport and education now exist in new relationships within other cultural settings. New pedagogies are required for a social responsibility for men as footballers as much as for their responsibilities as brothers, fathers, and partners.

Within both sport and schools, adults are needed to help young men develop new narratives of the self and of the self in relation to others. In particular, there is a need for a form of general education to develop new narratives of personal responsibility, narratives that promote accountability, respect for others, and self-monitoring within and between individuals and groups. To do this, both teaching and coaching will need to develop a new language of possible pedagogies.

Notes
1. "Football," as used in this chapter, applies to the game developed and played exclusively in Australia. However we assume that the issues raised apply equally to other codes of football both in Australia and in other "football"-playing countries throughout the world. We thus invite readers to consider how the narratives and analysis apply to players of soccer, gridiron, rugby, etc.
2. Another example of this link between the narrative of the ANZAC legend and Australian Rules football occurred on April 25, 2000. Players from the St. Kilda Football Club, a team in the elite-level Australian Football League, all attended a commemorative, dawn service to honour servicemen and servicewomen who had died in combat. This information was provided by the team coach at the time, Tim Watson, during an interview on ABC radio-Adelaide on April 29, 2000.
3. The Port Adelaide Football Club is arguably the most successful senior football club, not only in South Australia but Australia-wide. Since playing its first game in 1870, the club has gone on to win an Australian record of thirty-six SANFL premierships, including six in a row, and achieve the honour of being Champions of Australia on four occasions. See http://www.portmagpies.com.au/about.htm.
4. A small basic car from the 1950s/60s.
5. Metal and concrete power poles.
6. A soprano female pop singer during the 1970s.
7. A socially unworthy person who is an embarrassment to self, family, and friends.
8. The Australian Bureau of Statistics (1998) documents that, in 1995–96, 144,800 males from 5 to 15 years of age participated in Australian Rules football. This constituted 11 percent of the cohort of all children in this grouping.

Chapter 9

Sites of Asian American Masculinities in School:
"In-citing" Difference

Kevin K. Kumashiro

I can imagine attending school today as an Asian American youth. And I can imagine experiencing various forms of oppression based on my race, gender, and sexuality (Kumashiro 1999b). As I walk to different sites or places in school, I can imagine ways in which my race, gender, and sexuality influence how I self-identify, what I study and learn, and why I interact with others in different ways depending on the situation. In particular, I can imagine that others read and treat me in racialized, gendered, and sexualized ways, that they devalue what they see as my Asian American masculinity, and that I enact different Asian American masculinities in response. Of course, the forms of Asian American masculinity that I exhibit are not unrelated to the stereotypes and representations of Asian American masculinities that colour the lenses through which others read me and other Asian Americans. And these stereotypes and representations of Asian American masculinities are not unrelated to the ways in which race, gender, sexuality, and their intersections have historically been imagined, represented, and treated. Different conceptualizations of and attitudes toward Asian American masculinities reflect different discourses of what it means to be masculine, sexually normal, and Asian American. One might wonder, therefore, what forms of Asian American masculinity play out in school, and what their origins are.

In this chapter, I draw on educational research, cultural texts, and personal experience as I examine the multiple and contradictory ways in which Asian Americans both express their genders and are read by others in gendered ways in school. It is as if while walking through a school I look at four different sites—classrooms, hallways, locker rooms, and organized student activities—and examine how fourteen different stereotypes, representations, and self-representations cite (or reflect) different discourses of masculinity, including such discourses as hypomasculinity, hypermasculinity, deviant heterosexuality, White masculinity, Black masculinity, "traditional Asian" masculinity, Orientalism, and butch lesbianism. I do not wish to imply that these are the only sites in which Asian American masculinities play out, or that these are the only stereotypes and representations of Asian Americans, or that these are the only discourses that Asian American masculinities cite, but I do think the examples I discuss in this chapter provide a helpful starting point for examining the complexities of Asian American masculinities. I will argue that responses against the gendered racisms confronting Asian Americans can be both harmful and helpful, and that possibilities for change lie in articulations of identity that, paradoxically, both claim and trouble different notions of Asian American masculinity. I conclude with implications for education, and suggest that educators need to teach themselves and others to read identities in ways that look, not for repetition of normative discourses, but for resignification and difference.

In Classrooms: Hypo-, Hyper-, and Deviant Masculinities

As I imagine looking around the typical classroom, I see at least two stereotypes of Asian American students and at least two representations of Asian Americans in the curriculum, all of which cite a hypomasculinity, a hypermasculinity, or a deviantly heterosexual masculinity.

In terms of their academic abilities and performance, Asian American students are often stereotyped in one of two ways. First, they are seen as academic failures: as recent immigrants who have not learned the ways of American culture, not acquired English language skills, and not assimilated into the community. They are "unassimilable foreigners" (Lee, S. 1996) whose special needs, like bilingual education, drain the resources that would otherwise go to the "American" (i.e., White) students (U.S. Commission on Civil Rights 1992). Not surprisingly, by threatening the privilege of "White America," they constitute the "yellow peril," the fear of

Asian invasion and conquest. What is important, here, is the recognition that the yellow-peril stereotype is not only racialized, but also gendered. Its use of such sexual metaphors as penetration, domination, invasion, and conquest suggest that the threat that Asians pose to the minds and bodies of Whites is a masculinized threat (Okihiro 1994), a threat that is overly or dangerously masculine. Thus, the yellow peril, as embodied in the "foreigner" stereotype, and in comparison to the White American norm, attributes a hyper-masculinity to Asian Americans.

In contrast, Asian American students are also stereotyped as academic successes. They are the "model minority" students, "academic superstars" who excel in math and science and are "exemplars of the American dream of success" (Lee, S. 1996, 2). "Characterized as hardworking, disciplined, academically inclined" (McKay and Wong 1996, 586), they are (insidiously) cited as proof that schools are not racist institutions, and that if the other students of colour would only work as hard as Asian American students, then they too could succeed. This stereotype offers a justification for the racial hierarchy in U.S. society. But like the yellow-peril stereotype, the model-minority stereotype is not only racialized, but also gendered. Asian American boys, in particular, are stereotyped as "nerds," as students who spend too much time at the computer and not enough time socializing, playing sports, dating girls, and doing things that "normal" or "real" boys are supposed to do. As a result, Asian American boys are marginalized not only because of their race, but also because of their gender. In contrast to the masculinized threat of the yellow peril, the model minority symbolizes "a feminized position of passivity and malleability" (Okihiro 1994, 142). The model minority student, in other words, is feminized, is attributed a hypo-masculinity.

I do not wish to oversimplify the hyper-hypo dichotomy, because the model minority and the yellow peril are "not poles, denoting opposite relationships along a single line, but in fact form a circular relationship that moves in either direction" (Okihiro 1994, 142). The model minority, after all, if too successful, threatens the privileges of White students and, thus, becomes its own yellow peril. Furthermore, the struggling English speaker can be seen as weak and feminized, whereas the high-achieving student can be seen as dominating and masculinized. Contradictions abound in these stereotypes. My point, then, is that these different stereotypes are indeed gendered, but in contradictory and multiple ways.

Asian American students are not the only ones who are racialized and gendered in the classroom. So, too, are the Asian Americans who appear in the curriculum. Asian Americans are represented in at least two ways in historical research (I will briefly discuss representations of Asian Americans in literature in the next section). First, especially in historical writings on the United States in the second half of the twentieth century, Asians and Asian Americans are represented as both hyper- and hypo-masculine. They are a strong military enemy who enacts much violence on a U.S. territory (namely, Pearl Harbor) during World War II, and who actually defeats the U.S. military during the Vietnam War. But they are also a weak ally who needs help in a war against communists during the Korean War, and a persecuted population that needs to take refuge following the Vietnam War. Thus, on the one hand, government propaganda and Hollywood movies reflect a masculinized representation of Asians (Gee 1988), and government and military policies actualize this fear of yellow peril through the Japanese American internment camps and resettlement policies in the 1940s, and through the restricted immigration and distributed settlement of Southeast Asian refugees in the 1970s and 1980s. On the other hand, Asians and Asian Americans are degradingly feminized, especially in popular culture, where Asian-looking men appear in cartoons and movies as caricatures, like the sinister though effeminate villain, Fu Manchu; and even Asian-looking women appear in movies as caricatures, like the "dragon ladies" who are devious and sinister, though mysterious and graceful. This juxtaposition of hyper- and hypo-masculinity is not surprising: one way that U.S. society maintains the privilege of White Americans is to represent and, in doing so, define other racial groups as deviant in comparison (Omi and Winant 1994). Asian American masculinities, then, can never be the norm, and will always and already be too masculine, or not masculine enough.

These deviant masculinities of Asian Americans are not separable from the sexualities of Asian Americans. This brings us to the second way in which Asian Americans are represented in the curriculum, especially in historical writings of Asian American men in the United States in the early 1900s. Examining the written histories of Chinese Americans, Ting (1995) argues that the "bachelor society" trope, common in representations of early Chinese American communities, "insists on both the absence of Chinese women in the U.S. and the exclusive heterosexuality of Chinese immigrant men" (277). So, although the bachelor-society trope emphasizes the heterosexuality of the Chinese immigrant men, it does so in a way that implies that theirs was not a "normal" heterosexuality. In the eyes of both the dominant society and the historians, Chinese American men have what she calls a "deviant heterosexuality," one characterized by a homosocial living arrangement and by sexual activity (with female prostitutes) that is neither conjugal nor procreative. Only with the assimilation of the Chinese American men, i.e., with the creation of Chinese American communities that resemble mainstream White America's family-centred communities, did Chinese American men come to be seen as having "overcome" this deviant heterosexuality and achieve normalcy. (So, too, with Chinese American women, because only with the immigration of wives did Chinese American women start to engage in "normal," i.e., conjugal and procreative sex, instead of "abnormal" or prostitutive sex.) Thus, the bachelor-society trope, which centres on a White heterosexuality, frames our understandings of early Chinese Americans' sexuality. We understand Chinese American history only through the lens of White heterosexism, which means that, in comparison, Asian American heterosexuality and its concomitant masculinity are already deviant.

In Hallways and Playgrounds: White, Black, and "Traditional Asian" Masculinities

The process of asserting the privilege and dominance of the masculinities of other racial groups by defining Asian American masculinities as deviant happens not only in classrooms. As I step out into hallways and playgrounds, I see even more images of Asian American masculinities playing out among Asian American students. In particular, I see Asian American students trying to distance themselves from the stereotypes and representations described above by enacting other forms of masculinity, especially masculinities that typically characterize certain racial groups, such as White masculinities, Black masculinities, and "traditional Asian" masculinities.

I see at least three forms of masculinities being embraced among Asian American boys. One responds to the stereotype that Asian American boys are wimps. Similar to the "nerd" stereotype, but focusing more on personality, this stereotype assumes that Asian American boys are weak, passive, subservient, shy, not athletic, not aggressive, not leaders, and overall, "effeminate." They are "defenceless, eager-to-please, and helpful" (Connolly 1998, 125) and they are "quiet and 'little' and therefore needing to be befriended and looked after"—all "characteristics often associated with femininity" (121). They even stick to themselves and "play together in the corner" (131) and thus fail to prove their "masculinity" in conventional ways, namely, through aggressiveness, competitiveness, and excellence in a number of public arenas (Kimmel 1994). Some have argued that theirs is an Asian form of masculinity that draws on Confucian ethics (Sung 1985); some have argued that their tendency to stay together "in the corner" is a response to racism and sexism (Lei 2000); and some have argued that their sense of masculinity is based more on collectivity rather than individual competitiveness (Connolly 1998). Whatever the case, this stereotype is reflected not only in educational research, but also in Asian American novels (e.g., Kingston 1975) and the popular press (e.g., Nishioka 2000), and is cited as one reason why many Asian American females find Asian American males sexually undesirable.

Some Asian American male writers have responded by condemning the notion that they are "womanly, effeminate, devoid of all the traditionally masculine qualities of originality, daring, physical courage, creativity" (Chin and Chan 1972, as cited in Kim 1998, 271). They distance themselves from anything feminine or queer, and insist that they are, indeed, "masculine." Ironically, both this claim of masculinity and the stereotype to which it responds function to privilege White American masculinity, because the claim that Asian American boys are as masculine as White boys, like the stereotype that Asian American boys are not as masculine as White boys, has meaning only because White American masculinity is the norm, the ideal, the standard against which other colours of masculinity are judged.

Whiteness is not always the ideal. A second form of masculinity expressed by Asian American boys is of "young, testosterone-driven men, wearing hip-hop style, baggy jeans and loose T-shirts" (Nishioka 2000). Here, they seem to reflect the dress, speech, behaviour, and norms of urban Black American youth culture, the "vanguard of hip-hop culture" (Davis 1999, 49). Many Asian American boys are also joining Asian gangs (Fernandez 2000). These gangs are increasingly shifting "toward the African American and Latino gang models (using formal gang names, claiming territory)" (Ima and Nidorf 1998, 100), and are "becoming increasingly more like [African American and Latino] delinquent youth in terms of violence and gang-related behavior" (102). Images of these Asian American hip-hopsters and gangsters (see, e.g., Nakasako 1998) seem to reflect the tough, aggressive, street-smart image of Black American male youth in the popular media, such as in rap music videos or movies of inner-city life (e.g., the movie *Dangerous Minds* 1995). This is not to say that Black American boys are all gangsters, or that this is the only form of masculinity exhibited among Black American males. Nevertheless, popular media images of Black American males attribute to them what might be called an "urban Black" masculinity, and other boys sometimes also aspire to this masculinity.

Paradoxically, "Black males are both adored and loathed in American schools" (Davis 1999, 49). According to the stereotype, theirs is a masculinity that helps them survive in a dangerous world; theirs is a masculinity that requires greater-than-normal levels of aggression, defiance, and strength in the face of adversity; and, in these ways, theirs is a hypermasculinity. Not surprisingly, theirs is a masculinity that, in its toughness, is itself often seen as a threat, such as when Black American males come to symbolize "all that is dangerous in the world" (Williams 1995, 241). This dangerousness applies not only to crime. Black American men are also stereotyped as being dangerous sexually, which helps to explain both the castration that often accompanied lynchings (Wiegman 1993) and the notion that they all have large penises. As Fanon (1970) put it, "the Negro is eclipsed. He is turned into a penis. He *is* a penis" (120). Recognizing that some Asian Americans similarly stereotype Asian American male gangsters as dangerous, both as criminals and as sexual "players" (Nakasako 1998), it is not hard to see that Asian American masculinities cite a range of masculinities, not only White, but also Black.

In fact, Asian American masculinities cite masculinities traditionally associated with a range of racial groups. Drawing on martial-arts films and television shows with such Asian male actors as Bruce Lee, Jackie Chan, Jet Li, and Sammo Hung, a third form of masculinity responds to the stereotype that Asian American boys know or should know martial arts. Although the actors differ in their degrees of hardness, display of the male body, and vulnerability (Tasker 1997), they are unified in their participation in a practice that many believe typifies "traditional" Asian culture. And not only mainstream society believes this stereotype: in their search back in time to see how things used to be, some Asian Americans engage in an "imaginative rediscovery" (Hall 1990) in hopes of finding a truly "Asian" form of masculinity. Within some Asian cultures, that search could take them to times when man was a strong silent warrior, as embodied in the swordsman. Arguably, the swordsman could be seen as an ancestor to the modern-day martial artist, just as swordplay films can be seen as ancestors to today's martial arts films (Tasker 1997). Thus, whether imposed by others or claimed as their own, Asian American masculinities that centre on martial artistry cite what might be called a "traditional" Asian masculinity.

Up to this point I have focused on Asian American boys. However, masculinities can be exhibited by Asian American girls as well. Historically, Asian American females have been stereotyped as ultra-feminine, passive, subservient, quiet, mysterious, exotic, and erotic, through images such as the geisha girl and the "lotus blossom," and in movies, characters such as Suzy Wong (Gee 1988). But they have also been portrayed, simultaneously, as masculine, bringing to mind the devious "dragon lady," or more recently, the stern and blunt character, Ling, on the television show *Ally McBeal*. Asian American girls are increasingly visible in youth gangs (Ima and Nidorf 1998). And, as depicted by Kelly Hu in the television show *Martial Law*, Asian American females can be martial arts experts. One could argue that Asian Americans like Kelly Hu are not "being" masculine or appropriating Asian masculinity, but rather are redefining what it means to be feminine (and, by implication, what it means to be masculine). Whatever the case, they are exhibiting qualities that many define as traditionally Asian male characteristics, and in doing so, showing that Asian American females can blend traditionally "masculine" qualities (strength, martial arts expertise) with traditionally "feminine" ones (beauty, sensuality).

It is important to note that certain characteristics are easier to blend than others. Some characteristics, after all, are contradictory. This brings us to a subgroup of Asian American girls, namely, butch (or masculine) lesbians. Perhaps the most common stereotype of Asian American lesbians is that they do not exist. Within the mainstream U.S. imagination, Asian and Asian American women are passive, subservient to men, sexually skillful, and ultrafeminine (Cho 1997). Within "traditional" Asian cultures, they are supposed to be good daughters, wives, and mothers; and, because being a wife and mother requires marrying a man and having children, they are supposed to be heterosexual, or at least, to perform heterosexuality. Conversely, many in Asian American communities have asserted that being lesbian, gay, or bisexual is a "White thing," a "White disease" (Wat 1996). The popular media reinforces this notion with portrayals of queers (i.e., of gay, lesbian, bisexual, transgender, and questioning individuals) who are almost always White American. Furthermore, mainstream society often stereotypes queers as deviantly gendered: gay men as male-though-feminine and lesbians as female-though-masculine. If lesbians are supposed to be White, and if lesbians are supposed to be butch, and if Asian American women are supposed to be ultrafeminine and heterosexual, being queer *and* Asian American *and* female becomes an impossible contradiction in terms (Lee, J. 1996). It is so difficult for some to comprehend a butch queer Asian American woman when they see one, that they resort to the stereotype of Asian Americans to which they can most easily assimilate the queerly gendered person in front of them, namely, the stereotype of the effeminate Asian American man. Thus, when describing an incident in which a butch Asian American lesbian was mistaken as a man when using the women's restroom, Eng and Hom (1998) argue that "it is precisely mainstream stereotypes of an effeminized Asian American male (homo)sexuality that affect the ways in which the Asian American lesbian goes unseen and unrecognized" (1). What is important, here, is the recognition that certain intersections of identities resist queer readings. The identity of the "Asian American female" is already heteronormative (i.e., presumes and requires heterosexuality), which means that she can be masculine, but only so long as her heterosexual-femininity is not compromised.

In Locker Rooms: Multiple Orientalisms

As I continue to imagine walking around the school, peering into the boys' locker room I see multiple ways of reading the Asian American male body—from the male body in general, to the queer male body, to the transgender body—all of which cite Orientalism and racialized heterosexism.

According to Okihiro (1994), the Orientalization of Asia can be traced back two thousand years to when the earliest European explorers began crafting tales of a mystical "Orient," a place where the landscape, the food, even the bodies of the (in)human inhabitants were described as fundamentally different from their own. By subordinating Asia within an imagined patriarchal relationship between the feminized East and the masculinized West, Europeans convinced themselves that they had a moral responsibility to make Asia more civilized. Paraphrasing Said (1978), Okihiro (1994) argues that Orientalism "was an engendered subordination, by which European men aroused, penetrated, and possessed a passive, dark, and vacuous 'Eastern bride'" (11). This gendered form of racism, in which Asianness is marginalized, in part, by being associated with the feminine Other, whereas whiteness is privileged by being associated with the masculine norm, plays out in the United States today. And this U.S. Orientalism is what some of the stereotypes of Asian Americans cite.

I have already noted that Asian American males are feminized in U.S. society. However, U.S. Orientalism feminizes not just the Asian American males' personalities and behaviours, but also their bodies. Asian

American males are often stereotyped as having smaller bodies, and being shorter, thinner, less muscular, and less broad than White American males; in particular, their genitalia are stereotyped as being smaller. This is perhaps not surprising. In a patriarchal and White-dominated society where the penis symbolizes male power and where Whiteness is the norm, the Asian male can be denied power when "defined by a striking absence down there" (Fung 1996, 186). With less of a penis, the Asian male is less of a man.

In response, some Asian American males have asserted that they can look "as masculine" as their White counterparts. The recently popularized calendars (Mendez 1995) and greeting cards (Chen 1995) of muscular, tall, "hunky" Asian American male models demonstrate that some Asian American men do indeed embody popular society's image of what Connell (1995) calls "exemplary masculinity." Some even claim that the popularity and sex-symbol status of some Asian American actors attest to the fact that Asian American men can be "masculine." However, as was the case with the Asian American male writers mentioned earlier, the masculinity being claimed is a White masculinity. The body shape and size being aspired to represent the body that typifies White male models, and for that matter, many of the popular Asian American male actors are of mixed racial heritage and very "White looking," and thus pass more easily as White American. As one Asian American man put it, "there are some Asian descended men out there like Keanu Reeves and Dean Cain, but they are very white-looking, and they don't identify at all with their Asian culture" (Editors 1997, 29). With the notion that Asian male bodies can embody "exemplary masculinity," White masculinity remains the norm, Asian masculinity remains marginalized, and Orientalism continues to operate uncontested.

It is interesting that when one considers Asian American boys who are queer, Orientalism takes on an entirely different dimension. Whereas mainstream society stereotypes Asian American boys as feminine, and thus, sexually undesirable, many in queer communities stereotype Asian American boys as feminine, and thus, sexually hyperdesirable (Kumashiro 1999b). Those with a queer Asian fetish yearn for the "mysteriousness" and "boyishness" of queer Asian American males, expecting them to be "exotic creatures blending childlike simplicity with a smoldering sexuality open to entreaties from the West" (Hagland 1998, 279). They appropriate the Orientalist lens, stereotyping Asian American males as "feminine" or the "woman" of the relationship, and desiring them for their femininity.

There is something significant about this blending of Asian American male queerness and Asian American male femininity. This brings us to transgenderism among Asian American boys (I use the term "transgender" to mean not just one who identifies as another gender, such as a male who identifies as female, but more broadly, one who exhibits characteristics traditionally associated with another gender, such as a boy who acts or appears "like a girl"). Growing in popularity among some young queer Asian American male communities is the gay beauty pageant that involves cross-dressing (Guillermo 1995; McLaughlin 1997). Also increasing is the number of young Asian American males who identify as transvestites (cross-dressers) or as transexuals or transgenders (both male-to-female and female-to-male) and who are speaking out (Tran 1998). This increased visibility of transgender Asian American males demonstrates that many queer Asian American males embrace femininity and "womanly" characteristics. Perhaps they do so as a way to resist White-normative and heterosexist notions of "masculinity" and to embrace queer Asian ones. After all, historically in a number of Asian cultures, expressions of queer sexuality have gone hand-in-hand with expressions of gender nonconformity, so that for males, being gay and being effeminate and womanly (in terms of behaviour, dress, sexual activity, and so on) are synonymous. For example, in some Asian and Pacific Island cultures, the term for "homosexual" is the same term as that for "transgender" (using my broad definition of transgender), such as in Chinese (Ma and Stewart 1997), Vietnamese (McLaughlin 1997), Filipino (Manalansan 1995), and Hawai'ian (Hall and Kauanui 1996) cultures. In these instances, queer Asian American male masculinities are quite the opposite of the straight White American norm. Thus, although embracing the "opposite" can perpetuate stereotypes, it can also be a transgressive, activist move.

In Activist Spaces: Challenging the Politics of Representation

At the end of my tour I enter activist spaces, such as meetings and activities of student organizations. Here, I imagine seeing masculinities that are harder to pin down. They are harder to label and categorize because they refuse to cite only one of the masculinities that are traditionally cited in stereotypes, representations, and self-representations. By refusing to cite a normative masculinity, these kinds of masculinities are exactly the kinds that bring about changes in oppression. Let me explain.

I argued that, in each of the three sites visited earlier, different Asian American masculinities cite different discourses of masculinities, some centred on hypo/hyper/deviant masculinities, some centered on racialized masculinities, and some centered on Orientalist notions of race, gender, and sexuality. Although they cited different discourses, I argued that they all took part in a similar process—the citational process—and thus all engaged in some form of repeating the harmful, regulatory, and normative nature of each of these discourses. This should not be surprising because "masculinity" itself, in any form, is normative. As Munoz (1999) argues, "masculinity has been and continues to be a normative rubric that has policed the sex/gender system. I see very little advantage in recuperating the term *masculinity* because, as a category, masculinity has normalized heterosexual and masculinist privilege" (58) and, I would add, White privilege.

Even articulations of masculinity that sought to challenge some oppressions ironically reinscribed other structures of domination, albeit perhaps unintentionally. And this happened because responses to oppression often involve claiming identities that are already problematic. There are at least four responses to oppression that involve claiming problematic identities. One is internalizing oppression. Osajima (1993) writes that, often, "the oppressed internalize an identity that mirrors or echoes the images put forth by the dominant group. People come to accept and believe the myths and stereotypes about their group as part of their natural definitions of self" (83). When we believe the stereotypes that we are inferior to and less "masculine" or strong or sexually desirable than Whites, that we are the model minority, or that we are foreigners and not "Americans," we internalize the ways that mainstream U.S. society marginalizes us and we perpetuate the stereotypes ourselves. As individuals we might indeed be "good students," but when we believe that, as Asian Americans, we are supposed to be good students, then we comply with our own oppression.

A second response is identifying with the privileged. In contrast to internalization, this response involves rejecting the stereotypes and doing everything possible to distance the individual from them. Osajima (1993) tells us that "this generally manifests itself in a desire to become like or be accepted by members of the dominant group" (83). When we emulate White American boys in our appearance, behaviour, and values, we are identifying with the privileged, trying to be privileged ourselves, and in doing so, complying with the maintenance of structures of domination by failing to critique the harmfulness of the privilege-marginality hierarchy. This second response could also entail simply doing the opposite of what is expected. When we show that we are "strong," not wimpy; that we are "sexy," not asexual; that we are "masculine," not feminine, we are doing what Hall

(1988) calls "challenging the relations of representation" (224). As Yon (1999) explains, we are using "positive imagery to challenge and counter dominant and pervasive negative representations" (5). Such a response can help us fit in or raise our self-esteem, but it can also be problematic because it is always and already framed by the terms of the dominant group. Trying to do what is "good" necessarily involves embracing the normative definition of "good."

Another way to challenge the relations of representation leads to a third response to oppression: rediscovering an essential identity and culture. Such a response entails looking past the "fake," and looking for the "real" (Kim 1998); looking past the stereotypes, and looking for our "true" identity and culture. As Hall (1990) explains, this "imaginative rediscovery" entails finding and expressing "the common historical experiences and shared cultural codes which provide us, as 'one people,' with stable, unchanging and continuous frames of reference and meaning, beneath the shifting divisions and vicissitudes of our actual history. This 'oneness,' underlying all the other, more superficial differences, is the truth, the essence" of, say, the Asian experience, or of Asian masculinity (223). When we look to history to see what Asian men "used to be" (such as the warrior), when we look to "traditional Asian cultures" to see what Asian men are "supposed to be" (such as the ruler of the household), and when we embrace traditions as "our own" (such as pageants that blend queer sexuality with queer gender expressions), we move away from mainstream society's definition of who we are. Although such a process can help us take pride in our heritage, it can also be problematic when we recognize that cultures constantly change, that they vary from place to place and time to time, and that naming a "traditional Asian culture" is quite impossible (Yanagisako 1985). Furthermore, even if we could do so, we do not escape normative identities. Consider, for example, Chan's (1998) college-level course on "Contemporary Asian American Men's Issues," in which he says this of his students:

> It seems that...these male students were more interested in changing the ways in which Asian American men are represented in popular culture than [in] revisioning or redefining the ways in which masculinities are constructed by alternative models of masculinity, such as learning from Asian American gay men. With the advent of Hong Kong movie stars, I believe that some Asian American men would rather appropriate "imported" models of masculinity than challenge prevailing notions of heteromasculinity. (103)

The reification of an "Asian masculinity" can go hand in hand with heterosexism, as well as with patriarchy, inasmuch as "traditional Asian" men are often stereotyped as "stern and misogynist" (Nishioka 2000), locked in traditional gender roles, and even abusive towards their wives.

So, is there a way to respond to oppression without complying with the normative nature of prevailing discourses of masculinity? I believe a fourth response heads in this direction, a response that involves embracing multiplicity and inciting difference. There is not just one way to be masculine (there are multiple discourses of masculinity); there is not a best way to be masculine (because any discourse of masculinity is normative in some ways); there is not an essentially Asian way to be masculine (because it is not clear what that would mean); and there is not a limitation on how one can express masculinity (because different sites can call for different masculinities, perhaps simultaneously, and because differently gendered bodies can express different masculinities, perhaps even contradictory ones simultaneously). So, the work of disrupting the "normative rubric that has policed the sex/gender system" (Munoz 1999, 58) involves challenging "not just the *relations* but also the *politics* of representation" (Yon 1999, 5). New representations and expressions of Asian American masculinities need not aim to make Asian American masculinities into good things. They need not aim to reclaim masculinity for Asian Americans, especially Asian American men. They need not say, "I am as good as you." Rather, they can disrupt the notions held by both mainstream U.S. society and Asian America about Asian American masculinities. They can disrupt what it means to be masculine. They can disrupt what it means to be "good."

Such disruptions are possible not by asserting one's own masculinity, or more accurately, only one aspect of one's masculinities, but by playing around with one's multiple and contradictory masculinities. Asian Americans can exhibit multiple masculinities, perform contradictory ones simultaneously, and alternate between "negative" ones and "positive" ones. They can juxtapose masculine qualities with feminine ones, attribute "masculinity" to women and queers and "femininity" to men, and express value as well as critique towards the same discourse of masculinity. In sum, they can work to simultaneously claim and trouble their own Asian American masculinities.

I suspect that Asian American activists who work against multiple forms of oppression do just this kind of work. They work to change racism, sexism, and homophobia, as well as other forms of oppression. They identify strongly with the need to resist complying with one form of oppression while working against another. They work to take pride in their own identities while helping others in their fights against oppression. And they do all of that paradoxically.

Aguilar-San Juan (1998) illustrates some of these points in her discussion of queer Asian American activism. She tells us that we need to claim identities in order to trouble the discourses that give them meaning: "ironically, we need to fix ourselves as a stable (read: knowable, nameable, solid) community in order to point a finger at the practices and ideas that deny us that stability from the start" (38). She tells us that we need to resist claiming for ourselves or imposing on others singular identities that are already normative, such as identities of the mainstream:

> I do not want to be implicated in what seems a condescending gesture of showing lesbians in the Philippines the "true" path to freedom. This is a gesture I have associated with those U.S. feminists who reinscribe colonialist relations by subordinating the experience of Filipina feminists to the rubric of Third World feminism, thereby preserving the evidently neutral territory of feminism for themselves. (29)

She also tells us that we need to resist trying to discover each of our different essences, and then including them as something "as good" as the mainstream, without first critiquing why certain identities were defined as "better" in the first place: "incorporating a marginalized perspective in a larger work that does not ask *why certain perspectives are marginalized to begin with* is not sufficient" (32). After all, "no matter how inclusive we try to be—as editors of collections or as activists in social movements—at some point the line we draw must be exclusive of someone" (33). Finally, she tells us that even the spaces we call "home," spaces where we expect, say, our racial identities to be affirmed, can function to exclude some individuals (such as women and queers), as is the case with "traditional Asian" communities that are patriarchal and heterosexist. Even the Asian body can be a site that excludes some, such as when it is normalized and dimorphically gendered: "the exclusion of TGs [transgenders] from queer Asian America—whether by intent or by oversight—indicates to me that the body is not necessarily the site of home" (36). Changing oppression, then, "requires vigilance regarding the notions of home and experiences, especially regarding the ways these concepts may close off further discussion about who's in and who's out of the community and why" (37).

Activist efforts to change oppression, in other words, involve not just changing what kinds of Asian American masculinities are out there, and how many are out there, but also changing the political significance of these masculinities, i.e., their ability to reinforce or trouble oppression or to do both. And we do that by troubling—i.e., by critiquing and transforming—the processes by which different, normative discourses of masculinity are cited. Little research has been done on Asian American students who are activists; thus, I have few examples from which to draw. Future research should further explore this topic.

Implications for Educators

The responsibility for change does not lie solely with Asian Americans. How we express our racial, gender, and sexual identities is not the only factor at play. Educators, too, have a responsibility to work against the racism, sexism, and heterosexism confronting Asian American students. And they can do so by changing the ways we *read* different masculinities. They can change, in other words, what discourses we see different people, bodies, acts, and so forth to be citing.

The problem is that we often desire repetition (Britzman 1998). We often desire seeing what we expect to see, thinking what we have always thought, learning what we have already learned. We desire knowledge and experiences that affirm our prior knowledges and identities. After all, we are comforted when we can make sense of the situation in which we find ourselves; we are proud when we learn something that tells us that we are smart or good people; we are encouraged when we interact with someone in ways that benefitted from our expectations of who that person is and what that person is like. Not surprisingly, when we read about Asian Americans, when we see them in locker rooms, or when we interact with them in hallways, we look for repetition of the discourses of masculinity that we have already learned. We look, in other words, to see our stereotypes and expectations of Asian Americans play out. And because any situation, text, person, or performance is complex, and always reinforces some stereotypes and contradicts others, we should not be surprised when we pay attention to the ways in which stereotypes are confirmed rather than disconfirmed. Disconfirming knowledge, after all, tells us that the very ways in which we make sense of the world are partial, and perhaps even harmful. Disconfirming knowledge is discomforting, and can lead us into crisis, which we resist.

But education is not about repetition. Education is about difference. Education, in other words, "takes place precisely only through a crisis" (Felman 1995, 55). Therefore, the role of educators is to teach students to read in ways that work against repetition; to teach students to always look for difference, to look beyond what they expect; to trouble their own knowledges and identities. In other words, students need to work to resignify Asian American masculinities, to trouble the discourses they cite, and not to repeat the same harmful citational processes over and over (Kumashiro 1999a). Educators can teach themselves and their students to read, think, interact, and identify in ways that work toward resignification, not repetition. This is the direction in which education needs to go.

References

AAUW Educational Foundation and National Education Association. 1992. *The American Association of University Women Report: How schools shortchange girls.* New York: Marlowe & Company.

Aguilar-San Juan, K. 1998. Going home: Enacting justice in queer Asian America. In *Q&A: Queer in Asian America*, ed. D. Eng and A. Hom, 25–40. Philadelphia: Temple University Press.

Alberton, P., and G. Reid. (Director and script writer). 2000. *Dark and lovely, soft and free.* Brazil: Franmi Productions.

Alloway, N., and P. Gilbert, eds. 1997. *Boys and literacy: Professional development units.* Carlton, Australia: Curriculum Corporation.

Anyon, J. 1984. Intersections of gender and class: Accommodation and resistance by working class and affluent females to contradictory sex role ideologies. *Journal of Education* 166(1): 25–48.

Arnot, M. 1997. Personal communication.

Askew, C., and S. Ross. 1988. *Boys don't cry: Boys and sexism in education.* Milton Keynes, UK: Open University Press.

Australian Bureau of Statistics. 1998. Special article–Participation in sport and physical activities. Cat. No. 1301.0. Reproduced from *Yearbook Australia.*

Bastian, M., and J. Parpart, eds. 1999. *Great ideas for teaching about Africa.* Boulder, CO: Westview.

Bennett, C. 1996. The boys with the wrong stuff. *Guardian*, 6 November, 17.

Berger, I., and E. White. 1999. *Women in sub-Saharan Africa: Restoring women to history.* Bloomington, IN: Indiana University Press.

Berrill, D., and W. Martino. 2002. Pedophiles and deviants: Exploring issues of masculinity, sexuality and normalisation in male teacher candidates' lives. In *Getting ready for Benjamin: Preparing teachers for sexual diversity in the classroom*, ed. R. Kissen, 59–70. Lanham, MD: Rowman & Littlefield.

Biddulph, S. 1995. *Manhood: An action plan for changing men's lives.* 2d ed. Sydney: Finch.

———. 1997. *Raising boys.* Sydney: Finch.

Blacklock, M. 1936. Certain aspects of the welfare of women and children in the colonies. *Annals of Tropical Medicine and Parasitology* 30(4): 221–64.

Bloch, M., J. Beoku-Betts, and B. Tabachnick, eds. 1998. *Women and education in sub-Saharan Africa: Power, opportunities, and constraints.* Boulder, CO: Lynne Reiner.

Bly, R. 1990. *Iron John: A book about men.* Reading, MA: Addison-Wesley.

Boswell, A., and J. Spade. 1996. Fraternities and collegiate rape culture: Why are some fraternities more dangerous for women? *Gender & Society* 10: 133–47.

Bourke, J. 1999. *An intimate history of killing: Face-to-face killing in twentieth-century warfare*. London: Granta Books.

Bozzoli, B. 1983. Marxism, feminism and South African studies. *Journal of Southern African Studies* 9(2): 139–71.

Bradford Education Social Work Services. 1994. *Dealing with bullying: Guidelines for schools*. Shipley, UK: Bradford Education.

Britzman, D. 1995. Is there a queer pedagogy? Or stop reading straight. *Educational Theory* 45: 357–81.

———. 1998. *Lost subjects, contested objects: Toward a psychoanalytic inquiry of learning*. Albany, NY: SUNY Press.

Brod, H., and M. Kaufman. 1994. *Theorising masculinities*. Thousand Oaks, CA: Sage.

Brohm, J-M. 1978. *Sport, a prison of measured time: Essays*. Translated by I. Fraser. London: Ink Links Ltd.

Brown, P. 1989. Schooling for inequality? Ordinary kids in the school and the labour market. In *School, work and equality*, ed. B. Cosin, M. Flude, and M. Hales, 238–57. London: Hodder and Stoughton.

Browne, R., and R. Fletcher, eds. 1995. *Boys in schools: Addressing the real issues–Behaviour, values and relationships*. Lane Cove, NSW: Finch.

Buchbinder, D. 1994. *Masculinities and identities*. Carlton, VIC: Melbourne University Press.

Buckingham, D., and J. Sefton-Green. 1994. *Cultural studies goes to school. Reading and teaching popular media*. London: Taylor & Francis.

Butler, J. 1990. *Gender trouble: Feminism and the subversion of identity*. New York: Routledge.

———. 1993. *Bodies that matter*. New York & London: Routledge.

Canaan, J. 1991. Is "doing nothing" just boys' play? Integrating feminist and cultural perspectives on working class young men's masculinity. In *Off centre: Feminism and cultural studies*, ed. S. Franklin, C. Lury, and J. Stacey, 109–25. London: Harper Collins Academic.

Capp, G. 2000. In a class of his own. *The West Australian*, 24 May.

Carvel, J. 1996. Blunkett plans to tackle "laddism." *Guardian*, 1 November.

Chambers, D. 1983. Symbolic equipment and the objects of leisure images. *Leisure Studies* 2(3): 301–15.

Chan, C. 1996. Combating heterosexism in educational institutions: Structural changes and strategies. In *Preventing heterosexism and homophobia*, ed. E. Rothblum and L. Bond, 20–35. Thousand Oaks, CA: Sage.

Chan, J. 1998. Contemporary Asian American men's issues. In *Teaching Asian America: Diversity and the problem of community*, ed. L. Hirabayashi, 93–102. Lanham, MD: Rowman and Littlefield.

Chen, L. 1995. Make that a double a. men. *A. Magazine*, February/March.

Chin, F., and J. Chan. 1972. Racist love. In *Seeing through shuck*, ed. R. Kostelanetz, 65–79. New York: Ballantine Books.

Chisholm, L., ed. 1996. *Out-of-school youth report: Policy provision for out-of-school and out-of-work youth*. Johannesburg: Education Policy Unit, University of the Witwatersrand.

Chisholm, L., and S. Vally. 1996. *The culture of learning and teaching in Gauteng schools*. Johannesburg: Gauteng Ministry of Education.

Chitty, C. 1999. *State schools: New labour and the conservative legacy*. London: Woburn Press.

Cho, S. 1997. Asian Pacific American women and racialized sexual harassment. In *Making more waves: New writing by Asian American women*, ed. E. Kim, L. Villanueva, and Asian Women United in California, 164–73. Boston: Beacon Press.

Cohen, M. 1998. "A habit of healthy idleness": Boys' underachievement in historical perspective. In *Failing boys? Issues in gender and achievement*; ed. D. Epstein, J. Elwood, V. Hey, and J. Maw, 19–34. Buckingham, UK: Open University Press.

Cohen, P. 1984. Against the new vocationalism. In *Schooling for the dole? The new vocationalism*, ed. I. Bates, J. Clarke, P. Cohen, D. Finn, R. Moore, and P. Willis, 104–70. London: MacMillan.

Commitments Collective. 1980. Anti-sexist commitments for men .... *Anti-Sexist Men's Newsletter* 9.

Connell, R. 1985. Theorising gender. *Sociology* 19: 260–72.

———. 1987. *Gender and power*. Cambridge: Polity Press.

———. 1989. Cool guys, swots and wimps: The interplay of masculinity and education. *Oxford Review of Education* 15(3): 291–303.

———. 1993. Disruptions: Improper masculinities and schooling. In *Beyond silenced voices: Class, race, and gender in United States schools*, ed. L. Weis and M. Fine, 191–208. Albany, NY: SUNY Press.

———. 1996. Teaching the boys: New research on masculinity, and gender strategies for schools. *Teachers College Record* (USA) 98(2): 206–35.

———. 1997. *Arms and the man: Using the new research on masculinity to understand violence and promote peace in the contemporary world*. Paper presented at Women and a Culture of Peace, Norwegian National Commission for UNESCO. Oslo, Norway, 24–28 September.

———. 1998. Symposium on R. W. Connell's Masculinities: Men's gender politics. *Gender and Society* 12: 469–77.

———. 2000. *The men and the boys*. St. Leonards: Allen & Unwin.

Connell, R., D. Ashenden, S. Kessler, and G. Dowsett. 1982. *Making the difference: Schools, families and social divisions*. Sydney: Allen & Unwin.

Connell, R., D. Butland, J. Fisher, and L. Walker. 1997. *Gender issues in communicating road safety messages to boys: An examination of research literature and current educational approaches*. Sydney: Roads and Traffic Authority.

Connolly, P. 1998. *Racism, gender identities and young children: Social relations in a multi-ethnic inner-city primary school.* London: Routledge.

Cornwall, A., and N. Lindisfarne, eds. 1994. *Dislocating masculinity: Comparative ethnographies.* London: Routledge.

Corrigan P., and D. Sayer. 1985. *The great arch: English state formation as cultural revolution.* Oxford: Basil Blackwell.

Council on Scientific Affairs, American Medical Association. 1992. Violence against women: Relevance for medical practitioners. *Journal of the American Medical Association* 267: 3184–95.

Culley, M., and C. Portuges. 1985. *Gendered subjects: The dynamics of feminist teaching.* Boston: Routledge and Kegan Paul.

Cunneen, C., M. Findlay, R. Lynch, and V. Tupper. 1985. *Dynamics of collective conflict: Riots at the Bathurst bike races.* North Ryde, NSW: Law Book Company.

Dangerous Minds. 1995. Produced by J. Bruckheimer and D. Simpson. Directed by J. Smith. Hollywood Pictures.

Dankwort, J. 1992–93. Violence against women: Varying perceptions and intervention practices with woman abusers. *Intervention* 92: 34–49.

Davies, B. 1993. *Shards of glass: Children, reading and writing beyond gendered identities.* St. Leonards, NSW: Allen and Unwin.

Davies, B., and R. Hunt. 1994. Classroom competencies and marginal positioning. *British Journal of Sociology of Education* 15(3): 389–408.

Davis, J. 1999. Forbidden fruit: Black males' constructions of transgressive sexualities in middle school. In *Queering elementary education: Advancing the dialogue about sexualities and schooling*, ed. W. Letts and J. Sears, 49–59. Lanham, MD: Rowman and Littlefield.

Davis, P., and D. Riesenfeld (Producer/Director). 1993. *In darkest Hollywood: Cinema and apartheid.* Vancouver: Villon Films.

Davison, K. 1996. *Manly expectations: Memories of masculinities in school.* Masters thesis, Simon Fraser University, Burnaby, British Columbia.

———. 2000a. Masculinities, sexualities and the student body: "Sorting" gender identities in school. In *Experiencing difference*, ed. C. James, 44–52. Halifax, NS: Fernwood Press.

———. 2000b. Boys' bodies in school: Physical education. *The Journal of Men's Studies* 8(2): 255–66.

Deacon, R., R. Morrell, and J. Prinsloo. 1999. Discipline and homophobia in South African schools: The limits of legislated transformation. In *A dangerous knowing: Sexuality, pedagogy and popular culture*, ed. D. Epstein and J. Sears, 164–81. London: Cassell.

DeKeseredy, W. 1990. Male peer support and woman abuse: The current state of knowledge. *Sociological Focus* 23(6): 129–39.

DeKeseredy, W., and M. Schwartz. 1993. Male peer support and women abuse: An expansion of DeKeseredy's model. In *Issues in intimate violence*, ed. R. Bergen, 83–96. Thousand Oaks, CA: Sage.

Delamont, S. 1990. *Sex roles and the school*. 2d ed. London: Routledge.
Denborough, D. 1995. Step-by-step: Developing respectful and effective ways of working with young men to reduce violence. In *Men's ways of being*, ed. C. McLean, M. Carey, and C. White, 91–115. Boulder, CO: Westview Press.
Department of Education (DEC). 1997. Campaign on the culture of teaching and learning. Working document. Republic of South Africa: Author.
Dickinson, M., ed. 1993. *Our world*. Washington, DC: National Geographic Society.
Dobash, Rebecca Emerson, and Russell Dobash. 1992. *Women, violence and social change*. London: Routledge.
Dore, C. 2000. NZ talks up dollar union. *The Australian*, 4 April.
Durham, M. 1991. *Sex and politics: The family and morality in the Thatcher years*. Basingstoke, UK: Macmillan Education.
Editors. 1997. Guy talk. Roundtable discussion. *A. Magazine* (February/March): 26–31.
Edleson, J. 1990. Judging the success of interventions with men who batter. In *Family violence: Research and public policy issues*, ed. D. Besharov, 130–45. Washington, DC: AEI Press.
Edleson, J., and M. Syers. 1990. The relative effectiveness of group treatment with men who batter. *Social Work Research and Abstracts* 26: 10-17.
Edleson, J., and R. Tolman. 1992. *Intervention for men who batter: An ecological approach*. Newbury Park, CA: Sage.
Education Service Advisory Committee. 1990. *Violence to staff in the education sector*. London: HMSO.
Edwards, S., and J. Hearn. 2005. Working against men's "domestic violence": *Priority policies and practices for men in intervention, prevention and societal change*. Strasbourg: Council of Europe.
Egan, C. 2000. Good sorts, bad sports. *The Weekend Australian*, 10 June 10, 29.
Early Learning Resource Unit (ELRU) and Quaker Peace Centre (for Western Cape Education Department). 1999. *Baseline study of research done on anti-crime initiatives at school level*. Cape Town, Republic of South Africa.
Eng, D., and A. Hom. 1998. Introduction: Q&A: Notes on a queer Asian America. In *Q&A: Queer in Asian America*, ed. D. Eng and A. Hom, 1–21. Philadelphia: Temple University Press.
Epprecht, M. 2001. Class acts I: Resources and ideas for un-teaching about Africa. *Canadian Journal of African Studies* 35(2): 340–5.
Epstein, D. 1997a. Boyz' own stories: Masculinities and sexualities in schools. *Gender and Education* 9: 105–16.
———. 1997b. What's in a ban? The popular media, Romeo and Juliet and compulsory heterosexuality. In *Border patrols: Policing the boundaries of heterosexuality*, ed. D. Steinberg, D. Epstein, and R. Johnson, 183–203. London: Cassell.
Epstein, D., and R. Johnson. 1998. *Schooling sexualities*. Buckingham, UK: Open University Press.

Epstein, D., J. Elwood, V. Hey, and J. Maw, eds. 1998. *Failing boys?: Issues in gender and achievement*. Buckingham, UK: Open University Press.

Everatt, D., and E. Sisulu, eds. 1992. *Black youth in crisis: Facing the future*. Braamfontein, RSA: Raven Press.

Fanon, F. 1970. *Black skin, white masks*. London: Paladin.

Felman, S. 1995. Education and crisis, or the vicissitudes of teaching. In *Trauma: Explorations in memory*, ed. C. Caruth, 13–60. Baltimore, MD: The Johns Hopkins University Press.

Fenwick, M. 1996. "Tough guy eh?": The gangster-figure in *Drum*. *Journal of Southern African Studies* 22(4): 617–32.

Fernandez, L. 2000. Indo-American youth in gangs defy stereotypes. *San Jose Mercury News*, 9 April.

Fine, S. 2001. Schools told to fix boys' low grades. *The Globe and Mail*, 27 August, A1.

Fletcher, R. 1995. Looking to fathers. In *Boys in schools: Addressing the real issues—behaviour, values and relationships*, ed. R. Browne and R. Fletcher, 114–23. Sydney: Finch.

Fletcher, R., D. Hamilton, and P. Hewitson. 1997. *Fathers talking about risky driving to their teenage sons*. The Men's Health Project, Family Action Centre. Newcastle, NSW: University of Newcastle.

Foley, D. 1990. *Learning capitalist culture: Deep in the heart of Tejas*. Philadelphia: University of Pennsylvania Press.

Foucault, M. 1978. *The history of sexuality*. Vol. 1. Translated by R. Hurley. New York: Vintage.

———. 1981. *The history of sexuality*. Vol. 1. Translated by R. Hurley. Harmondsworth, UK: Penguin.

———. 1982. The subject and power. *Critical Inquiry* 8: 777–95.

———. 1984. Preface to *The history of sexuality*. Vol. 2. In *The Foucault reader*, ed. P. Rabinow. London: Penguin.

———. 1988a. Technologies of the self. In *Technologies of the Self*, ed. L. Martin, H. Gutman, and P. Hutton, 9–15. Ahmerst, MA: The University of Massachusetts Press.

———. 1988b. The political technology of individuals. In *Technologies of the Self*, ed. L. Martin, H. Gutman, and P. Hutton, 16–49. Ahmerst, MA: The University of Massachusetts Press.

———. 1993. About the beginning of the hermeneutics of the self. *Political Theory* 21: 198–227.

Fox Keller, E. 1982. Feminism and science. *Signs* 7(3): 589–602.

Frank, B. 1987. Hegemonic heterosexual masculinity. *Studies in Political Economy* 24: 159–70.

———. 1990. *Everyday masculinities*. Ph.D. diss., Dalhousie University, Halifax, Nova Scotia.

———. 1993. Straight/strait jackets for masculinity: Educating for "real men." *Atlantis: A Women's Studies Journal* 18: 47–59.

———. 1994. Queer selves/queer in schools: Young men and sexualities. In *Sex in schools: Canadian education & sexual regulation*, ed. S. Prentice, 44–59. Toronto: Our Schools/Our Selves Education Foundation.

———. 1997. Masculinity meets postmodernism: Theorizing the "man made" man. *Canadian Folklore Canadien* 19(1): 15–33.

Frank, B., M. Kehler, T. Lovell, and K. Davison. 2003. A tangle of trouble: Boys and schooling, future directions. *Educational Review* 55(2): 119–33.

Frank, B., and K. Davison, eds. 2000. Special Issue: Boys, men, masculinity, and education. *The Journal of Men's Studies* 8(2).

———. 2001. Masculinities and schooling: Challenging present practices and "panics." *Exceptionality Education Canada* 10(1 and 2): 63–74.

Freund, B. 1996. The violence in Natal. In *Political economy and identities in KwaZulu-Natal*, ed. R. Morrell, 179–95. Durban: Indicator Press.

Fung, R. 1996. Looking for my penis: The eroticized Asian in gay video porn. In *Asian American sexualities: Dimensions of the gay and lesbian experience*, ed. R. Leong, 181–98. New York: Routledge.

Gatens, M. 1996. *Imaginary bodies: Ethics, power and corporeality*. London: Routledge.

Gee, D. (Director), and Asian Women United (Producer). 1988. *Slaying the dragon*. Videocassette. Available from National Asian American Telecommunications Association, San Francisco.

Gibb, H., ed./trans. 1983 [1929]. *Ibn Battuta: Travels in Asia and Africa, 1325–1354*. London: Routledge.

Giddens, A. 1994. *Beyond left and right*. Cambridge, UK: Polity Press.

Gilbert, R., and P. Gilbert. 1998. *Masculinity goes to school*. London: Routledge.

Gillan, E., and E. Samson. 2000. The zero tolerance campaigns. In *Home truths about domestic violence*, ed. J. Hanmer and C. Itzen with S. Quaid and D. Wigglesworth, 340–55. London: Routledge.

Ginpil, S., and R. Attewell. 1994. *A comparison of fatal crashes involving male and female car drivers*. Canberra: Federal Office of Road Safety, Australian Government Publishing Service.

Godenzi, A., M. Schwartz, and W. DeKeseredy. 2001. Toward a gendered social bond/male peer support theory of university women abuse. *Critical Criminology* 10: 1–16.

Goffman, J. 1984. *Batterers anonymous: Self-help counselling for men who batter*. San Bernardino, CA: BA Press.

Gondolf, E. 1985. *Men who batter: An integrated approach for stopping wife abuse*. Holmes Beach, FL: Learning Publications.

———. 1989. Foreword. In *Treating men who batter: Theory, practice and programs*, ed. P. Caesar and L. Hamberger. New York: Springer.

———. 1993. Male batterers. In *Family violence: Prevention and treatment*, ed. R. Hampton, T. Gullotta, G. Adams, E. Potter III, and R. Weisberg, 230–57. Newbury Park, CA: Sage.

———. 1998. Multi-site evaluation of batterer intervention systems. Paper delivered at the Program Evaluation and Family Violence Research Conference, Durham, New Hampshire. Cited in A. Mullender and S. Burton. 2001. Dealing with perpetrators. In *What works in reducing domestic violence?* ed. J. Taylor-Browne, 59–94. London: Whiting and Birch.

Gondolf, E., and D. Russell. 1986. The case against anger control treatment programs for batterers. *Response* 9(3): 2–5.

Green, D. 1999. *Gender violence in Africa: African women's responses*. New York: St. Martin's Press.

Griffin, C., and S. Lees, eds. 1997. Special Issue on Masculinities in Education. *Gender and Education* 9(1): 5–253.

Guillermo, E. 1995. Going GAPA: A different kind of beauty contest. *Asian Week*, 8 September.

Hagland, P. 1998. "Undressing the Oriental boy": The gay Asian in the social imaginary of the gay white male. In *Looking queer: Body image and identity in lesbian, bisexual, gay, and transgender communities*, ed. D. Atkins, 277–94. New York: Harrington Park Press.

Halifax Men For Change. 1994. *Healthy relationships*. Halifax, NS: Men For Change Press.

Hall, L., and J. Kauanui. 1996. Same-sex sexuality in Pacific literature. In *Asian American sexualities: Dimensions of the gay and lesbian experience*, ed. R. Leong, 113–8. New York: Routledge.

Hall, S. 1988. New ethnicities. *Black film, British cinema*. ICA document no. 7. London: ICA.

———. 1990. Cultural identity and diaspora. In *Identity: Community, culture, difference*, ed. J. Rutherford, 222–37. London: Lawrence and Wishart.

Hanmer, J. 1996. Women and violence: Commonalities and diversities. In *Violence and gender relations: Theories and interventions*, ed. B. Fawcett, B. Featherstone, J. Hearn, and C. Toft, 7–21. London: Sage.

Hanmer, J., and S. Saunders. 1984. *Well-founded fear*. London: Hutchinson.

Hanmer, J., J. Hearn, C. Dillon, T. Kayani, and P. Todd. 1995. *Violence to women from known men: Policy development, interagency approaches and good practice*. Bradford, UK: Violence, Abuse and Gender Relations Research Unit, University of Bradford. Available from Research Centre on Violence, Abuse and Gender Relations, Leeds Metropolitan University.

Harris, J. 1998. *The nurture assumption: Why children turn out the way they do*. New York: Free Press.

Haug, F., et al. 1987. *Female sexualization: A collective work of memory*. Translated by E. Carter. London: Verso.

Hay, M., ed. 2000. *African novels in the classroom*. Boulder, CO: Lynne Rienner.

Haywood, C., and M. Mac an Ghaill. 1995. The sexual politics of the curriculum: Contesting values. *International Studies in Sociology of Education* 5(2): 221–36.

———. 1997. Materialism and deconstructivism: Education and the epistemology of identity. *Cambridge Journal of Education* 27(2): 261–72.
Hearn J. 1987. *The gender of oppression: Men, masculinity and the critique of Marxism.* New York: St. Martin's Press.
———. 1990. "Child abuse" and men's violence. In *Taking child abuse seriously*, ed. Violence Against Children Study Group, 63–85. London: Unwin Hyman.
———. 1993. The politics of essentialism and the analysis of the men's movement(s). *Feminism and Psychology* 3(3): 405–9.
———. 1996a. Men and men's violence to known women: The "lure" and "lack" of cultural studies approaches. Paper presented at Cultural Studies at the Crossroads Conference, Tampere, Finland.
———. 1996b. Men's violence to known women: Men's accounts and men's policy developments. In *Violence and gender relations*, ed. B. Fawcett, B. Featherstone, J. Hearn, and C. Toft, 99–114. London: Sage.
———. 1998a. Men will be men: The ambiguity of men's support for men who have been violent to known women. In *Men, gender divisions and welfare*, ed. J. Popay, J. Hearn, and J. Edwards, 147–80. London: Routledge.
———. 1998b. *The violences of men.* London: Sage.
———. 1999. Educating men against violence to women. Special Issue. Teaching about violence against women: International perspectives. *Women's Studies Quarterly* 27(1 and 2): 140–51.
Hearn, J., and D. Collinson. 1994. Theorizing unities and differences between men and between masculinities. In *Theorizing masculinities*, ed. H. Brod and M. Kaufman, 97–118. Thousand Oaks, CA: Sage Publications.
Heiskanen, M., and M. Piispa. 1998. *Faith, hope, battering: A survey of men's violence against women in Finland.* Helsinki: Statistics Finland/Council for Equality.
Hemson, C. 2001. Ukubhekezela or Ukuzithemba–Durban's African life savers. In *Changing men in Southern Africa*, ed. R. Morrell, 57–74. Pietermaritzburg: University of Natal Press.
Henderson, M. 1972. *The young driver.* New South Wales Traffic Accident Research Unit, Department of Motor Transport, New South Wales.
Hickey, C., L. Fitzclarence, and R. Matthews. 2000. *Where the boys are: Masculinity/sport/education.* Geelong, VIC: DCEC and Deakin University Press.
Hirson, B. 1979. *Year of fire, year of ash.* London: Zed.
Hobsbawm, E. 1972. *Bandits.* Harmondsworth, UK: Penguin.
Holmes, M., and C. Lundy. 1990. Group work for abusive men: A profeminist response. *Canada's Mental Health.* December: 12–7.
hooks, b. 1989. Toward a revolutionary feminist pedagogy. In *Talking back: Thinking black.* Boston: South End Press.
Hyslop, J. 1999. *The classroom struggle: Policy and resistance in South Africa 1940–1990.* Pietermaritzburg: University of Natal Press.

Ifeka-Moller, C. 1973. A reply to Judith van Allen. *Canadian Journal of African Studies* 7(2): 317–8.
Ima, K., and J. Nidorf. 1998. Characteristics of Southeast Asian delinquents: Toward an understanding. In *Struggling to be heard: The unmet needs of Asian Pacific American children*, ed. V. Pang and L. Cheng, 89–104. Albany, NY: SUNY Press.
Imms, W. 2000. Multiple masculinities and the schooling of boys. *Canadian Journal of Education* 25(2): 152–65.
Jackson, D. 1992. Riding for joy. *Achilles Heel* (Summer): 18–38.
Jackson, S. 2003. Batterer intervention programs. In *Batterer intervention programs: Where do we go from here?* ed. S. Jackson, L. Feder, D. Forde, R. Davis, C. Maxwell, and B. Taylor. Washington, DC: National Institute of Justice. Available at: http://www.ncjrs.org/txtfiles1/nij/195079.txt
Jackson, S., L. Feder, D. Forde, R. Davis, C. Maxwell, and B. Taylor. 2003. *Batterer intervention programs: Where do we go from here?* Washington, DC: National Institute of Justice. Available at: http://www.ncjrs.org/txtfiles1/nij/195079.txt
Jenkins, A. 1990. *Invitations to responsibility*. Adelaide: Dulwich Centre Publications.
Jenny, C., T. Roeseler, and K. Poyer. 1994. Are children at risk for sexual abuse by homosexuals? *Pediatrics* 94: 41-4.
Jones, L. 1991. The Minnesota school curriculum project: A state-wide domestic violence prevention project in secondary schools. In *Dating violence: Young women in danger*, ed. B. Levy, 258–66. Seattle, WA: Seal.
Jopson, D. 2004. Sex and the team player. *The Age*, 6 March, Insight 4. Last retrieved Oct. 11, 2006 from www.theage.com.au/articles/2004/03/05/1078464638396.html
Kandylaki, A. 1996. *Male youth and sexual abuse*. Ph.D. diss., University of Bradford, Bradford, England.
Kaufman, M. 1987. The triad of men's violence. In *Beyond patriarchy: Essays by men on pleasure, power and change*, ed. M. Kaufman, 1–29. Toronto: Oxford University Press.
———. 1994. Men, feminism, and mens' contradictory experiences of power. In *Theorizing masculinities*, ed. H. Brod and M. Kaufman, 142–63. Thousand Oaks, CA: Sage.
Keddie, A. 2005. On fighting and football: Gender justice and theories of identity construction. *International Journal of Qualitative Studies in Education* 18(4): 425–44.
Kehler, M. 2000. High school masculinity and gender politics: Submerged voices, emerging choices. Ph.D. diss., Michigan State University.
———. 2004. Masculinities and resistance: High school boys (un)doing boy. *Taboo* 8(3): 97–113.
Kehler, M., and W. Martino. In press. Questioning Masculinities: Interrogating Boys' Capacities for Self-Problematization in Schools. *Canadian Journal of Education* 30(1).

Kehler, M., K. Davison, and B. Frank. 2005. Contradictions and tensions of the practice of masculinities in school: Interrogating "Good Buddy Talk." *Journal of Curriculum Theorizing* 21(3): 3–16.

Kehler, M., and C. Greig. 2005. Boys can read: Exploring the socially literate practices of high school young men. *International Journal of Inclusive Education* 9(4): 351–70.

Kennedy, L., and J-C Tomas. 2004. Players front police for grilling over alleged assault. *The Age*, 4 March, 7. Last retrieved Oct. 11, 2006 from www.theage.com.au/cgi-bin/common/popupPrintArticle.pl?path=/articles/2004/03/03/1078295452322.html

Kenway, J. 1995. Masculinities in schools: Under siege, on the defensive and under reconstruction? *Discourse: Studies in the Cultural Politics of Education* 16: 59–79.

———. 1996. Reasserting masculinity in Australian schools. *Women's Studies International Forum* 9: 447–66.

Kenway, J., and L. Fitzclarence. 1997. Masculinity, violence and schooling: Challenging "poisonous pedagogies." *Gender and Education* 9(1): 117–34.

Kenway, J., and S. Willis. 1998. *Girls, boys and feminism*. St. Leonards, NSW: Allen & Unwin.

Kerley, N. 2000. Footy's modern mind games. *Sunday Mail*, 30 April.

Kessler, S., D. Ashenden, R. Connell, and G. Dowsett. 1985. Gender relations in secondary schooling. *Sociology of Education* 58: 34–48.

Kim, D. 1998. The strange love of Frank Chin. In *Q&A: Queer in Asian America*, ed. D. Eng and A. Hom, 270–303. Philadelphia: Temple University Press.

Kimmel, M. 1994. Masculinity as homophobia: Fear, shame, and silence in the construction of gender identity. In *Theorizing masculinities*, ed. H. Brod and M. Kaufman, 119–41. Thousand Oaks, CA: Sage.

———, ed. 1995. *The politics of manhood: Profeminist men respond to the mythopoetic men's movement (and the mythopoetic leaders answer)*. Philadelphia: Temple University Press.

———. 1997. *Manhood in America: A cultural history*. New York: Free Press.

Kimmel, M., and M. Messner. 1989. *Men's lives*. New York: Macmillan Publishing Company.

Kindlon, D., and M. Thompson. 1999. *Raising Cain: Protecting the emotional life of boys*. New York: Ballantine Books.

King, J. 1997. *The football factory*. London: Vintage.

Kingston, M. 1975. *The woman warrior: Memoirs of a childhood among ghosts*. New York: Random House.

Krug, E., L. Dahlberg, J. Mercy, A. Zwi, and R. Lozano, eds. 2002. *World report on violence and health*. Geneva: World Health Organization.

Kumashiro, K. 1999a. "Barbie," "big dicks," and "faggots": Paradox, performativity, and anti-oppressive pedagogy. *JCT: Journal of Curriculum Theorizing* 15(1): 27–42.

———. 1999b. Supplementing normalcy and otherness: Queer Asian American men reflect on stereotypes, identity, and oppression. *Qualitative Studies in Education* 12(5): 491–508.

Lee, J. 1996. Why Suzie Wong is not a lesbian: Asian and Asian American lesbian and bisexual women and femme/butch/gender identities. In *Queer studies: A lesbian, gay, bisexual, and transgender anthology*, ed. B. Beemyn and M. Eliason, 115–32. New York: New York University Press.

Lee, S. 1996. *Unraveling the "model minority" stereotype: Listening to Asian American youth.* New York: Teachers College Press.

Lei, J. 2000. (Un)Necessary toughness: Those "loud Black girls" and those "quiet Asian boys." Paper presented at Swarthmore College, Swarthmore, Pennsylvania, 16 March.

Letts W., and J. Sears. 1999. *Queering elementary education.* Lanham, MD: Rowman & Littlefield.

Levy, B. 1984. *Skills for violence-free relationships.* Santa Monica, CA: Southern California Coalition for Battered Women.

Lichter, C. 2002. "What about the boys?": Unraveling the yarn about boys, literacy and masculinity. Masters thesis, Mount Saint Vincent University, Halifax, Nova Scotia.

Lindsay, L., and S. Miescher, eds. 2003. *Men and masculinities in modern Africa.* Portsmouth, NH: Heinemann.

Lingard, B., and P. Douglas. 1999. *Men engaging feminisms: Pro-feminism, backlashes and schooling.* Buckingham, UK: Open University Press.

Local Government Act. 1988. (UK). London: HMSO.

Lorber, J. 1994. *Paradoxes of gender.* New Haven, CT: Yale University Press.

Lubelska, C. 1991. Teaching methods in women's studies: Challenging the mainstream. In *Out of the margins: Women's studies in the nineties*, ed. J. Aaron and S. Walby, 41–8. Philadelphia: The Falmer Press.

Luxton, M. 1993. Dreams and dilemmas: Feminist musings on "the man question." In *Men and masculinities: A critical anthology*, ed. T. Haddad, 348–74. Toronto: Canadian Scholars' Press.

Ma, M., and C. Stewart. 1997. *There is no name for this.* Videocassette. Available from Asian and Pacific Islander Wellness Center, San Francisco.

Mac an Ghaill, M. 1994a. *The making of men: Masculinities, sexualities and schooling.* Buckingham, UK: Open University Press.

——. 1994b. The making of Black English masculinities. In *Theorizing Masculinities*, ed. H. Brod and M. Kaufman, 183–99. Thousand Oaks, CA: Sage.

——. 1999. *Contemporary racisms and ethnicities: Social and cultural transformations.* Buckingham, UK: Open University Press.

Mac an Ghaill, M., and C. Haywood. 2000. Emerging young heterosexual masculinities. Paper presented at the Centre for Gender and Women's Studies, University of Newcastle, Newcastle upon Tyne, England.

Maccoby, E., and C. Jacklin. 1975. *The psychology of sex differences.* Stanford, CA: Stanford University Press.

MacKinnon, C. 1983. Feminism, Marxism, method and the state: Towards feminist jurisprudence. *Signs* 8(4): 635–58.

MacLeod, J. 1987. *Ain't no makin' it: Leveled aspirations in a low income neighborhood.* Boulder, CO: Westview Press.
———. 1995. *Ain't no makin' it: Aspirations and attainment in a low-income neighborhood.* Boulder, CO: Westview Press.
Mager, A. 1998. Youth organisations and the construction of masculine identities in the Ciskei and Transkei, 1945–1960. *Journal of Southern African Studies* 24(4): 653–67.
Mager, D., and R. Sulek. 1997. Teaching about homophobia at a historically black university: A role play for undergraduate students. In *Overcoming heterosexism and homophobia: Strategies that work,* ed. J. Sears and W. Williams, 182–96. New York: Columbia University Press.
Mahlobo, V. 2000. The effect of violence on academic achievement: The case study of Amandlethu Secondary School. Masters of Education thesis, University of Natal, Durban, Republic of South Africa.
Mahoney, P. 1985. *School for the boys?* London: Hutchinson.
———. 1988. Oppressive pedagogy: The importance of process in women's studies. *Women's Studies International Forum* 11: 103–8.
———. 1998. Girls will be girls and boys will be first. In *Failing boys? Issues in gender and achievement,* ed. D. Epstein, J. Elwood, V. Hey, and J. Maw, 37–55. Buckingham, UK: Open University Press.
Manalansan IV, M. 1995. Speaking of AIDS: Language and the Filipino "gay" experience in America. In *Discrepant histories: Translocal essays on Filipino cultures,* ed. V. Rafael, 193–220. Manila, Philippines: Anvil Publishing.
Mannheim, K. 1952. *Essays on the sociology of knowledge.* London: Routledge and Kegan Paul.
Marks, M. 2001. *Young warriors: Youth politics, identity and violence in South Africa.* Johannesburg: Witwatersrand University Press.
Marsh, C., and N. Hyde. 1990. *Road safety education in Australian schools: A study of dissemination, implementation and exemplary practice.* Report CR 89. Canberra: Federal Office of Road Safety.
Martino, W. 1996. *Boys and literacy: Addressing the links between masculinity and learning.* Paper presented at the Gender Network Conference for the DSE, Sydney, Australia.
———. 1997. "A bunch of arseholes": Exploring the politics of masculinity for adolescent boys in schools. *Social Alternatives* 16(3): 31–43.
———. 1999. "It's ok to be gay!": Interrupting straight thinking in the English classroom. In *Teaching Queerly,* ed. W. Letts and J. Sears, 137–50. Boulder, CO: Rowman & Littlefield.
———. 2000. Mucking around in class, giving crap, and acting cool: Adolescent boys enacting masculinities at school. *Canadian Journal of Education* 25(2): 102–12.
———. 2001. "Powerful people aren't usually real kind, friendly, open people!": Boys interrogating masculinities at school. In *What about the boys?,* ed. W. Martino and B. Meyenn, 82–95. Buckingham, UK: Open University Press.

Martino, W., and B. Meyenn, eds. 2001. *What about the boys?* Buckingham, UK: Open University Press.

Martino, W. and M. Pallotta-Chiarolli. 2001. *Boys' stuff: Boys talking about what matters.* Sydney: Allen & Unwin.

———. 2003. *So what's a boy? Issues of masculinity and schooling.* Buckingham, UK: Open University Press.

Matthews, B. 2000. Brave Hird rekindles Anzac spirit. *The Herald-Sun,* 26 April 84.

Maylam, P., ed. 1995. Special issue on teaching. *South African Historical Journal* 33.

McKay, S., and S. Wong. 1996. Multiple discourses, multiple identities: Investment and agency in second-language learning among Chinese adolescent immigrant students. *Harvard Educational Review* 66(3): 577–608.

McLaren, P., and C. Lankshear, eds. 1994. *Politics of liberation: Paths from Freire.* New York: Routledge.

McLaughlin, K. 1997. Vietnamese views on gays changing with the times. *San Jose Mercury,* 29 April 1A, 12A.

McRobbie, A. 1978. Working class girls and the culture of femininity. In *Women take issue,* ed. Women's Study Group Centre for Contemporary Cultural Studies, 96–108. London: Hutchinson.

Meena, R., ed. 1992. *Gender in Southern Africa: Conceptual and theoretical issues.* Harare, Zimbabwe: SAPES.

Mendez, C. 1995. Those controversial, crazy calendar boys. *Asian Week,* 27 January.

Mercer, K. 1994. *Welcome to the jungle.* New York & London: Routledge.

Messerschmidt, J. 1993. *Masculinities and crime: Critique and reconceptualisation of theory.* Lanham, MD: Rowman and Littlefield.

Messner, M. 1988. Sports and male domination: The female athlete as contested ideological terrain. *Sociology of Sport Journal* 5: 197–211.

———. 1989. Boyhood, organized sports, and the construction of masculinities. In *Men's lives,* ed. M. Kimmel and M. Messner, 141–54. Boston: Allen & Bacon.

———. 1991. Masculinities and athletic careers. In *The social construction of gender,* ed. J. Lorber and S. Farrell, 147–62. Thousand Oaks, CA: Sage.

———. 1992. *Power at play: Sports and the problem of masculinity.* Boston: Beacon Press.

———. 1997. *Politics of masculinities: Men in movements.* Thousand Oaks, CA: Sage.

———. 1998. The limits of "the male sex role": An analysis of the men's liberation and men's rights movements' discourse. *Gender and Society* 12: 255–76.

Messner, M., and D. Sabo, eds. 1990. *Sport, men, and the gender order: Critical feminist perspectives.* Champaign, IL: Human Kinetics Books.

Messner, M., and D. Sabo. 1994. *Sex, violence and power in sports: Rethinking masculinity.* Freedom, CA: Crossing Press.

Miedzian, M. 1992. *Boys will be boys: Breaking the link between masculinity and violence.* London: Virago.

Mills, M. 2000. Issues in implementing boys' programs in schools: Male teachers and empowerment. *Gender and Education* 12(2): 221–38.

Mills, M., and B. Lingard. 1997. Masculinity politics, myths and boys' schooling. *British Journal of Educational Studies* 45: 276–92.

Mirrlees-Black, C. 1994. *Estimating the extent of domestic violence: Findings from the 1992 BCS*. Home Office Research Bulletin No. 37. London: Home Office Research and Statistics Department.

Mkhize, Z. 2000. The effects of education policy change on the practice of corporal punishment in a rural school in KwaZulu-Natal: The case of Amaqadi Community Primary School. Masters of Education Research Report, University of Natal, Durban, Republic of South Africa.

Mobonda, H. 1992. Which North American past for Congolese students? *Journal of American History* 79(2): 472–6.

Mokwena, S. 1991. The era of the Jackrollers: Contextualising the rise of youth gangs in Soweto. Unpublished paper. Project for the Study of Violence Seminar, University of the Witwatersrand, Johannesburg, Republic of South Africa.

Moller, V. 1990. *Lost generation found: Black youth at leisure*. Durban: Indicator Project South Africa.

Mooney, J. 1994. The prevalence and social distribution of domestic violence: An analysis of theory and method. Ph.D. diss., Middlesex University.

Morrell, R. 1998a. Of boys and men: Masculinity and gender in Southern African studies. *Journal of Southern African Studies* 24(4): 605–30.

———. 1998b. Gender and education: The place of masculinity in South African schools. *South African Journal of Education* 18(4): 218–25.

———., ed. 1998c. Special edition on masculinities. *Journal of Southern African Studies* 24(4).

———. 2001a. Corporal punishment and masculinity in South African schools. *Men and Masculinities* 4(2): 140–57.

———., ed. 2001b. *Changing men in Southern Africa*. Pietermaritzburg: University of Natal Press.

Morrell, R., and L. Moletsane. 2002. Inequality and fear: Learning and working inside Bantu education schools. In *The history of education under apartheid, 1948–1994: The doors of culture and learning shall be opened*, ed. P. Kallaway, 224–42. New York/Cape Town: Peter Lang/Pearson Education, South Africa.

Moyana, T. 1988. *Education, liberation, and the creative act*. Harare, Zimbabwe: Zimbabwe Publishing House.

Munoz, J. 1999. *Disidentifications: Queers of color and the performance of politics*. Minneapolis, MN: University of Minnesota Press.

Murray, S., and W. Roscoe, eds. 1998. *Boy wives and female husbands: Studies in African homosexualities*. New York: St. Martin's Press.

Nakasako, S. (Director and Producer). 1998. *Kelly loves Tony*. Videocassette. Available from National Asian American Telecommunications Association, San Francisco.

Nayak, A., and M-J. Kehily. 1996. Playing it straight: Masculinities, homophobias and schooling. *Journal of Gender Studies* 5: 211–30.
Nayak, A., and M. Kehily. 1997. Lads and laughter: Humour and the production of heterosexual hierarchies. *Gender and Education* 9(1): 69–87.
Nfah-Abbenyi, J. 1997. *Gender in African women's writing: Identity, sexuality, and difference.* Bloomington, IN: Indiana University Press.
Niehaus, I. 2000. Towards a dubious liberation: Masculinity, sexuality and power in South African Lowveld schools, 1953–1999. *Journal of Southern African Studies* 26(3): 387–407.
Nilan, P. 2000. "You're hopeless I swear to God": Shifting masculinities in classroom talk. *Gender and Education* 12(1): 53–68.
Nishioka, J. 2000. A threatened manhood: Exploring the myth of the angry Asian male. *Asian Week*, 3 February.
Nkosi, T. 1987. *The time of the comrades.* Johannesburg: Skotaville.
Nnaemeka, O., ed. 1998. *Sisterhood, feminisms and power: From Africa to the diaspora.* Trenton, NJ/Asmara, Eritrea: Africa World Press.
Nzegwu, N. 1998. Chasing shadows: The misplaced search for matriarchy. *Canadian Journal of African Studies* 32(3): 594–622.
OECD. 1994. *OECD road transport research programme: Improving road safety by attitude modification.* Paris: Author.
———. 1996. *Effectiveness of road safety education programmes.* Paris: Author.
Office for Standards in Education (OFSTED). 1996. *The gender divide: Performance differences between boys and girls.* London: HMSO.
Okihiro, G. 1994. *Margins and mainstreams: Asians in American history and culture.* Seattle, WA: University of Washington Press.
Omi, M., and H. Winant. 1994. *Racial formation in the United States: From the 1960s to the 1990s.* 2d ed. New York: Routledge.
Open School. 1986. *Two dogs and freedom: Children of the townships speak out.* Braamfontein, RSA: Ravan in conjunction with the Open School.
Orr, D. 1993. Toward a critical rethinking of feminist pedagogical praxis and resistant male students. *Canadian Journal of Education* 18: 239–54.
Osajima, K. 1993. The hidden injuries of race. In *Bearing dreams, shaping visions: Asian Pacific American perspectives,* ed. L. Revilla, G. Nomura, S. Wong, and S. Hune, 81–91. Pullman, WA: Washington State University Press.
Pallotta-Chiarolli, M. 1997. "We want to address boys' education but...". In *Will boys be boys? Boys' education in the context of gender reform,* ed. J. Kenway, 65–8. Australian Curriculum Association Publication.
Pascoe, R. 1996. *The winter game: Over 100 years of Australian football.* Melbourne: Mandarin.
Patterson, A. 1997. Setting limits to English. In *Constructing critical literacies,* ed. S. Muspratt, A. Luke, and P. Freebody, 335–52. Sydney: Allen & Unwin.
Pattman, R. 2001. Learning to be men at a teachers' college in Zimbabwe. In *Changing men in Southern Africa,* ed. R. Morrell, 225–38. Pietermaritzburg, RSA: University of Natal Press.

Pearce, L. 2000. Hird the hero has a medal to prove it. *The Age- Sport*, 26 April, 1.
Pease, B. 2000. *Recreating men: Postmodern masculinity politics*. London: Sage.
Pence, E., and M. Paymar. 1990. *Power and control: Tactics of men who batter: An educational curriculum*. Duluth, MN: Minnesota Program Development.
Pinnock, D. 1997. *Gangs, rituals and rites of passage*. Cape Town: Africa Sun Press/Institute of Criminology, University of Cape Town.
Pirog-Good, M., and J. Stets-Kealey. 1985. Male batterers and battering prevention programs: A national survey. *Response* 8: 8–12.
Plummer, D. 1999. *One of the boys: Masculinity, homophobia and modern manhood*. New York, London & Oxford: Harrington Park Press.
Pollock, W. 1999. *Real boys: Rescuing our sons from the myth of boyhood*. New York: Henry Holt and Company.
Potts, D. 1996. *Why do men commit most crime? Focusing on masculinity in a prison group*. Wakefield, UK: West Yorkshire Probation Services/HM Prison Service.
Poynting, S., G. Noble, and P. Tabar. 1999. "If anyone called me a Wog, they wouldn't be speaking to me alone": Protest masculinity and Lebanese youth in Western Sydney. Special Issue: Australian masculinities. *Journal of Interdisciplinary Gender Studies* 3(2): 76–94.
Prichard, G. 2004. Bulldog defends DNA refusal. *The Sunday Age*, 7 March 11. Last retrieved Oct. 11, 2006 from www.theage.com.au/articles/2004/03/06/1078464696348.html?from=storyrhs
Quill, D., J. Wynne, W. Lacy, T. Myers, H. Riches, M. Wright, and J. Hearn, eds. 1993. *Offender victim mediation handbook*. Leeds, UK: Care and Justice/West Yorkshire Probation Service.
Quinn Patton, M. 1990. *Qualitative evaluation and research methods*. London: Sage.
Ratele, K. 2001. Between "Ouens": Everyday makings of black masculinity. In *Changing men in Southern Africa*, ed. R. Morrell, 239–53. Pietermaritzburg, RSA: University of Natal Press.
Redman, P. 1996. Empowering men to disempower themselves: Heterosexual masculinities, HIV and the contradictions of anti-oppressive education. In *Understanding masculinities*, ed. M. Mac an Ghaill, 168–81. Buckingham, UK: Open University Press.
Redman, P., and M. Mac an Ghaill. 1996. Schooling sexualities: Heterosexual masculinities, schooling, and the unconscious. *Discourse* 17(2): 243–56.
Redman, P., D. Epstein, M. Kehily, and M. Mac an Ghaill. 2002. Boys bonding: Same-sex friendship, the unconscious and heterosexual discourse. *Discourse: Studies in the Cultural Politics of Education* 23(2): 179–91.
Reed, L. 1998. Zero tolerance: Gender performance and school failure. In *Failing boys? Issues in gender and achievement*, ed. D. Epstein, J. Elwood, V. Hey, and J. Maw, 56–76. Buckingham, UK: Open University Press.
Reid, J., S. Hunter, T. Clark, and C. Collett van Rooyen. 2000. Establishing levels of aggression and the impact of violence on high school learners in the Durban

area. Preliminary Report. CRISP, University of Natal, Durban, Republic of South Africa. Retrieved from: www.und.ac.za/und/cadds/Crisp/michiganrep.htm (At the time of publication, this site was not active.)

Renold, E. 2000. "Coming out": Gender, (hetero) sexuality and the primary school. *Gender and Education* 12(3): 309–26.

———. 2004. "Other boys": Negotiating non-hegemonic masculinities in the primary school. *Gender and Education* 16(2): 247–66.

Respect. 2000. *Statement of principles and minimum standards of practice*. London: Author.

Rich, A. 1980. Compulsory heterosexuality and lesbian existence. *Signs* 54: 631–60.

Richardson, D. 1996. *Theorising heterosexuality: Telling it straight*. Buckingham, UK: Open University Press.

Robinson, K. 2005. Reinforcing hegemonic masculinities through sexual harassment issues of identity, power and popularity in secondary schools. *Gender and Education* 17(1): 19–37.

Rolls, G., R. Hall, and M. McDonald. 1991. *Accident risk and behavioural problems of young drivers*. Basingstoke, UK: AA Foundation for Road Safety Research.

Rothe, J. 1986. *Young drivers involved in injury-producing crashes: What they say about life and the accidents*. Vancouver: Insurance Corporation of British Columbia.

Rotundo, A. 1998. Boy culture. In *The children's culture reader*, ed. H. Jenkins, 337–62. New York: New York University Press.

Roulston, K., and M. Mills. 2000. Male teachers in feminised learning areas: Marching to the beat of the men's movement drums? *Oxford Review of Education* 26: 221–37.

Roads and Traffic Authority (R.T.A.). 1994. *Driving with attitude*. Sydney: Author.

———. 1996. *The driving experience*. Sydney: Author.

Rubin, G. 1984. Thinking sex: Notes for a radical theory of the politics of sexuality. In *Pleasure and danger: Exploring female sexuality*, ed. C. Vance, 267–319. London: Pandora.

Sabo, D., and D. Frederick. 1995. *Men's health and illness: Gender, power, and the body*. Thousand Oaks, CA: Sage.

Sadker, M., and D. Sadker. 1986. Sexism in the classroom: From grade school to graduate school. *Phi Delta Kappan* 67: 512–5.

———. 1994. *Failing at fairness: How our schools cheat girls*. New York: Touchstone.

Said, E. 1978. *Orientalism*. New York: Vintage Books.

Salisbury, J., and D. Jackson. 1996. *Challenging macho values: Practical ways of working with adolescent boys*. London: The Falmer Press.

Saunders, D. 1989. Cognitive and behavioral interventions with men who batter: Application and outcome. In *Treating men who batter: Theory, practice and programs*, ed. P. Caesar and L. Hamberger, 77–100. New York: Springer.

Scarnecchia, T. 1997. Mai Chaza's Guta re Jehova (City of God): Gender, healing and urban identity in an African Independent Church. *Journal of Southern African Studies* 23(1): 87–105.

Schrumpf, F., D. Crawford, and R. Bodine. 1997. *Peer mediation: Conflict resolution in schools. Student manual.* Champaign, IL: Research Press.

Schwartz, M., W. DeKeseredy, D. Tait, and S. Alvi. 2001. Male peer support and a feminist routine activities approach to explaining sexual assault. *Justice Quarterly* 12: 9–31.

Sedgwick, E. 1991/1989. *Epistemology of the closet.* London: Harvester Wheatsheaf.

———. 1995. "Gosh, Boy George, you must be awfully secure in your masculinity." In *Constructing masculinity*, ed. M. Berger, B. Wallis, S. Watson, and C. Weems, 11–20. New York: Routledge.

Seekings, J. 1993. *Heroes or villains? Youth politics in the 1980s.* Johannesburg: Ravan.

Segal, L. 1990. *Slow motion: Changing masculinities, changing men.* London: Virago.

Seidler, V. 1989. *Rediscovering masculinity: Reason, language and sexuality.* London: Routledge.

Sethna, C. 1993. Comrades or _____ ? Women graduate students look at the presence of male graduate students in feminist academe. *Gender and Education* 5: 139–55.

Sharp, G. 1985. Constitutive abstraction and social practice. *Arena* 70: 48–83.

Sharp, G., and D. White. 1968. Features of the intellectually trained. *Arena* 15: 30–3.

Sheehan, M. 1994. *Alcohol controls and drunk/driving: The social context.* Canberra: Federal Office of Road Safety.

Silverman, K. 1992. *Male subjectivity at the margins.* New York: Routledge.

Simpson, M. 1994. *Male impersonators: Men performing masculinity.* New York: Routledge.

Sitas, A. 1991. The comrades. *Reality* 23(3): 6–8.

Skeggs, B. 1991. Challenging masculinity and using sexuality. *British Journal of Sociology of Education* 12: 127–40.

Skelton, C. 1994. Sex, male teachers and young children. *Gender and Education* 6(1): 87–93.

———. 1998. Feminism and research into masculinities and schooling. *Gender and Education* 10(2): 217–27.

———. 2001. Typical boys? Theorizing masculinity in educational settings. In *Investigating gender: Contemporary perspectives in education*, ed. B. Francis and C. Skelton, 164–76. Buckingham: Open University Press.

Snyder, M. 2000. Women and African development. *Choice* (February): 1037–51.

Squirrell, G. 1989. In passing...teachers and sexual orientation. In *Teachers, gender and careers*, ed. S. Acker, 87–106. New York, Philadelphia & London: The Falmer Press.

Stanko, E., D. Crisp, C. Hale, and H. Lucraft. 1997. *Counting the costs: Estimating the impact of domestic violence in the London Borough of Hackney*. Swindon, UK: Crime Concern.

Stark, E., and A. Flitcraft. 1996. *Women at risk: Domestic violence and women's health*. Thousand Oaks, CA: Sage.

Steinberg, D., D. Epstein, and R. Johnson. 1997. *Border patrols: Policing the boundaries of heterosexuality*. London: Cassell.

Stoddart, B. 1986. *Saturday afternoon fever: Sport in the Australian culture*. North Ryde, NSW: Angus & Robertson.

Strange, P. 1983. *It'll make a man of you ... A feminist view of the arms race*. Nottingham, UK: Mushroom.

Sung, B. 1985. Bicultural conflicts in Chinese immigrant children. *Journal of Comparative Family Studies* 16(2): 255–69.

Tasker, Y. 1997. Fists of fury: Discourses of race and masculinity in the martial arts cinema. In *Race and the subject of masculinities*, ed. H. Stecopoulos and M. Uebel, 315–36. Durham, NC: Duke University Press.

Tattum, D., and D. Lane, eds. 1993. *Understanding and managing bullying*. London: Heinemann.

Thorne, B. 1990. Children and gender: Constructions of difference. In *Theoretical perspectives on gender*, ed. D. Rhode, 100–13. New Haven, CT: Yale University Press.

———. 1993. *Gender play: Girls and boys in school*. New Brunswick, NJ: Rutgers University Press.

Ting, J. 1995. Bachelor society: Deviant heterosexuality and Asian American historiography. In *Privileging positions: The sites of Asian American studies*, ed. G. Okihiro, M. Alquizola, D. Rony, and K. Wong, 271–9. Pullman, WA: Washington State University Press.

Tolman, R., and L. Bennett. 1990. A review of quantitative research on men who batter. *Journal of Interpersonal Violence* 5: 87–118.

Tran, D. 1998. Transgender/transsexual roundtable. In *Q&A: Queer in Asian America*, ed. D. Eng and A. Hom, 227–43. Philadelphia: Temple University Press.

U.S. Commission on Civil Rights. 1992. *Civil rights issues facing Asian Americans in the 1990s*. Washington, DC: Author.

Unterhalter, E. 2000. The work of the nation: Heroic adventures and masculinity in South African autobiographical writing of the anti-apartheid struggle. *The European Journal of Development Research* 12(2): 157–78.

Van Allen, J. 1972. Sitting on a man: Colonialism and the lost political institutions of Igbo women. *Canadian Journal of African Studies* 6(2): 165–81.

Waldron, I. 1976. Why do women live longer than men? *Social Science and Medicine* 10(7–8): 349–62.

Walker, K. 1998. "I'm not friends the way she's friends": Ideological and behavioral constructions of masculinity in men's friendships. In *Men's lives*, ed. M. Kimmel and M. Messner, 223–36. Boston: Allyn & Bacon.

Walker, L. 1989. *Australian maid: Sex, schooling and social class*. Ph.D. diss., Macquarie University.

———. 1993. Girls, schooling and subcultures of resistance. In *Youth subcultures: Theory, history and the Australian experience*, ed. R. White, 144–50. Hobart: National Clearing House for Youth Studies.

———. 1998a. Chivalrous masculinity among juvenile offenders in Western Sydney: A new perspective on young working class men and crime. *Current Issues in Criminal Justice* 9(3): 279–93.

———. 1998b. Under the bonnet: Car culture, technological dominance and young men of the working class. *Journal of Interdisciplinary Gender Studies* 3(2): 23–43.

———. 1999a. *Masculinity, motor vehicles and government intervention: An ethnographic and case study analysis of working class male youth in Western Sydney*. Canberra: Federal Office of Road Safety.

———. 1999b. Hydraulic sexuality and hegemonic masculinity: Young working-class men and car culture. In *Australian youth subcultures: On the margins and in the mainstream*, ed. R. White, 178–87. Hobart, TAS: Australian Clearing House for Youth Studies.

Walkerdine, V. 1990. *Schoolgirl fictions*. London: Verso.

Walvin, J., and J. Mangan, eds. 1987. *Manliness and morality: Middle-class masculinity in Britain and America, 1800–1940*. Manchester, UK: Manchester University Press.

Wat, E. 1996. Preserving the paradox: Stories from a Gay-Loh. In *Asian American sexualities: Dimensions of the gay and lesbian experience*, ed. R. Leong, 71–80. New York: Routledge.

Weems, L. 1999. Pestalozzi, perversity, and the pedagogy of love. In *Teaching queerly*, ed. W. Letts and J. Sears, 27–36. Lanham, MD: Rowman & Littlefield.

Weiner, G. 1994. *Feminisms in education: An introduction*. Buckingham, UK: Open University Press.

Weis, L. 1990. *Working class without work: High school students in a de-industrialising economy*. New York: Routledge, Chapman & Hall.

Weis, L., and M. Fine, eds. 1993. *Beyond silenced voices: Class, race, and gender in United States schools*. Albany, NY: SUNY Press.

West, C., and D. Zimmerman. 1991. Doing gender. In *The social construction of gender*, ed. J. Lorber and S. Farrell, 13–37. Thousand Oaks, CA: Sage.

White Ribbon Campaign. n.d. *Men working to end men's violence against women. The Education & Action Kit*. Toronto: White Ribbon Campaign. Available at: www.whiteribbon.ca/educational_materials/#edkit

White, M. 1995. Schools as communities of acknowledgment. *The Dulwich Centre Newsletter*, 2 and 3.

White, R., ed. 1993. *Youth subcultures: Theory, history and the Australian experience*. Hobart, TAS: National Clearing House for Youth Studies.

Whitelaw, S., L. Hills, and J. De Rosa. 1999. Sexually aggressive and abusive behavior in schools. Special Issue. Teaching about violence against women: International perspectives. *Women's Studies Quarterly* 27(1 and 2): 203–11.

Whyld, J., D. Pickersgill, and D. Jackson, eds. 1990. *Update on anti-sexist work with boys and young men.* Caistor, UK: Whyld Publishing Co-op.

Wiegman, R. 1993. The anatomy of lynching. In *American sexual politics: Sex, gender, and race since the Civil War*, ed. J. Fout and M. Tantillo, 223–45. Chicago: University of Chicago Press.

Wilkinson, G. 2004. Sex storm. *The Herald Sun*, 5 March 1.

Wilkinson, I. 2004. Soccer players face rape allegations. *The Sunday Age*, 7 March 11. Last retrieved Oct. 11, 2006 from www.theage.com.au/articles/2004/03/06/1078464696336.html?from=storyrhs

Williams, P. 1995. Meditations on masculinity. In *Constructing masculinity*, ed. M. Berger, B. Wallis, and S. Watson, 238–49. New York: Routledge.

Willis, P. 1977. *Learning to labour: How working class kids get working class jobs.* New York: Columbia University Press.

———. 1978. *Profane culture.* London: Routledge and Kegan Paul.

Wilson, C. 2004. Saints join unhappy club: Players in sex probe. *The Age*, 17 March 1.

Wolpe, A., O. Quinlan, and L. Martinez. 1997. *Gender equity in education: A report of the gender equity task team.* Pretoria, RSA: Department of Education.

Women's Studies Quarterly. 1993. Special Issue. Feminist Pedagogy: An update, 21.

Wood, K., and R. Jewkes. 1997. Violence, rape and sexual coercion: Everyday love in a South African township. *Gender and Development* 5(2): 41–6.

———. 2001. "Dangerous" love: Reflections on violence among Xhosa township youth. In *Changing men in Southern Africa*, ed. R. Morrell, 317–36. Pietermaritzburg, RSA: University of Natal Press.

Wragg, T. 1997. Oh boy! *Times Educational Supplement*, 16 May 4.

Xaba, T. 2001. Masculinities in a transitional society: The rise and fall of the Young Lions. In *Changing men in Southern Africa*, ed. R. Morrell, 105–24. Pietermaritzburg, RSA: University of Natal Press.

Yanagisako, S. 1985. *Transforming the past: Tradition and kinship among Japanese Americans.* Stanford, CA: Stanford University Press.

Yates, L. 1997. Gender equity and the boys debate: What sort of challenge is it? *British Journal of Sociology of Education* 18: 337–41.

Yon, D. 1999. The end of innocence: Multiculturalism, anti-racism, and pedagogy in global times. *JCT: Journal of Curriculum Theorizing* 15(4): 5–12.

Zeleza, P. 1993. Gendering African history. *Africa Development* 18(1): 99–117.

———. 1997. *Manufacturing African studies and crises.* Dakar, Senegal: CODESRIA.

Index

A
abuse, 75
   emotional, 75
   psychological, 75
   sexual, 88
   see also violence
academic underachievement, 11, 12
acceptance of violence by girls, 83–84
age-related differences, 5–6
AIDS, 54, 59, 71
alcohol, *see* social problems
American Association of University Women (AAUW), 93
analysis
   cost benefit, 79
   of abuse, 79
   of controlling behaviour, 79
   of violence, 79
anger control, 79
anti-violence education, 125–126
ANZAC (Australian and New Zealand Army Corp), 133, 134, 135
ANZAC Day (April 25), 133, 134, 137, 138
ANZAC myth, 133
Asian American
   novels, 158
   popular press, 158
Asian American boys
   effeminate characteristics in, 157–158, 161
Asian American girls
   feminine and masculine characteristics of, 160–161

Asian Americans
   in school, 154
   in the curriculum, 156
Asian American students
   as academic failures, 154
   as academic successes, 155
   as unassimilable foreigners, 154
Australian Rules football, 5, 130, 131, 143

B
belonging, 137, 138, 141–142, 147, 150; *see also* "groupness"
bicycles, 119–121
bodies, 9, 17–18, 86, 98–99, 107, 124
"boy culture", 129, 132, 145, 146, 148–150
   male entitlement in, 150
   stoicism in, 146
"boys, the", *see* "the boys"
"boys will be boys", 83, 150
bravery, 47, 79, 129, 130
bullying
   guidelines for dealing with, 83
   racialized bullying, 83
   sexual harassment, 83

C
campaigns, 88–89
   need for advertising, 89
   poster, 88
   walk from Windsor to Toronto, 89
   White Ribbon—Montreal Massacre, 89

cars, *see* motor vehicles
Central High, 102–103, 105
children's culture, 147
Chinese Americans, 156–157
   heterosexuality of, 156
class
   masculinity and road safety, 117
coaching, 130, 148
colonialism, 60, 72
   see also postcolonialism
common sense
   gender, 9
competition, 106–107
   with girls, 51
competitive football, 141–142
conversations
   about male-centered activities, 102–103
   arts versus sports, 102–103
   casual, 102–103
   power over, 104
   small talk, 102, 103
corporal punishment, 43, 82
counter-hegemonic masculinity practice, 96–97
crashes, 111, 114
crime, 36, 40, 43–47
critical literacy, 126–127
cultural difference, 114–115
curricular activities
   hockey, 95
   school government, 95
   theatre, 95
curricular programs
   arts and sports in, 105–106
   extracurricular programs, 105–106
curriculum, 86, 87, 88
   feminist alternative, 69–70, 72
   violence in, 84

D
deviance, *see* social problems
discourses of masculinity, 154, 163, 164, 166
diversity, 116-117

drugs, *see* social problems
drunk driving, *see* social problems

E
education
   about violence, 75
   against men's violence, 83–84
   of boys and men, 75
   early-age education, 82
   gendered violence, 82
   innocence, 82
   in families, 77
   of girls and women, 93
   through policy development, 77
   see also self-education; sex education
effeminate characteristics in Asian American boys, 157–158, 161
emotional awareness, 150
empowerment of students, 68–69
essentialist categories, 165
ethnographic project, 117
ethnicity, 8, 9
Eurocentrism, 68
evaluation of research results, 80
even-handedness, 116
expectations
   of how to act, 107
exposure, 113

F
femininity, 10, 161–162
feminism, 3, 14
   third world, 63, 67, 167
feminist insight, 146
feminist theory and practice, 10, 76
football, 5, 106, 130, 131, 132–135, 143–145, 149, 151
Foucauldian analysis, 15

G
Gallipoli, battle of, 134, 145
gangs
   African American, Asian, Latino, 158

South African, 42, 47–49
gay, 87, 100, 109
gender
    as analytic concept, 65
    as threatening, 72
    in Asian American masculinity, 155
    oppression based on, 155
    equity, 62, 63
    self-identification according to, 155
    treachery, 30–31
    treatment because of, 155
gender awareness
    teaching male teachers, 88
gender divisions
    as "natural", 112–113
    curriculum, 86
    physical education, 86
    staff, 86
gendered racism, *see* racism
gendered violence, 126
gender gap, 96
gender issues, 111, 127
    among teachers, 128
    in road safety, 112
gender politics, *see* politics
gender relations, 81
girls in cars, 127
girls supporting hegemonic masculinity, 47, 107, 135
"groupness"
    belonging, 131
    bonding of "brothers (and sisters) in arms", 131
groups
    see men in groups

H
"hallway hangers", 97–98
"Hattrick hug", 98–99
hegemonic masculinity, 5, 17, 33, 44, 47–48, 52, 56, 59, 61, 72, 80, 98–99, 115, 116, 119, 125, 132, 149
    feminist insight into, 144
heterosexism, 7, 68, 104, 168
    racialized, 161–163

heterosexual privilege, 29–31, 54, 55
heterosexuality, 7, 86–87, 104, 160–161
    deviant, 25, 154–157
HIV/AIDS, *see* AIDS
hockey, 95, 106
homophobia, 3, 7, 10, 14, 15–16, 18, 22–23, 25–26, 35, 36, 54, 55, 62, 71, 86–87, 166
homosexuality, 102
    assumed link to paedophilia, 6, 14–16, 18, 21–22, 25, 34
    "gay" as derogatory term, 87
hugs, *see* physicality; "Hattrick hug"
human factors, 112, 113

I
inappropriate behaviour
    teacher response to, 82–86
initiatives
    Education and Action Kit, 87
    White Ribbon Campaign, 87
    Skills for Violence-Free Relationships, 87
injury
    in sports, 129, 139, 141–144, 146
interaction
    male-male, 98–99
interrupting sexism, 84–86

L
learner's licence, 121, 123
lesbians, butch
    Asian American, 160–161

M
male drivers, 111–128
male teachers, 27–34
male identity, 81–82
male models
    Asian and White, 161–162
martial arts, 159
masculinity
    as collective, 41
    as contextual, 114–115

as contradictory, 137, 155, 160–161
as violent, 38–39, 44–49, 75–91
beliefs about, 100
Black, 154, 157–159
deviant, 154, 156
deviantly heterosexual, 154
hyper-, 154–155
hypo-, 154–155
"rules of", 99
traditional Asian, 154, 157, 159, 165, 167
White, 154, 157–158, 162
see also hegemonic masculinity
media
education through, 90
"memory work", 131
men as victims, 27, 53
men in groups
support for each other, 78, 133
male peer support, 78
military campaigns, 131, 133–134
military myths, 129, 131
misogyny, 3, 10, 25, 35, 36, 39, 53, 61–62, 66–67, 71
model minority stereotype, 157
Montreal Massacre, see campaigns
moral panic, ii–iii, 18
motor vehicles
as rite of passage to manhood, 119–120
interest in, 102, 119–121
muscular intellectualness, 8

N

naturalized/normalized heterosexuality, 10, 15, 19, 21, 24, 29, 86–87, 167; see also heterosexism,
non-violent educational environments, 82–83

O

oppression, 164, 167, 168
identifying with the privileged, 164
inciting difference, 166
rediscovering identity, 165

Orientalism, 161, 162

P

parents and schooling, 25–26
patriarchal privilege, 5, 66–67
pedagogy, 78
as dangerous, 28
see also curriculum
peer approval, 48, 49
peer associations, 129
peer groups, 114, 132, 140, 147, 148–150
abuse in, 135
bicycle culture in, 119–121
peer support, 78, 79, 83
penis size
in Black Americans, 159
in Asians, 162
personal is political, 77
physical education, 86
physicality
high five, 99, 101
hugging, 100, 101
physical interaction, 98, 99
touchy feely, 98
pleasure and pain, 130, 132, 143
policies against violence
criminal justice system reforms, 75
safe housing, 75
support of victims/survivors, 75
women-centred services, 75
women's refuge and rape crisis movements, 75
policing heterosexuality, 7, 14, 17–20, 25
politics
anti-sexist, 78
countersexist, 95
gender politics, 95, 99, 101, 102, 108, 109
men's profeminist, 78
positivism, 112
postcolonialism, 112
power relations, 3, 5, 85
practical initiatives, 90

problem of men's violence against
     women, 54, 76
profeminist resocialization, 79
programs
   men's, 79
protest masculinity, 122
punishment
   as a form of violence, 82
   corporal punishment, 82
   abolition of, 82
   application of, 82
   detention, 82
   discipline, 82
   impact of, 82

Q
queerness, 160–163, 165–166, 167
queer theory, 1, 63, 64, 99

R
race
   and class convergence, 35, 68
   in Asian American masculinity, 153
   oppression based on, 153
   self-identification according to, 153
   treatment because of, 153
   see also ethnicity
racism, 14, 17, 24, 67, 166, 168
   gendered, 9–10, 154, 155, 161
relational politics in sports, 130
relationships with girls and women,
     49–56, 77
remasculinization, 2, 88
   of schooling, 2, 13
representations, 154, 157, 163
road casualty research, 114
road casualty statistics, 112
road safety research, 111–112
role models for boys, 27, 30, 33–34

S
school,
     as arena for development of violence,
        81
     as business model, 2, 27
     as social process, 3
school violence, 61, 70; see also violence
Section 28 (Local Government Act), 6,
     12
self-education, 76, 90
self-representations, 154, 163
sex difference, 112–113
sex education, 88
sex roles, 113, 125
sexism, 94, 108, 166–167, 168
   in school, 93
sexist language, 65, 66, 101–102
sexual abuse, 88
   of females, gang bang, 152
sexual harassment, 61
sexuality, 6, 18
   in Asian American masculinity, 153
   normalization, 10, 15, 16, 25, 87; see
        also naturalized
   oppression based on, 153
   self-identification according to, 153
   treatment because of, 153
shame, 146
skills for violence-free relationships, 87
social factors in sports, 130
social interaction, 140
social power, 3–5, 8, 22, 32
social problems
   alcohol, 114, 116, 125
   drugs, 46, 114, 116, 125
   drunk driving, 114, 126
   sports, 5, 49
   see also conversations, arts versus
        sports; curricular programs, arts
        and sports in; injury in; rela-
        tional politics in sports; social
        factors in sports; wars and sport;
        physical education
stereotyping, 116, 161–163
subcultures, 114, 115
suppression of emotions, 149

T
tacit approval, 85
target groups, 116

teacher education, 14, 17, 23–24
ten commitments
    by men's anti-sexist collective, 78
    "the boys", 93–96, 108, 109
    "the brothers", 97–98
transgenderism, 167
    among Asian American males, 162–163
    cross-dressing, 163
    homosexuality, 163

U

underachievement of boys, 1–2, 88
United Kingdom schools, 2, 5, 88
university education, 14, 93–109

V

violence, 61, 70, 75–76, 77, 79, 80, 82–4, 85, 88, 89, 90
    against women teachers, 84
    coercive sex, 75
    different kinds of, 76
    girls' acceptance of, 83–84
    interconnections of sexuality and, 88
    men's against women, men, self, children, 53, 54, 66, 89
    physical, 76
    rape, 51–52, 75
    sexual harassment, 61, 75
    teaching of, 85
    what is, 76
    see also abuse

W

war, 131
    and sport, 134
    World War II, 156
    Vietnam, 156
    Korean, 156
White Ribbon, *see* campaigns
women's history, 66
World Health Organization (WHO)
    report on violence, 75
working class, 122, 128
working on cars and bikes, 119–120

Y

Yellow peril, 154–15
    stereotype, 155
Young Lions, 38
youth, as problem, 38

Z

Zulu Christians, 48